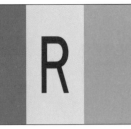

Rwanda

St. Kitts and Nevis

St. Lucia

Sa'udi Arabia

Senegal

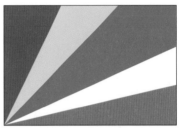

Seychelles

Slovenia

Solomon Islands

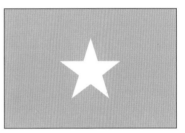

Somalia

Junior Worldmark Encyclopedia of the Nations

Junior Worldmark Encyclopedia of the Nations

Junior Worldmark Encyclopedia of the Nations

Third Edition

VOLUME 7

Qatar to
South Africa

GALE GROUP

™

THOMSON LEARNING

*Detroit • New York • San Diego • San Francisco
Boston • New Haven, Conn. • Waterville, Maine
London • Munich*

JUNIOR WORLDMARK ENCYCLOPEDIA OF THE NATIONS, THIRD EDITION

Timothy L. Gall and Susan Bevan Gall, *Editors*
Karen Hanson, Jennifer Jackson, Sarah Kunz, and Barbara Walker Dickinson, *Associate Editors*
Bram Lambrecht and Brian Rajewski, *Graphics and Layout*
Jennifer Wallace, *Editorial Assistant*
Janet Fenn and Matthew Markovich, *Proofreaders*
Maryland Cartographics, Inc., *Cartographers*

U•X•L Staff

Julie Carnagie, *U•X•L Senior Editor*
Carol DeKane Nagel, *U•X•L Managing Editor*
Thomas L. Romig, *U•X•L Publisher*
Evi Seoud, *Assistant Manager, Composition Purchasing and Electronic Prepress*
Rita Wimberley, *Senior Buyer*
Cynthia Baldwin, *Product Design Manager*
Barbara J. Yarrow, *Graphic Services Supervisor*
Mary Krzewinski, *Cover Designer*
Margaret Chamberlain, *Permissions Specialist (Pictures)*

Copyright © 2002
U•X•L
An Imprint of The Gale Group

Library of Congress Cataloging-in-Publication Data

Junior worldmark encyclopedia of the nations / [Timothy L. Gall and Susan Bevan Gall].
    p. cm.
      Includes bibliographical references.
      Contents: v. 1. Afghanistan to Brunei Darussalam -- v. 2. Bulgaria to Czech Republic
v. 3. Denmark to Guyana -- v. 4. Haiti to Kyrgyzstan -- v. 5. Laos to Myanmar -- v. 6.
Namibia to Portugal -- v. 7. Qatar to South Africa -- v. 8. Spain to Tuvalu -- v. 9. Uganda
to Zimbabwe.
      ISBN 0-7876-5366-7 (set : hardcover) -- ISBN 0-7876-5367-5 (v. 1) -- ISBN
0-7876-5368-3 (v. 2) -- ISBN 0-7876-5369-1 (v. 3) -- ISBN 0-7876-5370-5 (v. 4) --
ISBN 0-7876-5371-3 (v. 5) -- ISBN 0-7876-5372-1 (v. 6) -- ISBN 0-7876-5373-X (v. 7)
-- ISBN 0-7876-5374-8 (v. 8) -- ISBN 0-7876-5375-6 (v. 9)
      1. Geography--Encyclopedias, Juvenile. 2. History--Encyclopedias, Juvenile. 3.
Economics--Encyclopedias, Juvenile. 4. Political science--Encyclopedias, Juvenile. 5.
United Nations--Encyclopedias, Juvenile. [1. Geography--Encyclopedias.] I. Gall,
Timothy L. II. Gall, Susan B.

G63 .J86 2001
903--dc21   2001044239

CONTENTS

Guide to Country Articles

Every country profile in this encyclopedia includes the same 35 headings. Also included in every profile is a map (showing the country and its location in the world), the country's flag and seal, and a table of data on the country. The country articles are organized alphabetically in nine volumes. A glossary of terms is included in each of the nine volumes. This glossary defines many of the specialized terms used throughout the encyclopedia. A keyword index to all nine volumes appears at the end of Volume 9.

Flag color symbols

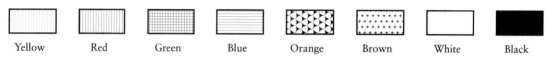

Yellow   Red   Green   Blue   Orange   Brown   White   Black

Alphabetical listing of sections

Agriculture	21
Armed Forces	16
Bibliography	35
Climate	3
Domesticated Animals	22
Economy	17
Education	31
Energy and Power	27
Environment	5
Ethnic Groups	8
Famous People	34
Fishing	23
Foreign Trade	26
Forestry	24
Government	13
Health	29
History	12
Housing	30
Income	18
Industry	19
Judicial System	15
Labor	20
Languages	9
Location and Size	1
Media	32
Migration	7
Mining	25
Plants and Animals	4
Political Parties	14
Population	6
Religions	10
Social Development	28
Topography	2
Tourism/Recreation	33
Transportation	11

Sections listed numerically

1	Location and Size
2	Topography
3	Climate
4	Plants and Animals
5	Environment
6	Population
7	Migration
8	Ethnic Groups
9	Languages
10	Religions
11	Transportation
12	History
13	Government
14	Political Parties
15	Judicial System
16	Armed Forces
17	Economy
18	Income
19	Industry
20	Labor
21	Agriculture
22	Domesticated Animals
23	Fishing
24	Forestry
25	Mining
26	Foreign Trade
27	Energy and Power
28	Social Development
29	Health
30	Housing
31	Education
32	Media
33	Tourism/Recreation
34	Famous People
35	Bibliography

Abbreviations and acronyms to know

GMT= Greenwich mean time. The prime, or Greenwich, meridian passes through Greenwich, England (near London), and marks the center of the initial time zone for the world. The standard time of all 24 time zones relate to Greenwich mean time. Every profile contains a map showing the country and its location in the world.

These abbreviations are used in references to famous people:
b.=born
d.=died
fl.=flourished (lived and worked)
r.=reigned (for kings, queens, and similar monarchs)

A dollar sign ($) stands for US$ unless otherwise indicated.

QATAR

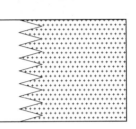

State of Qatar

Dawlat Qatar

CAPITAL: Doha (Ad-Dawhah).

FLAG: Maroon with white serrated border at the hoist.

ANTHEM: *Qatar National Anthem.*

MONETARY UNIT: The Qatar riyal (QR) of 100 dirhams was introduced on 13 May 1973. There are coins of 1, 5, 10, 25, and 50 dirhams, and notes of 1, 5, 10, 50, 100, and 500 riyals. QR1 = \$0.2747 (or \$1 = QR3.64).

WEIGHTS AND MEASURES: The metric system is the legal standard, although some British measures are still in use.

HOLIDAYS: Emir's Succession Day, 22 February; Independence Day, 3 September. Muslim religious holidays include 'Id al-Fitr, 'Id al-'Adha', and Milad an-Nabi.

TIME: 3 PM = noon GMT.

1 LOCATION AND SIZE

The State of Qatar, a peninsula projecting northward into the Persian Gulf, has an area of 11,000 square kilometers (4,247 square miles), slightly smaller than the state of Connecticut. Qatar also includes a number of islands.

Qatar's capital city, Doha, is located on the Persian Gulf coast.

2 TOPOGRAPHY

The terrain is generally flat and sandy, rising gradually from the east to a central limestone plateau. Extensive salt flats at the base of the peninsula support the theory that Qatar was once an island.

3 CLIMATE

Qatar's summer is extremely hot. Mean temperatures in June are 42°C (108°F), dropping to 15°C (59°F) in winter. Rainfall is minimal.

4 PLANTS AND ANIMALS

Vegetation is generally sparse. Jerboas (desert rats) and an occasional fox are found. Birds include the flamingo, cormorant, osprey, kestrel, plover, and lark. Reptiles include monitors (large lizards) and land snakes.

5 ENVIRONMENT

Conservation of oil supplies, preservation of the natural wildlife heritage, and increasing the water supply through

Geographic Profile

Geographic Features

Size ranking: 157 of 192
Highest elevation: 103 meters (338 feet) at Qurayn
    Aba al Bawl
Lowest elevation: Sea level at the Persian Gulf

Land Use†

Arable land:	1%
Permanent crops:	0%
Permanent pastures:	5%
Forests:	0%
Other:	94%

Weather††

Average annual precipitation: less than 7.5 centimeters
    (3 inches)
Average temperature in January: 15°C (59°F)
Average temperature in June: 42°C (108°F)

†*Arable land:* Land used for temporary crops, like meadows for mowing or pasture, gardens, and greenhouses. *Permanent crops:* Land cultivated with crops that occupy its use for long periods, such as cocoa, coffee, rubber, fruit and nut orchards, and vineyards. *Permanent pastures:* Land used permanently for forage crops. *Forests:* Land containing stands of trees. *Other:* Any land not specified, including built-on areas, roads, and barren land.

††The measurements for precipitation and average temperature were taken at weather stations closest to the country's largest city. Precipitation and average temperature can vary significantly within a country, due to factors such as latitude, altitude, coastal proximity, and wind patterns.

desalination (removing salt) are high on Qatar's environmental priority list. In 1984 an Environmental Protection Committee was formed. As of 1987, the hawksbill and green sea turtle were considered endangered species, and protection was afforded to a group of rare white oryx (type of antelope).

6 POPULATION

The 2000 population was estimated at 749,542. Average population density was about 51 persons per square kilometer (132 per square mile) in 2000. During the 1990s, the population grew by an average of 4.4% a year. A population of 874,000 is projected for 2005.

According to United Nations estimates, Qatar's population had the world's highest ratio of males to females in 1998: there were 191 men for every 100 women.

7 MIGRATION

In 1993, the number of immigrant workers was about 85,000, including Pakistanis, Indians, and Iranians. In 1999, the net immigration rate was about 20.1 immigrants per 1,000 population.

8 ETHNIC GROUPS

The native population (about 100,000) descends from Bedouin tribes who migrated to Qatar in the 1700s. Pakistanis (18%), Indians (18%), Iranians (10%), and Gulf and Palestinian Arabs (40%) are among the leading immigrant groups.

9 LANGUAGES

Arabic is the national language, but English is widely spoken, and Farsi is used by smaller groups in Doha, the capital city.

10 RELIGIONS

Islam is the official religion of Qatar and is practiced by the great majority (95%) of the people. The Qataris are mainly Sunni Muslims of the Wahhabi sect. There also are small populations of Christians, Hindus, and Baha'is.

11 TRANSPORTATION

As of 1995 there were an estimated 1,230 kilometers (764 miles) of highways, of which 90% were paved. That year, there were 95,000 passenger cars and 83,600 commercial vehicles registered.

Doha International Airport is served by more than a dozen international airlines. In 1997, 1.2 million passengers were carried on scheduled domestic and international flights.

Qatar maintains modern deepwater ports at Doha and Umm Sa'id. In 1998, the merchant fleet consisted of 22 vessels with 713,014 gross registered tons.

12 HISTORY

The ath-Thani family, forebears of the present rulers, arrived in Qatar in the eighteenth century from what is now Sa'udi Arabia. During the same century, the al-Khalifah family, who currently rule Bahrain, arrived from Kuwait.

In 1868, the Perpetual Maritime Truce terminated the Bahraini claim to Qatar in exchange for a tribute payment (payment by one ruler of a nation to another to acknowledge submission). In 1872, however, Qatar fell under Ottoman occupation, and Turkish rule lasted until the outbreak of World War I (1914–18). Qatar then established its independence. In 1916, it signed a treaty with the United Kingdom providing for British protection in exchange for a central role for the United Kingdom in Qatar's foreign affairs. High-quality oil was discovered at

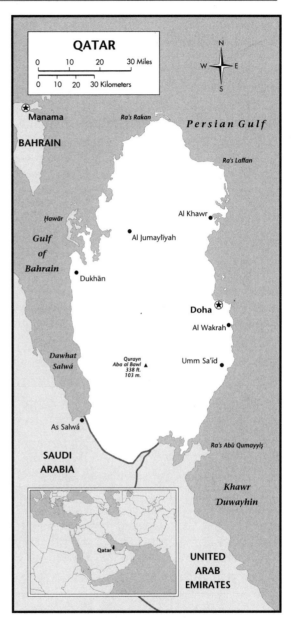

LOCATION: 26°23′ to 24°31′N; 50°43′ to 51°41′E.
BOUNDARY LENGTHS: Persian Gulf coastline, 563 kilometers (350 miles); United Arab Emirates, 45 kilometers (28 miles); Sa'udi Arabia, 60 kilometers (38 miles). **TERRITORIAL SEA LIMIT:** 3 miles.

Dukhan in 1940, but full-scale use of the discovery did not begin until 1949.

In January 1968, the United Kingdom announced its intention to withdraw its forces from the Persian Gulf states by the end of 1971. On 3 September 1971, the independent State of Qatar was declared. A new treaty of friendship and cooperation was signed with the United Kingdom, and Qatar was soon admitted to membership in the 20-member Arab League (also known as the League of Arab States) and the United Nations.

On 22 February 1972, Sheikh Khalifa bin Hamad ath-Thani seized power in a peaceful coup, deposing his cousin, Sheikh Ahmad. Since his accession, Sheikh Khalifa has pursued a vigorous program of economic and social reforms, including the transfer of royal income to the state.

Qatar's boundary disputes with Bahrain disrupted relations between the two countries in the mid-1980s. In December 1992, a minor dispute with Sa'udi Arabia was resolved with a boundary agreement.

In February 1995, Sheikh Hamad seized power from his father, Sheikh Khalifa. Sheikh Khalifa had put government revenues in his own bank accounts and paid for government services out of those funds. When Sheikh Hamad took over the government, his father froze the bank accounts, which disabled Qatar's treasury.

In 1996, Sheikh Khalifa set up a government in exile in nearby United Arab Emirates. The hostile transfer of power has led to problems among the members

Photo credit: EPD/Government of Qatar.

Name:	Sheikh Hamad bin Khalifa al-Thani
Position:	Emir of a traditional monarchy
Took office:	27 June 1995 (deposed his father in a bloodless coup)
Birthplace:	Doha, Qatar
Birth date:	1950
Education:	Royal Military Academy, Sandhurst, U.K., 1971
Of interest:	Sheikh Hamad is generally seen as more decisive and assertive than his father, the former emir.

of the Gulf Cooperation Council. Budget problems from the lost revenue have caused Sheikh Hamad to cut government spending.

The government will need to spend money in order to develop huge offshore natural gas reserves. The former emir still claims to be the legitimate ruler, however

Sheikh Hamad continues to rule despite outside threats.

Sheikh Hamad is encouraging political openness, allowing women to vote and run for office in 1999. A constitutional committee has been set up which will establish an elected parliament.

13 GOVERNMENT

Qatar is a monarchy ruled by an emir (ruler of an Islamic country). A Basic Law, including a bill of rights, provides for a nine-member executive Council of Ministers (cabinet) and a 30-member legislative Advisory Council. No electoral system has been instituted, and no provisions for voting have been established.

14 POLITICAL PARTIES

There are no organized political parties.

15 JUDICIAL SYSTEM

The legal system is based on the Shari'ah (canonical Muslim law). The Basic Law of 1970, however, provided for the creation of an independent judiciary, including the Court of Appeal, which has final jurisdiction in civil and criminal matters; the Higher Criminal Court, which judges major criminal cases; the Lower Criminal Court; the Civil Court; and the Labor Court, which judges claims involving employees and their employers.

16 ARMED FORCES

The Qatar security force consists of 8,500 army, 1,800 naval, and 1,500 air force

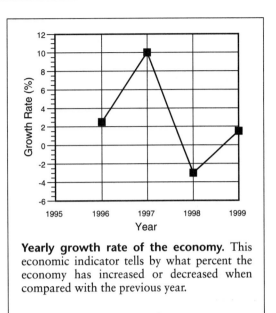

Yearly growth rate of the economy. This economic indicator tells by what percent the economy has increased or decreased when compared with the previous year.

personnel. Defense spending may have been as high as $940 million in 1999.

17 ECONOMY

Until recent decades, the Qatar peninsula was an impoverished area with a scant living provided by pearl diving, fishing, and nomadic herding. In 1940, oil was discovered at Dukhan, and since then it has dominated the Qatari economy. The recent discovery of a vast field of natural gas promises to add a new dimension to the economy. The economy performed sluggishly in the early 1990s but recovered somewhat by 1995 because of a surge in oil prices.

18 INCOME

In 1998, Qatar's gross domestic product (GDP) was $12 billion, or about $17,100 per person. During the same year, the average annual decline of GDP was 3%.

19 INDUSTRY

In 1995, Qatar Iron and Steel Co. (70% government-owned) produced 614,000 tons of crude steel; Qatar Fertilizer Co. (70%) produced 653,900 tons of ammonia and 886,000 tons of urea; and Qatar National Cement Co. made 580,000 tons of cement. Qatar Petrochemical Co. (80%) produces ethylene, polyethylene, and sulfur.

20 LABOR

About 70% of the economically active population is engaged in industry (largely oil-related), commerce, and services. Of the remainder, about 10% work in the agricultural sector (producing about 1% of the gross national product, or GNP) and another 20% in government.

21 AGRICULTURE

As of 1997, only 1.5% (17,000 hectares/42,000 acres) of total land area was under cultivation. In 1998, 15,000 tons of dates were produced, mostly for local consumption. Rice also is grown for the domestic market.

22 DOMESTICATED ANIMALS

According to 1998 estimates, Qatar had 14,000 head of cattle, 200,000 sheep, 172,000 goats, and 47,000 camels. Output in 1998 included about 14,000 tons of mutton and 4,000 tons of poultry.

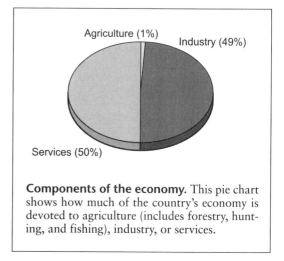

Components of the economy. This pie chart shows how much of the country's economy is devoted to agriculture (includes forestry, hunting, and fishing), industry, or services.

23 FISHING

Fish and shellfish production in 1997 totaled 5,034 tons (down from 8,136 tons in 1991).

24 FORESTRY

There are no forests in Qatar.

25 MINING

Aside from petroleum and natural gas, Qatar has few exploitable minerals. In 1996, 900,000 tons of limestone and 61,000 tons of sulfur were produced.

26 FOREIGN TRADE

Exports in 1998 were petroleum products (accounting for 75%), natural and manufactured gas (5.2%), fertilizers (3.8%), and steel (3.7%). The main destinations of exports are Japan, Singapore, Korea, and the US.

Selected Social Indicators

The statistics below are estimates for the period 1996 to 2000. For comparison purposes, data for the United States and averages for low-income countries and high-income countries are also given.

Indicator	Qatar	Low-income countries	High-income countries	United States
Per capita gross national product (GNP)†	$17,000	$1,870	$25,690	$31,910
Population growth rate	3.4%	2.1%	0.7%	1.1%
People per square kilometer of land	51	73	29	30
Life expectancy in years	75	59	78	77
Number of physicians per 1,000 people	1	1.0	2.5	2.5
Number of pupils per teacher (primary school)	9	41	17	14
Illiteracy rate (15 years and older)	18%	34%	<5%	3%
Television sets per 1,000 people	309	85	693	844
Energy consumed per capita (kg of oil equivalent)	12,248	550	5,366	7,937

† The GNP is the total dollar value of all goods and services produced by a country in a year. The per capita GNP is calculated by dividing a country's GNP by its population and adjusting for relative purchasing power. About 15% of the world's 6.1 billion people live in high-income countries, while 40% live in low-income countries.

n.a. = data not available   > = greater than   < = less than

Sources: World Bank. *World Development Indicators.* Washington, D.C.: The World Bank, 2001; Central Intelligence Agency. *The World Factbook.* Washington, D.C.: Government Printing Office, 2000.

Imports amounted to $4.2 billion in 1999. Main imports include food, industrial supplies, machinery, and transport equipment. The most important suppliers are Japan, the United Kingdom, the United States, and France.

27 ENERGY AND POWER

Qatar's substantial oil reserves, estimated at 3.7 billion barrels in 1999, dominate the country's economy. Production was 782,000 barrels per day in 1998. Qatar's gas reserves (world's third largest) are estimated at 300 trillion cubic feet (8.5 trillion cubic meters); output was estimated at 630 billion cubic feet (17.8 billion cubic meters) in 1997. Qatar's electrical power production in 1998 reached 6.7 billion kilowatt hours.

28 SOCIAL DEVELOPMENT

The Ministry of Labor and Social Affairs provides help to orphans, widows, and other Qatari nationals in need of assistance. Both law and Islamic customs closely restrict the activities of Qatari women, who are largely limited to roles within the home. Non-Muslims may experience discrimination in employment and education. Recent democratic reforms have allowed both men and women to vote. Corporal punishment is allowed by law.

29 HEALTH

In 1992, there was about one doctor for every 1,000 people. In 1991, 100% of the population had access to health care services and safe water. Life expectancy was 75 years in 2000.

30 HOUSING

A "popular housing" scheme provides dwellings through interest-free loans and repayment on easy terms.

31 EDUCATION

Adult illiteracy in 2000 stood at about 18%. Education is compulsory and free for all residents 6–16 years of age; books, meals, transportation, clothing, and boarding facilities (if required) also are free. As of 1996, there were 174 schools with 5,864 teachers and 52,631 pupils at the primary level; secondary level schools had 3,858 teachers and 38,594 pupils.

The leading higher educational institution is the University of Qatar. Enrollment in all higher level institutions in 1997 was 8,475 pupils with 643 teaching staff.

32 MEDIA

There were an estimated 111,200 telephones in 1995. Radio transmissions include 12 hours per day of English-language service, with a French–language service instituted in 1985. Two television channels transmit mostly in Arabic. In 1997 there were 268 radios and 309 television sets per 1,000 population.

Publications available in Qatar (with 1999 circulation figures) include the daily newspapers *Al-'Arab* (25,000), *Ar-Rayah* (25,000), *Al-Sharq* (40,000), *Al-Usbun* (15,000), and *Gulf Times* (15,000). Official censorship of the print media was lifted in 1995.

33 TOURISM AND RECREATION

Most visitors to Qatar are business travelers; a convention center managed by the Sheraton Hotel Group opened in 1982. Qatar's remoteness and a ban on alcohol have kept tourism weak. In 1997, there were 435,000 tourist arrivals at hotels. Rooms numbered 1,998, with a 78% occupancy rate.

34 FAMOUS QATARIS

Sheikh Khalifa bin Hamad ath-Thani (b.1932) was emir (leader of an Islamic state) of Qatar from 1972 to 1995. His heir-apparent Sheikh Hamad bin Khalifa al-Thani (b.1948) became emir in June 1995 following a weak takeover that ousted his father.

35 BIBLIOGRAPHY

Abu Saud, Abeer. *Qatari Women, Past and Present.* New York: Longman, 1984.

Augustin, Byron. *Qatar.* New York: Children's Press, 1997.

Robison, Gordon. *Bahrain, Kuwait & Qatar.* Hawthorn, Vic.; London: Lonely Planet, 2000.

Zahlan, Rosemarie Said. *The Creation of Qatar.* London: Croom Helm, 1979.

ROMANIA

Romania

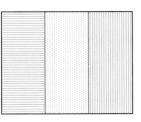

CAPITAL: Bucharest (Bucuresti).

FLAG: The national flag, adopted in 1965, is a tricolor of blue, yellow, and red vertical stripes.

ANTHEM: *Trei culori (Three Colors).*

MONETARY UNIT: The leu (L) is a paper currency of 100 bani. There are coins of 25 bani and 1, 3, 5, 10, 20, 50, and 100 lei, and notes of 10, 25, 50, 100, 200, 500, 1,000, and 5,000 lei. L1 = $0.00005 (or $1 = L17,996.4).

WEIGHTS AND MEASURES: The metric system is the legal standard.

HOLIDAYS: New Year's Day, 1 January; International Labor Day, 1–2 May; Liberation Day, 23 August; National Day, 1 December; Christmas Day, 25 December.

TIME: 2 PM = noon GMT.

1 LOCATION AND SIZE

Situated in eastern Europe, north of the Balkan Peninsula, Romania has a total area of 237,500 square kilometers (91,699 square miles), slightly smaller than the state of Oregon. Its total boundary length is 2,744 kilometers (1,702 miles). Romania's capital city, Bucharest, is located in the south central part of the country.

2 TOPOGRAPHY

The backbone of Romania is formed by the Carpathian Mountains, which swing southeastward and then westward through the country. The southern limb of this arc-shaped system is known as the Transylvanian Alps, whose compact, rugged peaks rise to 2,543 meters (8,343 feet) in Mt. Moldoveanu, Romania's highest mountain. On the eastern and southern fringes of the Carpathian arc are low plateaus and plains. On the inside of the Carpathian arc is the Transylvanian Basin, a hilly region divided by the wide, deep valleys of the Mures and Somes rivers. Between the lower Danube (Dunùrea) and the Black Sea is an eroded plateau with average elevations of 400–600 meters (1,310–1,970 feet).

An earthquake that struck Romania on 4 March 1977 left more than 34,000 families homeless. The shock, measuring 7.2 on the open-ended Richter scale, was the most severe in Europe since a series of shocks in October–November 1940, also in Romania.

3 CLIMATE

Romania is exposed to northerly cold winds in the winter and moderate westerly winds from the Atlantic Ocean in the summer. Average January temperatures range from –4°C to 0°C (25–32°F). During the summer, the highest temperatures are recorded in the Danube (Dunùrea) River Valley (24°C/75°F). Precipitation averages between 100 and 125 centimeters (about 40 and 50 inches) annually in the mountains and about 38 centimeters (15 inches) in the delta.

4 PLANTS AND ANIMALS

Natural vegetation consists mainly of grasslands in the northeast lowlands. The Carpathian mountains are covered with forests, with deciduous trees at lower elevations and conifers at altitudes above 1,070–1,220 meters (3,500–4,000 feet). Alpine meadows occupy the highest parts of the mountains.

Wild animals, including the Carpathian deer, wolves, hares, marten, brown bear, lynx, boar, and fox, are found in the Carpathians. Water birds flourish in the mouths of the Danube (Dunùrea) River area, and sturgeon abound in the waters of the lower Danube (Dunùrea) River. Carp, bream, and pike populate the lakes.

5 ENVIRONMENT

Rapid industrialization since World War II (1939–45) has caused widespread water and air pollution, particularly in the region where oil is refined. Acid rain originating in Hungary and radioactivity from the 1986 nuclear power plant accident at Chernobyl, Ukraine, pose additional environmental problems.

Geographic Profile

Geographic Features

Size ranking: 79 of 192
Highest elevation: 2,543 meters (8,343 feet) at Moldoveanu
Lowest elevation: Sea level at the Black Sea

Land Use

Arable land:	41%
Permanent crops:	3%
Permanent pastures:	21%
Forests:	29%
Other:	6%

Weather

Average annual precipitation: 57.8 centimeters (22.8 inches)
Average temperature in January: –2.7°C (27.1°F)
Average temperature in July: 23.3°C (73.9°F)

Air pollution is heaviest in the nation's cities where industry produces hazardous levels of sulfur dioxide. Romania uses 59% of its available water to support farming, and 33% for industrial purposes.

In 1994, two of Romania's mammal species, 18 of its bird species, and 67 plant types were endangered. Romania has 12 national parks.

6 POPULATION

According to the 2000 census, Romania's total population was 22.3 million. During the 1990s, Romania's population decreased by an average of 0.3% a year. A population of 22.3 million is projected for 2005. The average density in 2000 was 97 persons per square kilometer (251 per square mile). Bucharest, the capital and principal city, had a metropolitan population of 2.1 million in 2000.

ROMANIA

0   50   100 Miles

0   50   100 Kilometers

LOCATION: 48°15′06″ to 43°37′07″N; 20°15′44″ to 29°41′24″E. **BOUNDARY LENGTHS:** Ukraine, 531 kilometers (329 miles); Moldova, 450 kilometers (279 miles); Black Sea coastline, 234 kilometers (145 miles); Bulgaria, 608 kilometers (377 miles); Yugoslavia, 476 kilometers (295 miles); Hungary, 445 kilometers (277 miles). **TERRITORIAL SEA LIMIT:** 12 miles.

7 MIGRATION

Population shifts numbering in the millions occurred as a result of the two world wars and the 1947 communist takeover. In the late 1970s and early 1980s, labor unrest caused some 120,000 ethnic Germans to leave Romania between 1978 and 1988. Some 40,000 ethnic Hungarians fled in 1987 alone. In 1990, 80,346 people left: 78% to Germany, and 9% to Hungary. Approximately 44,160 Romanians emigrated in 1991 and 31,152 in 1992. In 1992, 103,787 Romanians were given asylum (political protection) in Germany, but in September of that year Germany returned 43,000 refugees, more than half of whom were Roma (Gypsies).

Since 1999, Romania has been an asylum for refugees from the war in Yugoslavia, offering to accept 6,000 Kosovars from Macedonia, although only 100 actually arrived.

8 ETHNIC GROUPS

Romanians constitute by far the majority group (89.1%, according to the 2000 census), but the population includes two important ethnic minorities: Hungarians (8.9% of the total population) and Germans (0.4%), both concentrated in the Transylvania region. The number of Roma (Gypsies), which is officially 401,087, may be as high as 2.3 million. Smaller minorities include Ukrainians, Turks, Russians, Serbs, Croats, Jews, Poles, Bulgarians, Czechs, Greeks, Armenians, Tatars, and Slovaks.

Since 1989, Roma have been targets of an organized campaign of violence throughout Romania.

9 LANGUAGES

Romanian is the official language. It is a Romance language derived from the Latin spoken in the Eastern Roman Empire. In the 2,000 years of its development, the language also was influenced by contacts with Slavonic, Albanian, Hungarian, Greek, and Turkish. Hungarian is spoken by a large percentage of the inhabitants of Transylvania.

Photo credit: AP/Wide World Photos.

A Roma (Gypsy) family is trying to make extra money selling snowflake flowers near one of the Bucharest revolution memorials.

10 RELIGIONS

The great majority of Romanians (estimated at 70% in 1998) are affiliated with the Romanian Orthodox Church.

There are 15 other legally recognized denominations. About 6% belonged to the Roman Catholic Church in 1998. There were about 17,500 Jews in 1988. Other denominations include the Reformed (Calvinist) Church of Romania, with an estimated 600,000 members; the German-minority Evangelical Church of the Augsburg Confession, 150,000; and the Unitarian Church (mostly Hungarian), 60,000.

There are small numbers of Baptists, Seventh-Day Adventists, Pentecostals, and Muslims.

11 TRANSPORTATION

The length of Romania's railroad network in 1996 was 11,376 kilometers (7,069 miles). There were 153,358 kilometers (95,297 miles) of roads at the end of 1996. In 1995, there were 2 million passenger cars and 370,000 commercial vehicles in use. Only the Danube (Dunùrea) and Prut rivers are suitable for inland navigation. The main Danube ports include Galaţi, Bràila, and Giurgiu. The Romanian merchant fleet is based in Constanta, the nation's chief Black Sea port. Romanian Air Transport (Transporturile Aeriene Române—TAROM) and Romanian Air Lines (Liniile Aeriene Române—LAR) are the primary air carriers. Otopeni International Airport, near Bucharest, is the nation's principal international air terminal.

12 HISTORY

Present-day Romania was known as the kingdom of Dacia at the end of the first millennium (1,000 years) BC. It reached the highest stage of its development toward the end of the first century AD, but fell to the Roman Emperor Trajan in AD 106. The withdrawal of the Romans in AD 271 left the Romanians a partly Christianized Dacian-Roman people, speaking Latin and living in towns and villages built in the Roman style.

In the following centuries, as Dacia was overrun by waves of invaders, the early Romanians are believed to have sought refuge in the mountains or to have migrated south of the Danube (Dunùrea) River. There the Dacian-Romanians, assimilating Slavic influences, became known by the seventh century as Vlachs (Walachians). The Vlachs apparently remained independent of their neighbors, but came under Mongol domination in the thirteenth century.

The kingdoms of Walachia and Moldavia were established in the late thirteenth and early fourteenth centuries. Walachia came under Turkish control in 1476 and Moldavia in 1513; thirteen years later, Transylvania, which had been under Hungarian control since 1003, also passed into Turkish hands.

The tide of Ottoman (Turkish) domination began to ebb under Russian pressure in the second half of the seventeenth century. The Congress of Paris in 1856 ended the Crimean War (1853–56), in which Russia fought against Turkey, Britain, and France. As a result, the self-rule of the principalities of Walachia and Moldavia was guaranteed. Russia was forced to return the southernmost part of Bessarabia to Moldavia.

At the Congress of Berlin in 1878, Romania obtained full independence from Turkey but returned southern Bessarabia to Russia. Under the rule of Carol I, Romania developed into a modern political state.

In World War I (1914–18), Romania joined the Allies, and as a result acquired Bessarabia from Russia, Bukovina from Austria, and Transylvania from Hungary. The establishment of a greatly expanded

Romania was confirmed in 1919–20 by the treaties of St. Germain, Trianon, and Neuilly. In 1930, Carol II, who had earlier renounced his right of succession, returned to Romania and established a royal dictatorship.

World War II

As economic conditions deteriorated, Fascism (a dictatorial and oppressive political philosophy) and anti-Semitism (discrimination toward Jews) became increasingly powerful. Carol II sought to satisfy both Germany and the Soviet Union. However, with Germany moving towards war with the Soviet Union, Romania would eventually have to pick sides. In 1940, Romania gave up territory to the Soviet Union, Hungary, and Bulgaria. In the same year, German troops entered Romania, and Romania joined the Axis (Germany and Italy) against the Allies in 1941 in World War II (1939–45).

Soviet forces drove into Romania in 1944. A coup (forced takeover) overthrew the wartime regime of General Ion Antonescu. Romania switched sides, joining the Allies against Germany. The Allies would eventually defeat Germany.

After World War II, a communist-led coalition government under Premier Petru Groza was set up. On 30 December 1947, the Romanian People's Republic was proclaimed.

In international affairs, Romania followed a distinctly pro-Soviet line, becoming a member of the alliance of socialist countries known as the Council for Mutual Economic Assistance (CMEA) and the Warsaw Pact for mutual defense.

Romania Under Ceausescu

During the 1960s, however, and especially after the emergence of Nicolae Ceausescu as Communist Party and national leader, Romania followed a more independent course, increasing its trade with Western nations. In 1968, Romania denounced the intervention by the Soviet Union in Czechoslovakia. In December 1973, President Ceausescu visited Washington, where he signed a joint declaration on economic, industrial, and technical cooperation with the United States.

In contrast to some other East European countries, there was relatively little political dissent in Romania during the first 30 years of communist rule. In 1977, however, about 35,000 miners in the Jiu Valley, west of Bucharest, went on strike because of economic grievances. In the early and mid-1980s, there were a number of work stoppages and strikes caused by food and energy shortages. In early 1987, Ceausescu indicated that Romania would not follow the reform trend initiated by Mikhail Gorbachev in the Soviet Union.

When the Securitate, Romania's dreaded secret police, attempted to deport Laszlo Toekes, a popular clergyman and leading spokesperson for the local Hungarians, thousands of people took to the streets. Troops were summoned, and two days of rioting ensued, during which several thousand citizens were killed.

Upon Ceausescu's return from a visit to Iran, he convened a mass rally at which he

Photo credit: AP/Wide World Photos.

Romanian citizens walk by the People's House in Bucharest. Former dictator Ceausescu built this huge palace during his ruling period. The building is open now to the Romanian public.

attempted to portray his opponents as advocating dictatorship. However, the rally turned into an anti-government demonstration, in which the army sided with the demonstrators. Ceausescu and his wife attempted to flee the country, but were detained, tried, and executed on 25 December 1989.

Political and Economic Reform

A hastily assembled Council of National Salvation took power. The council's president was Ion Iliescu, a former secretary of the Communist Party. In February 1990, Iliescu agreed to ban the Communist Party, replacing the 145-member Council of National Salvation with a 241-member Council of National Unity, which included members of opposition parties, national minorities, and former political prisoners.

Parliamentary elections were held in May 1990 against a background of continued civil unrest, especially in the Hungarian west. Iliescu was elected president, with about 85% of the votes, and was reelected in the general elections of September 1992.

Continued political instability and the slow pace of economic change have kept foreign investment quite low. Because of this, Romania has had to rely upon loans from Western sources, especially the International Monetary Fund (IMF), piling up foreign debt at the rate of about $1 billion a year.

Romanians began the 1990s as among the poorest people in Europe, and their economy only grew worse. Inflation for 1992 was 210%, and more than 300% for 1993, while unemployment was almost 10%. Most significantly, production fell for the first few years after the anti-communist revolution. By 1994, however, Romania began to turn its economy around. Presidential and parliamentary elections were held in November 1996. Emil Constantinescu of the Democratic Convention Alliance of Opposition Groups was elected as Romania's first post-communist leader. In March 1998, thousands of citizens protested in Bucharest against high unemployment and recent tax hikes.

In the 2000 presidential elections, Ion Iliescu was able to regain the presidency for the second time (Emil Constantinescu had been elected in 1996).

13 GOVERNMENT

The Council for National Unity enacted a new constitution for Romania in November 1991, but the document is similar to Soviet-era constitutions.

The present government has a directly elected president, who is head of state. The legislature is made up of two houses: the Senate, with 143 seats, and the Assembly of Deputies, with 341 seats. Although the legislature has the formal duty to propose and pass laws, in practice the bodies

Photo credit: EPD/Office of the President of Romania.

Name:	Ion Iliescu
Position:	President of a republic
Took office:	2001
Birthplace:	Oltenita, Romania
Birth date:	3 March 1930
Education:	Polytechnic Institute in Bucharest; Moscow Institute for Energy
Spouse:	Elena Iliescu (engineer, scientific researcher in the field of metal corrosion)
Of interest:	In the 1980s, Iliescu was president of the Kayak-Canoe Romanian Federation for several years. He speaks French, English, and Russian.

have been weak; so that much of the country's function appears still to be conducted by decrees and orders, as in the past.

Romania is divided into 40 counties, as well as the municipality of Bucharest.

14 POLITICAL PARTIES

After the overthrow of Nicolae Ceausescu in 1989, some 80 political parties appeared. The dominant party in the 1990 elections proved to be the National Salvation Front (NSF). Due to disagreements over supporting its leader, Ion Iliescu, the NSF has since split into the Party of Social Democracy in Romania (PSDR), the Democratic National Salvation Front, and the Front for National Salvation.

The second-largest party in the 1992 elections was a coalition, called the Democratic Convention of Romania (DCR), which incorporated such parties as the National Peasant Party Christian Democratic, the Movement of Civic Alliance, the Party of Civic Alliance, Liberal Party '93, and the Social Democratic Party.

Smaller parties include the Magyar Democratic Union, the Agrarian Democratic Party, the National Unity Party, Democratic National Salvation Front, and others. There are two ultra-nationalist parties, the Party of Romanian National Unity and the Greater Romania Party, and the Communists have been reborn as the Socialist Labor Party.

In the parliamentary election of November 1996, the DCR became the ruling party, with 53 seats in the Senate and 122 in the Chamber of Deputies. The PSDR, which lost the majority, held 41 and 91 seats, respectively.

By early 2000, the failure of the reformists to bring about promised economic recovery led to widespread disenchantment; Romania also had failed to achieve its major foreign policy goals: admittance to NATO and the EU. This allowed the ex–Communist Party leader, Iliescu, to win a decisive victory in the June 2000 elections.

15 JUDICIAL SYSTEM

The 1992 law on reorganization of the judiciary establishes a four-level legal system. The four levels consist of courts of first instance, intermediate appellate level courts, a Supreme Court, and a Constitutional Court. The Constitutional Court has responsibility for judicial review of constitutional issues. The intermediate appellate courts had not yet been established as of 1993 due to lack of personnel and funding.

16 ARMED FORCES

The revolution of 1989–90 destroyed the communist armed forces and security establishment. Reorganization continues. In 2000, the armed forces numbered about 207,000 officers and men: 106,000 in the army, 20,800 in the navy, and 43,500 in the air force, which had 367 combat aircraft and 16 attack helicopters.

Military service is compulsory, and all able-bodied men at the age of 20 may be drafted into the armed forces for 12–18 months. Romania's budgeted defense expenditures in 1996 were $650 million, or 2.5% of the gross domestic product (GDP).

17 ECONOMY

Before World War II (1939–45), the economy was mainly agricultural. Under the communists, industry was developed rapidly and surpassed agriculture in importance. Heavy industry, particularly machine-building, was emphasized as opposed to consumer goods. During the late 1970s and 1980s, the continued emphasis on industrial expansion and consequent neglect of agriculture led to food shortages and rationing.

The transition to a market economy also has proved extremely painful. By 1993, industrial output had fallen to 47% of the 1989 level. The domestic economy shrank by 38% between 1989 and 1992 before rising 1% in 1993. Foreign debt ($10 billion), unemployment (9%), and inflation (38.8%) all contributed to a struggling economy in 1996.

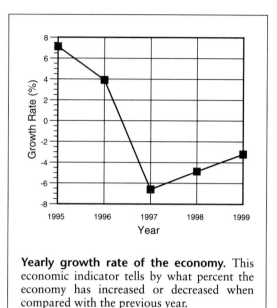

Yearly growth rate of the economy. This economic indicator tells by what percent the economy has increased or decreased when compared with the previous year.

18 INCOME

In 1998, the gross domestic product (GDP) was $90.6 billion, or about $4,050 per person. That year, the average inflation rate was 41%, resulting in a 3% decline in GDP in 1999.

19 INDUSTRY

In 1993, industrial production was at only 47% of the 1989 level. Industrial production increased during 1994–96. In 1995, it was 13% higher than in 1992. The leading industries are food and drink, metallurgy, electric power, chemicals and synthetic fibers, and machines and equipment. In 1996, industrial production increased the most in the processing and machine and electronics industries. Although industry continues to be the largest sector of the economy (51% of GDP in 1999), it is outmoded and in serious need of modernization.

Romanian industry manufactures steel, caustic soda, sulfuric acid, chemical fertilizers, automobiles, seagoing vessels, woven goods, artificial fibers, synthetic rubber, and footwear.

20 LABOR

An estimated 10.8 million people were employed in 1998, of whom 40% worked in agriculture; 21.3% were employed in industry (including mining and public utilities); 8.5% in trade, transportation, and communications; and the remainder in other sectors. Officially, unemployment was at 6.3% in 1998.

21 AGRICULTURE

Although under communism the emphasis had been on industrialization, Romania is still largely an agricultural country. Of

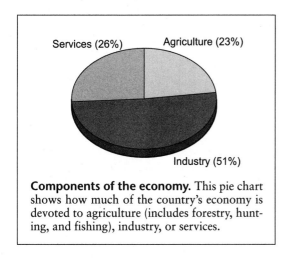

Components of the economy. This pie chart shows how much of the country's economy is devoted to agriculture (includes forestry, hunting, and fishing), industry, or services.

Pie chart labels: Services (26%), Agriculture (23%), Industry (51%)

total land area, 43% was devoted to agriculture in 1997, engaging 40% of the population and accounting for 23% of GDP in 1998. The Land Reform of 1991 returned 80% of agricultural land to private ownership. In 1996, private farms covered 44.6% of all agricultural land; associations of private producers farmed 25%; state farms operated 12.8%; and public land accounted for 17.6%.

The 1998 production totals (in thousands of tons) for major crops included wheat, 4,804; barley, 1,238; corn, 8,623; sugar beets, 2,361; and potatoes, 3,319. Romania also is an important grape producer. Grape production in 1999 was 874,000 tons.

22 DOMESTICATED ANIMALS

In 2000, Romania had 3.4 million hectares (8.4 million acres) of pastures. In 1998, there were 3.2 million head of cattle, 7 million hogs, 8.9 million sheep, and 67 million poultry.

Output of livestock products for 1998 comprised of 1.1 million tons of meat, 42,000 tons of cheese, 292,000 tons of eggs, and 9,000 tons of butter.

23 FISHING

About 80% of the fish comes from the Danube (Dunùrea) floodlands and delta and 20% from the Black Sea, with the rest from fishing operations in the Atlantic. In 1997, the total catch was 19,322 tons.

24 FORESTRY

Forests in 1999 represented 29% of the total area of Romania, and were found mainly in the Carpathian Mountains. The amount of timber to be cut is approved each year by the Romanian parliament. Roundwood production in 1998 was 14.9 million cubic meters. Most sawmills and wood products companies are only operating at 40–50% of capacity.

25 MINING

Output of coal, mainly of the lignite variety, was 36.5 million tons in 1996. In addition to fuels, Romania mines iron ore (650,000 tons in 1996), as well as copper, gold, silver, nonferrous metals, and uranium. Barite, bentonite, diatomite, feldspar, graphite, gypsum, kaolin, limestone, and other industrial minerals also were mined at about 60 deposits throughout the country.

26 FOREIGN TRADE

Exports in 1999 totaled $8.4 billion and imports $9.6 billion. The major export categories in 1998 were textiles, basic metals, minerals, and machinery and elec-

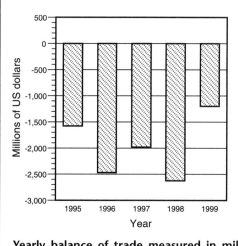

Yearly balance of trade measured in millions of US dollars. The balance of trade is the difference between what a country sells to other countries (its exports) and what it buys (its imports). If a country imports more than it exports, it has a negative balance of trade (a trade deficit). If exports exceed imports there is a positive balance of trade (a trade surplus).

tronic equipment, chemicals, and food products. About 80% of all imports are raw materials (oil, natural gas, and minerals).

Trade with the European Union countries, especially Germany, has increased greatly, mostly because of Romania's need for advanced technology and equipment. Italy, France, and the United States are other important trade partners.

27 ENERGY AND POWER

Electric power generation totaled 52.4 billion kilowatt hours in 1998. Before the 1989 revolution, there were frequent power shortages and strict energy rationing measures. Two nuclear reactors being built at Cernavoda, near Constanta, were scheduled to begin operation in 1985, but as of 1996, only one reactor was partially completed.

In 1998, oil output was only 132,000 barrels per day. Romania has had to import oil since 1979. A major fuel source is natural gas. Output fell from 37.4 billion cubic meters (1.32 trillion cubic feet) in 1987 to 15.3 billion cubic meters (540 billion cubic feet) in 1995. Reserves of natural gas were estimated at 400 billion cubic meters (14 trillion cubic feet) in 1996.

28 SOCIAL DEVELOPMENT

Social security covers all wage earners. Workers' compensation and unemployment insurance also are provided. Families with children under age 16 receive family allowances and a birth grant for each child. Legally, women have the same rights and privileges as men, although they face employment discrimination in Romania's harsh economic climate. Ethnic Hungarians are often subjected to discrimination.

29 HEALTH

In 1997, there were 1.8 doctors per 1,000 people. Through social insurance, all workers and employees, pensioners, and their dependents are covered for medical care and medicine.

The general health of the population has improved, with several previously serious diseases eliminated (recurrent fever, malaria) or greatly reduced (diphtheria, tuberculosis). In 1994, tuberculosis and measles were commonly reported. Major causes of death are communicable dis-

Selected Social Indicators

The statistics below are estimates for the period 1996 to 2000. For comparison purposes, data for the United States and averages for low-income countries and high-income countries are also given.

Indicator	Romania	Low-income countries	High-income countries	United States
Per capita gross national product (GNP)†	**$5,970**	$1,870	$25,690	$31,910
Population growth rate	**–0.2%**	2.1%	0.7%	1.1%
People per square kilometer of land	**97**	73	29	30
Life expectancy in years	**69**	59	78	77
Number of physicians per 1,000 people	**1.8**	1.0	2.5	2.5
Number of pupils per teacher (primary school)	**22**	41	17	14
Illiteracy rate (15 years and older)	**1.8%**	34%	<5%	3%
Television sets per 1,000 people	**312**	85	693	844
Energy consumed per capita (kg of oil equivalent)	**1,760**	550	5,366	7,937

† The GNP is the total dollar value of all goods and services produced by a country in a year. The per capita GNP is calculated by dividing a country's GNP by its population and adjusting for relative purchasing power. About 15% of the world's 6.1 billion people live in high-income countries, while 40% live in low-income countries.

n.a. = data not available   > = greater than   < = less than

Sources: World Bank. *World Development Indicators*. Washington, D.C.: The World Bank, 2001; Central Intelligence Agency. *The World Factbook*. Washington, D.C.: Government Printing Office, 2000.

eases, noncommunicable diseases, and injuries. Average life expectancy was 69 years in 2000.

30 HOUSING

Romanian housing suffered from the 1940 earthquake, war damage, neglect, and inadequate repair and maintenance after the war. An increase in the urban population caused by industrialization worsened the problem. Since 1987, construction of new housing units has fallen from 110,400 to 60,400 in 1989 and 28,000 in 1991. The total number of houses was 7.8 million in 1991.

31 EDUCATION

Average adult illiteracy was about 1.8% (males, 0.9% and females, 2.7%) in 2000.

Since 1968, 10 years of education has been required. Romania's educational system consists of preschool (ages 3–6), primary school (grades 1–4), gymnasium (grades 5–8), lyceum or college in two steps (each consisting of 2 years), vocational schools, higher education, and postgraduate education.

In 1997, there were 6,188 general education schools (primary schools and gymnasiums), with 1.4 million students and 71,829 teachers. The total number of secondary level students was 2.2 million with 175,958 teachers. Institutions of higher learning had 263,310 students and 26,310 instructors in the same year. There are universities in Bucharest, Brasov, Craiova, Galati, Iasi, Timisoara, and Cluj-Napoca.

32 MEDIA

There were 12 AM and 5 FM radio broadcasting stations and 130 TV stations broadcasting in 1999. For every 1,000 Romanians there were 317 radios, 312 television sets, and 9 mobile phones. There were 2.6 million telephone subscribers in 1995. In 1995 there were 76 daily newspapers with a total annual circulation of 7.5 million. The leading daily newspapers (with 1999 circulation figures) are *Adevarul* (100,000); *Romania Libera* (100,000); and *Libertatea* (150,000).

33 TOURISM AND RECREATION

The Carpathian Mountains, the Black Sea coast, and the Danube (Dunùrea) River region are being developed to attract and accommodate larger numbers of tourists. In 1997, visitor arrivals (including same day visitors) numbered 2.9 million; about 30% from the Republic of Moldova. Major tourist attractions include many old cities and towns (Brasov, Constanta, Sibiu, Sighişoara, Suceava, Timişoara, and others) and more than 120 health resorts and spas. Castle Dracula, the castle of Prince Vlad of Walachia, has been a tourist attraction since the 1970s. Popular sports are soccer, skiing, hiking, swimming, canoeing, wrestling, handball, and gymnastics. Between 1965 and 1984, Romanian athletes won 176 Olympic medals.

34 FAMOUS ROMANIANS

Perhaps the most famous historical figure in what is now Romania was Vlad (1431?–76), a prince of Walachia who resisted the Turkish invasion and was called Tepes ("the impaler") and Dracula ("son of the devil") because of his practice of impaling his enemies on stakes; he was made into a vampire by Bram Stoker in his novel *Dracula*.

The nation's greatest playwright was Ion Luca Caragiale (1852–1912). Playwright Eugène Ionesco (1912–94) settled in Paris in 1938. Romanian-born Elie Wiesel (b.1928), in the United States from 1956, is a writer on Jewish subjects, especially the Holocaust, and a winner of the Nobel Peace Prize in 1986.

Romanian-born Tristan Tzara (1896–1963), a literary and artistic critic who settled in Paris, was one of the founders of Dadaism. Sculpture was greatly advanced by Constantin Brâncusi (1876–1957). Famous musicians include violinist and composer Georges Enescu (1881–1955) and pianist Dinu Lipatti (1917–50). A prominent tennis player was Ilie Nastase (1946–94); gymnast Nadia Comaneci (b.1961) won three gold medals at the 1976 Olympics.

35 BIBLIOGRAPHY

Castellan, Georges. *A History of the Romanians.* New York: Columbia University Press, 1989.

Fischer-Galati, Stephen A. *Twentieth Century Romania.* 2d ed. New York: Columbia University Press, 1991.

Mooney, Bel. *The Voices of Silence.* New York: Delacorte Press, 1997. [fiction]

Popescu, Julian. *Romania.* Philadelphia: Chelsea House, 2000.

Romania in Pictures. Minneapolis: Lerner Publications, 1993.

Sheehan, Sean. *Romania.* New York: Marshall Cavendish, 1994.

Willis, Terrie. *Romania.* New York: Children's Press, 2000.

RUSSIA

Russian Federation

Rossiyskaya Federatsiya

CAPITAL: Moscow

FLAG: Equal horizontal bands of white (top), blue, and red.

ANTHEM: *Patriotic Song.*

MONETARY UNIT: The rouble (R) is a paper currency of 100 kopecks. There are coins of 1, 2, 3, 5, 10, 15, 20, and 50 kopecks and 1 rouble, and notes of 100, 200, 500, 1,000, 5,000, 10,000 and 50,000 roubles. R1 = $0.03731 (or $1 = R26.7996).

WEIGHTS AND MEASURES: The metric system is the legal standard.

HOLIDAYS: New Year's Day, 1–2 January; Christmas, 7 January; Women's Day, 8 March; Spring and Labor Day, 1–2 May; Victory Day, 9 May; State Sovereignty Day, 12 June; Socialist Revolution Day, 7 November.

TIME: 3 PM Moscow = noon GMT.

1 LOCATION AND SIZE

Russia is located in northeastern Europe and northern Asia. It is the largest country in the world—slightly more than 1.8 times the size of the United States, with a total area of 17,075,200 square kilometers (6,592,771 square miles). Russia's capital city, Moscow, is located in the eastern part of the country.

2 TOPOGRAPHY

The topography of Russia features a broad plain with low hills west of the Ural Mountains and vast coniferous forests and tundra in Siberia. Northernmost is the so-called arctic desert zone, which includes most of the islands of the Arctic Ocean and the seacoast of the Taymyr Peninsula (Poluostrov Taymyr).

South of the tundra is the vast forest zone, or taiga, covering half the country. Farther south is the forest-steppe zone, a narrow band bounded by the Great Russian plain and the West Siberian low country. There are uplands and mountains along the southern border region.

3 CLIMATE

Most of the country has a continental climate, with long, cold winters and brief summers. Temperatures in January range from 6°C (45°F), on the southeast shore of the Black Sea, to as low as –71°C (–96°F) in northeastern Siberia. The lowest temperatures of any of the world's inhabited regions are found in Siberia. Precipitation varies from 53 centimeters (21 inches) at Moscow to between 20 and 25 centimeters (8–10 inches) in eastern Siberia.

4 PLANTS AND ANIMALS

Vegetation ranges from an almost complete absence of plant cover in the arctic desert zone to spruce, pine, fir, and cedar and some deciduous trees in the forested areas, and oak, birch, and aspen in the forest-steppe areas.

Birds and mammals associated with the sea (sea calf, seal, and walrus) are found in the northernmost part of the country. The arctic fox, reindeer, white hare, and lemming inhabit the tundra. Wildlife in the taiga (forest zone) includes moose, Russian bear, reindeer, lynx, sable, squirrel, and among the birds, capercaillie, hazel-grouse, owl, and woodpecker. European wild boar, deer, roe deer, red deer, mink, and marten are found in the broadleaf woods.

5 ENVIRONMENT

Decades of poor management of natural resources by the Soviet government resulted in severe pollution of land, air, rivers, and seacoasts. Air pollution is especially bad in the Ural Mountains, where vast populations are exposed to hazardous emissions from metal-processing plants. About 75% of Russia's surface water is unsuitable for drinking. Lake Baikal (Ozero Baykal), the largest freshwater reservoir in the world, has been heavily polluted through agricultural and industrial development. In the mid-1990s, 17 mammal, 35 bird, and 123 plant species were listed as threatened.

Geographic Profile

Geographic Features

Size ranking: 1 of 192
Highest elevation: 5,642 meters (18,510 feet) at Mount Elbrus
Lowest elevation: –28 meters (–92 feet) at the Caspian Sea

Land Use

Arable land:	8%
Permanent crops:	0%
Permanent pastures:	4%
Forests:	46%
Other:	42%

Weather

Average annual precipitation (Moscow): 53 centimeters (21 inches)
Average temperature in January: –9.9°C (14.2°F)
Average temperature in July: 19°C (66.2°F)

6 POPULATION

The estimated population of Russia was 145 million in 2000. The population is projected at 144.3 million in 2005. The estimated population density in 1998 was nine persons per square kilometer (23 per square mile). The biggest city is Moscow, the capital, with an estimated population in 2000 of 9.3 million. That year, the population of St. Petersburg (formerly Leningrad) was 5.1 million.

7 MIGRATION

Since the breakup of the Union of Soviet Socialist Republics (USSR or Soviet Union) in 1991, Russians from other parts of the former Soviet Union have flooded the country. During 1989–95, 169,000 Russians returned from Azerbaijan and 296,000 from Kyrgyzstan. During 1991–95, 50,000 Russians returned from

LOCATION: 60°0′N; 30°0′E. **BOUNDARY LENGTHS:** Total land boundary lengths, 20,139 kilometers (12,514 miles); Azerbaijan, 284 kilometers (177 miles); Belarus, 959 kilometers (596 miles); China (southeast), 3,605 kilometers (2,240 miles); China (south), 40 kilometers (25 miles); Estonia, 290 kilometers (180.2 miles); Finland, 1,313 kilometers (816 miles); Georgia, 723 kilometers (450 miles); Kazakstan, 6,846 kilometers (4,254 miles); North Korea, 19 kilometers (12 miles); Latvia, 217 kilometers (135 miles); Lithuania, 227 kilometers (141 miles); Mongolia, 3,441 kilometers (2,138 miles); Norway, 167 kilometers (104 miles); Poland 432 kilometers (268 miles); Ukraine, 1,576 kilometers (980 miles); total coastline 37,653 kilometers (23,398 miles).

Belarus, 614,000 from Kazakstan, and 30,000 from Tajikistan. Another 400,000 have returned from Uzbekistan and 100,000 from Turkmenistan. Some 200,000 ethnic Germans have emigrated to Germany. As of mid-1996, there were still 75,000 Russians internally displaced from the 1986 nuclear accident at Chernobyl, Ukraine.

8 ETHNIC GROUPS

The most recent figures indicate 81.5% of the population was Russian. Minorities included Tatars, 3.8%; Ukrainians, 3%;

Photo credit: Susan D. Rock.

Pedestrians on St. Petersburg's busiest street, Nevsky Prospekt.

Chuvash, 1.2%; and a wide variety of other peoples.

9 LANGUAGES

Russian is a member of the eastern group of Slavic languages. It is highly inflected, with nouns, pronouns, and adjectives having six grammatical cases. The language has been written in the Cyrillic alphabet of 33 letters since about AD 1000. A variety of other Slavic, Finno–Ugric, Turkic, Mongol, Tungus, and Paleo–Asiatic languages also are spoken.

10 RELIGIONS

Russians are mostly Russian Orthodox, followed by Protestant and Roman Catholic, Jewish, and Muslim. Since the breakup of the former Soviet Union, thousands of churches have been reopened; freedom of religion was incorporated into the draft constitution of 1993.

11 TRANSPORTATION

Russia's transportation system is extensive, but much has fallen into disrepair.

Railroads have long been an important means of transportation in Russia. Railways in 1997 extended some 150,000 kilometers (93,210 miles). There were 948,000 kilometers (589,087 miles) of highways in 1995. Compared with other developed countries, Russia has few passenger cars on the road. Russia's ratio of population per car is four times that of Europe.

Marine transport has been important to Russia ever since the construction of St. Petersburg. Other important maritime ports include Novorossiysk, on the Black Sea; and Vladivostok and Nakhodka, both on the Sea of Japan. Major inland ports include Nizhniy Novgorod, Krasnoyarsk, Samara, Moscow, Rostov, and Volgograd. The merchant fleet consisted in 1998 of 617 ships. Almost three-fifths of the merchant fleet consists of cargo vessels.

12 HISTORY

The history of Russia is usually dated from the ninth century AD when a loose federation of the eastern Slavic tribes was achieved under the legendary Rurik, with its center at Kiev. By the eleventh century, it had united all the eastern Slavs. However, over the next two centuries, its dominance was eroded by other Slavic and non-Slavic groups.

Russia Under the Tsars

The Mongol conquest of Russia marked the fall of Kiev as a center of power. When Mongol power declined in the fourteenth and fifteenth centuries, it was Moscow that emerged as the new Russian capital. In 1547, Grand Duke Ivan IV was crowned as the first "Tsar (ruler) of All the Russias."

In 1618, the first of the Romanovs was crowned tsar. In the seventeenth century, Russia expanded across Siberia to the Pacific Ocean. Under Peter I (r.1682–1725), its power was extended to the Bal-

tic Sea, and the Russian capital was moved from Moscow to St. Petersburg. The Russians expanded their territory farther into Europe and Asia during the eighteenth century.

The French Emperor, Napoleon, attacked Russia in 1812. Despite significant advances, he was forced to withdraw from Russia and retreat across Europe in 1814. By the end of the Napoleonic wars in 1815, Russia had acquired Bessarabia (Moldova), Finland, and eastern Poland. In the nineteenth century, Russia completed its conquest of the Caucasus, Central Asia, and what became its Maritime Province (Vladivostok).

Alexander II (r.1855–81) emancipated (freed) the serfs (farm workers bound to a landowner) of Russia in 1861. He appeared to be embarking on a course of political reform involving elections when he was assassinated in 1881. His son, Alexander III (r.1881–94) ended political reform efforts and returned to absolute rule.

By the reign of the last tsar, Nicholas II (r.1894–1917), many had begun to oppose the powerful ruling tsars. A socialist revolutionary movement began in 1905. The Tsarist regime was weak from its defeat in the 1905 Russo-Japanese War. Revolutionary "soviets," or councils, seized power in parts of St. Petersburg and Moscow.

The government was able to appease (calm) the rebels by promising to form an elected Duma (parliament). Four Dumas were convened between 1906 and 1917. While the Third Duma made some

Photo credit: Susan D. Rock.

Lining up for snacks at a kiosk in a St. Petersburg park.

progress in economic and social reform, the tsar and his ministers kept firm control over the government.

It was Russia's disastrous involvement in World War I (1914–18) that led to the end of the monarchy. In response to a number of defeats by German forces and continued dictatorship by the tsar, riots broke out in the major cities in March 1917. The tsar attempted to dissolve the Fourth Duma but failed. "Soviets" again rose up in Petrograd (formerly St. Petersburg) and Moscow. Nicholas II was forced to abdicate (give up his ruling power) on 15 March 1917.

The Russian Bolshevik Revolution

A temporary government, based on the old Fourth Duma, was declared, but its authority was challenged. On the night of 6 November 1917, the Bolsheviks (extreme socialists), led by Vladimir Lenin, seized control of St. Petersburg. When the newly elected Constituent Assembly convened on 18 January 1918, it was prevented from meeting by Bolshevik forces. Lenin and the socialists took over the government.

After taking power, Lenin moved quickly to end Russia's involvement in World War I, signing a peace treaty in March 1918, and the Bolsheviks moved the capital back to Moscow. From 1918 to 1921, they fought a civil war against a large number of opponents, whom they defeated. Except for Finland, Poland, the Baltic states, and Bessarabia (Moldova), Lenin's forces succeeded in regaining the territories they had given up in the treaty of 1918.

The Bolshevik regime was based on a Marxist-Leninist ideology. They sought to overthrow the rule of the aristocracy (ruling class) and the bourgeoisie (middle class) in favor of the proletariat (working class). Theoretically, power in the Communist Party (the Bolshevik's political group) was vested in an elected party congress and smaller elected groups. In truth, the top party leadership—Lenin and his colleagues—maintained dictatorial control.

The Stalin Era and World War II

After Lenin died on 21 January 1924, a power struggle among the top communist leaders broke out. By 1928, Joseph Stalin had eliminated all his rivals and achieved full power. He ushered in a brutal period of political repression and forced industrialization and organization of agriculture into communes. Stalin's rule was especially harsh in the republics other than Russia. Scholars estimate that as many as 20 million Soviet citizens died during the 1928–38 period because of either famine or persecution by the state.

In August 1939, as World War II (1939–45) approached, the Soviets signed an agreement with Adolph Hitler's Nazis in Germany that divided Eastern Europe between them. But on 22 June 1941, Hitler's forces invaded the Soviet Union, advancing until they reached the outskirts of Moscow. With the help of massive arms shipments from the United States and other western European countries, Soviet forces were able to drive the Germans back.

By the end of World War II in May 1945, the Soviet Union had reconquered everything it lost to Germany in their 1939 pact. The Red Army (Communist Army) was in Eastern Europe. Stalin was able to establish satellite communist regimes in Poland, Czechoslovakia, Hungary, Romania, Bulgaria, and East Germany.

Khrushchev and the Cold War

Stalin died in 1953 and the power struggle to succeed him was eventually won by Nikita Khrushchev. Khrushchev ended the terror of the Stalin years. During Khrushchev's era, the "Cold War" (tension between countries involving diplomatic tactics, but no military force) with the United States intensified.

The Soviet Union launched an unmanned satellite before the United States had done so. This action encouraged a competitive "Space Race" between the two countries, which drew public attention and government spending through the 1960s. However, basic features of Stalin's system (Communist Party monopoly on power; centralized economy allowing for little private initiative; limited opportunities for free expression) remained until Mikhail Gorbachev came to power in March 1985.

The Breakup of the Soviet Union

Gorbachev sought to reform the communist system. However, he was unwilling to implement changes that would weaken Communist Party control. The intense division within the government on how to solve the problems faced by them led ultimately to the breakup of the nation into its separate republics in 1991.

For the first time since 1917, free multiparty elections were held in Russia in March 1990. On 12 June 1991, the first elections to the Russian presidency were won by Boris Yeltsin. On 8 December 1991, Yeltsin, together with the leaders of Ukraine and Belarus, formed the nucleus of the Commonwealth of Independent States (CIS). This spelled the end of the Union of Soviet Socialist Republics (USSR) later that month. Like the other former Soviet republics, Russia became an independent sovereign state.

barricaded themselves inside the parliament building, a state of emergency was declared for a brief period.

The referendum and parliamentary elections were held as planned. The electorate approved the new constitution, which called for a strong presidency. In the parliamentary elections, ten parties won seats. Both communist and nationalist forces won representation.

As Yeltsin tried to stabilize the government, nationalistic feelings grew in the republics inhabited by non-Russians. War broke out in December 1994 in Chechnya when the rebellious region in the Caucasus declared its independence. Russia's military was not able to subdue the region and withdrew. The bloody and unpopular conflict led Yeltsin to sign a peace treaty with Chechen leader Aslan Maskhadov in May 1997. The treaty agreed to wait five years for a final decision on Chechnya's status.

In a show of power on 23 March 1998, President Yeltsin dismissed the entire cabinet, including Prime Minister Chernomyrdin. Several ministers retained their positions, and Yeltsin's new picks consisted largely of young reformists not associated with Moscow's politics, such as Sergei Kiriyenko, who became the new prime minister. The Russian economy continued to sink, however, as did Yeltsin's authority. In August Yeltsin sought to reappoint Chernomyrdin as prime minister, but the legislature rejected the nomination.

In mid-1998 the International Monetary Fund agreed to loan Russia $11.2 billion. Despite the promised bailout, the

Photo credit: Susan D. Rock.

Jazz musicians perform near Red Square, Moscow.

In early 1992, Yeltsin sought to reform the economy, but prices rose rapidly and public opposition to his reforms grew. Much of Russian politics in 1993 consisted of bitter squabbling between Yeltsin and the legislature. No progress was made on drafting a new constitution to replace the much amended Soviet-era constitution that still governed Russia.

On 21 September 1993, Yeltsin dissolved the Supreme Soviet and introduced rule by presidential decree until new parliamentary elections and a referendum on his draft constitution could be held on 12 December. After anti-Yeltsin legislators

Photo credit: EPD/Office of the President.

Name:	Vladimir Putin
Position:	President of a federation
Took office:	7 May 2000
Birthplace:	St. Petersburg (formerly Leningrad)
Birth date:	7 October 1952
Education:	Leningrad State University, Law Department, Masters of Economics, 1975; Red Banner Intelligence School, studied spycraft and fluency in German
Spouse:	Lyudmila
Children:	Two daughters, Maria and Katerina
Of interest:	In a 1999 memoir, Putin stated that his paternal grandfather had been a cook for Lenin and Stalin. He has a black belt in judo.

13 GOVERNMENT

A new constitution for Russia was approved in a referendum held 12 December 1993. The constitution established a two-chamber legislature known as the Federal Assembly. The lower house (State Duma) consists of 450 elected deputies while the 178-member upper house (Council of the Federation) is composed of representatives of the provinces and autonomous republics that make up Russia. The president is elected separately for a five-year term.

The president appoints the cabinet members and other top government posts subject to confirmation by the legislature. The president may declare war or a state of emergency on his own authority. Impeachment of the president is provided for in the constitution, but is very difficult.

The State Duma has jurisdiction over the budget and economic policy. The Council has jurisdiction over issues affecting the provinces and autonomous republics, including border changes and the use of force within the Russian Federation.

14 POLITICAL PARTIES

After elections to the State Duma held in December 1999, the Communist Party held 120 of the 450 seats; other parties gaining seats were Unity, 73; Fatherland, 70; Union, 29; Yabloko, 20; and the Zhirinovskiy bloc, 19. Nonparty affiliates won 95 seats. A little more than one-third of the deputies were incumbents from the previous Duma.

stock market plunged as interest rates soared, and Russia moved to devalue its currency.

Yeltsin resigned in 1999, under allegations of financial mismanagement and ill health. Supported by the former president, Vladimir Putin, a former officer of the KGB, was elected to the presidency.

15 JUDICIAL SYSTEM

A Constitutional Court has been established to rule on disputes between the executive and legislative branches. The Supreme Court reviews charges brought against the executive and legislative branches. The High Court of Arbitration is the highest court for matters between businesses.

16 ARMED FORCES

Although equipment numbers and force structure are impressive, Russian armed forces have declined significantly since the breakup of the Soviet Union. The active Russian armed forces may number more than 1 million. The Russian army has 348,000 soldiers, of whom perhaps 185,000 are draftees. The air force claims 184,600 airmen. The Russian navy of 171,000 retains the vast majority of the combat capability of the former Soviet navy. It remains organized in four major fleets with regional and global missions. The fleets are stationed in Arctic Russia, four Baltic bases, three Black Sea bases, and Vladivostok.

Russia remains the world's second most formidable nation, when it comes to nuclear weapons, after the United States. The Strategic Deterrent Forces (149,000) control 711 silo-based and mobile intercontinental ballistic missiles (ICBMs) with warheads, and provide ground defense forces to defend ICBM launch sites and warhead storage facilities.

In addition to troops remaining in two Commonwealth of Independent States (CIS) member nations, Russia maintains major military missions or units in Cuba, Cambodia, Syria, Mongolia, Bosnia, and Vietnam. Russian units participate in four separate peacekeeping missions, two sponsored by the United Nations. Russia has assumed the treaty responsibilities of the former Soviet Union to reduce its strategic arsenal and conventional forces in Europe.

17 ECONOMY

Russia's economic situation has deteriorated steadily since the breakup of the Soviet Union in 1991. It is undergoing a transformation from a centrally planned economy to a market-oriented one, with limited public ownership. Services accounted for 53% of the gross domestic product (GDP) in 1999, while industry contributed 39%, and agriculture, 8%. There is a serious demand for goods that is not being met, especially for consumer goods. A stabilization plan started in 1995 tightened the budget, opened up trade, and lowered inflation. The inflation rate fell from 214% in 1994 to just 3% in 1997. Unemployment is around 8%, although payment of wages and pensions are usually not made.

18 INCOME

In 1998, the gross domestic product (GDP) was $593 million, or about $4,000 per person. That year, the average inflation rate was 84%, with the average annual decline of GDP at 5%.

19 INDUSTRY

Major manufacturing industries include crude steel, cars and trucks, aircraft, chemicals (including fertilizers), plastics,

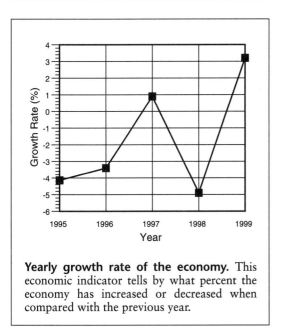

Yearly growth rate of the economy. This economic indicator tells by what percent the economy has increased or decreased when compared with the previous year.

cement and other building materials, paper, television sets, and appliances. Military production, which dominated industrial output in the former Soviet Union, is being replaced by other types of manufacturing, often consumer goods and food processing.

20 LABOR

In 1998, the nonagricultural labor force was estimated at 66.7 million. The 1995 figures for workers in sectors were: manufacturing and mining accounted for 25%; construction, 9.2%; commerce, 8.5%; transportation and communications, 7.8%; services, 27%; and other sectors, 22%. Women accounted for about 41% of the work force, but 56% of the unemployed in 1995. As reforms progress, the role of unions is expected to grow as a reaction to widespread unemployment.

21 AGRICULTURE

Russian agriculture (including pastures) covered 76% of the total land area in 1997. The 1998 harvest included (in millions of tons): potatoes, 31.3; wheat, 26.9; sugar beets, 10.8; barley, 9.8; vegetables, 12.1; oats, 4.6; sunflower seeds, 3; rye, 3.3; corn, 0.3; rice, 0.4; and soybeans, 0.3.

22 DOMESTICATED ANIMALS

Russia's pastures occupy about the same amount of land as those of all the other nations of Europe combined. As of 1999, the livestock population included: cattle, 28.6 million (including 13.5 million dairy cows); sheep, 18.2 million; and pigs, 16.4 million. Russia had 2.2 million horses, 405 million chickens, and 3 million turkeys in 1998.

The 1999 meat production included (in millions of tons): beef, 1.9; pork, 1.5; mutton, 0.15; and poultry, 0.64. In 1995, meat production dropped the most in one year since 1990. Beef and veal production now stands at 50% of the 1990s amount. Milk production in 1999 was estimated at 31.5 million tons, and egg production amounted to 32.5 billion.

23 FISHING

In 1997, Russia's fish production ranked seventh in the world. The total catch in 1997 was 4.7 million tons. The main commercial species are Alaska pollock, cod, scat, herring, salmon, and mackerel.

Overfishing and pollution of territorial waters have forced fishermen farther away from traditional fishing waters. Since 1990, there has been a shift away from

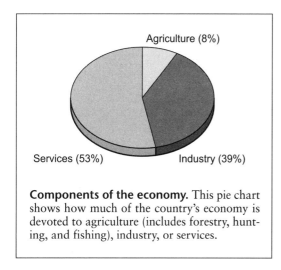

Agriculture (8%)

Services (53%)

Industry (39%)

Components of the economy. This pie chart shows how much of the country's economy is devoted to agriculture (includes forestry, hunting, and fishing), industry, or services.

processed to unprocessed fish products. As of 1996, 40% of fishing industry firms were losing money, and 60–70% of the onshore processing facilities were unused.

24 FORESTRY

Russia's forested areas are vast. In early 1995, an estimated 800 million hectares (2 billion acres) were forested—an area about as large as the total land area of Australia. The forests in Russia are 80% coniferous, consisting mainly of spruce, fir, larch, and pine in subarctic areas. Deciduous trees (oak, ash, maple, elm) grow farther south.

The timber cut in 1998 totaled 57 million cubic meters of roundwood. Production that year included, in millions of cubic meters: sawn timber, 16.5; plywood, 1.1; and particleboard, 1.47. Items made from pulp in 1996 included 2,300 tons of paper, 1,200 tons of cellulose, and 900 tons of cardboard.

25 MINING

Russia has plentiful and varied mineral resources. Mining activities are concentrated near the Arctic Circle (nickel, cobalt, phosphate, uranium, gold, tin, and mercury); in the Ural Mountains region (titanium, vanadium, nickel-cobalt, soda ash, asbestos, magnesite, vermiculite, talc, bauxite, copper, bismuth, beryllium, lead, zinc, and iron ore); and in Siberia (tungsten, molybdenum, fluorospar, mica, asbestos, diamond, talc, iron ore, gold, tin, lead, and zinc).

Iron ore production in 1996 amounted to 72.1 million tons; bauxite, 3.3 million tons; copper, 523,000 tons; nickel, 230,000 tons; and zinc, 126,000 tons. Russian gold production was estimated at 123,000 kilograms that year.

26 FOREIGN TRADE

Principal exports have traditionally been oil, gas, minerals, military equipment and weapons, gold, shipping, and transport services. Principal imports include machinery and equipment, consumer goods, medicines, meat, grain, sugar, and semifinished metal products. Exports in 1999 totaled $75.4 billion, while imports amounted to $48.2 billion. Ukraine, Germany, the United States, Belarus, and the Netherlands were the leading export markets in 1998. Ukraine, Germany, Kazakstan, the United States, and Italy were the leading import providers that year.

27 ENERGY AND POWER

Russia possesses enormous reserves of oil, natural gas, and coal. Oil production was

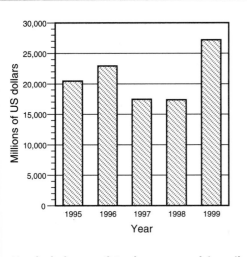

Yearly balance of trade measured in millions of US dollars. The balance of trade is the difference between what a country sells to other countries (its exports) and what it buys (its imports). If a country imports more than it exports, it has a negative balance of trade (a trade deficit). If exports exceed imports, there is a positive balance of trade (a trade surplus).

306.8 million tons in 1995 (about 6.2 million barrels per day), when Russia ranked third in total oil production (after Sa'udi Arabia and the United States). At the start of 2000, Russia had some 6.7 billion tons (or 4.8% of the world's) proven oil reserves.

In 1998, Russia produced 591.7 billion cubic meters of natural gas. Proven reserves at the start of 2000 totaled 48.1 trillion cubic meters (1,700 trillion cubic feet), or 34.5% of the world's total reserves.

Coal production in 1996 was estimated at 290 million tons. In 1995, natural gas contributed 51% to Russia's primary energy consumption; oil, 23.4%; coal, 19.1%; nuclear energy, 4.1%; and hydroelectric power, 2.4%.

28 SOCIAL DEVELOPMENT

The Russian Republic had enacted its own pension legislation in November 1990, before the collapse of the Soviet Union. While it followed the Soviet Union model in many respects, it linked pensions to a "minimum subsistence" figure instead of to the minimum wage. However, rapid price increases in 1992 pressured the Yeltsin government into once again tying pensions to the minimum wage.

Social security legislation was updated in 1992 and 1993 to provide medical care for all residents. Pensions also are provided for all employed and self-employed persons, and for independent farmers.

The constitution prohibits discrimination based on race, sex, religion, language, and social status. Despite the provisions, there is employment discrimination against minorities and women.

29 HEALTH

There were 3.8 physicians per 1,000 people in 2000, and 11.7 hospital beds. Average life expectancy was 66 years in 2000.

30 HOUSING

In the early 1990s, 50% of all privately owned urban housing had running water, 36% had central heating, 35% had sewer lines, and 17.2% had hot water. In 1990, Russia had 16.4 square meters of housing space per capita.

Selected Social Indicators

The statistics below are estimates for the period 1996 to 2000. For comparison purposes, data for the United States and averages for low-income countries and high-income countries are also given.

Indicator	**Russia**	Low-income countries	High-income countries	United States
Per capita gross national product (GNP)†	**$6,990**	$1,870	$25,690	$31,910
Population growth rate	**–0.3%**	2.1%	0.7%	1.1%
People per square kilometer of land	**9**	73	29	30
Life expectancy in years	**66**	59	78	77
Number of physicians per 1,000 people	**3.8**	1.0	2.5	2.5
Number of pupils per teacher (primary school)	**20**	41	17	14
Illiteracy rate (15 years and older)	**0.6%**	34%	<5%	3%
Television sets per 1,000 people	**421**	85	693	844
Energy consumed per capita (kg of oil equivalent)	**3,963**	550	5,366	7,937

† The GNP is the total dollar value of all goods and services produced by a country in a year. The per capita GNP is calculated by dividing a country's GNP by its population and adjusting for relative purchasing power. About 15% of the world's 6.1 billion people live in high-income countries, while 40% live in low-income countries.

n.a. = data not available   > = greater than   < = less than

Sources: World Bank. *World Development Indicators.* Washington, D.C.: The World Bank, 2001; Central Intelligence Agency. *The World Factbook.* Washington, D.C.: Government Printing Office, 2000.

31 EDUCATION

The 2000 adult illiteracy rate is estimated at about 0.6%. Education, mostly state-funded, also is compulsory for 10 years. In 1995, there were 66,235 primary schools and 7.8 million students, while secondary schools had 13.7 million students. The state provides a stipend for higher education. There were 4.5 million university students in 1995, 56% of them female.

32 MEDIA

Broadcasting is overseen by All-Russian State Television and Radio (Ostankino). In 1999 there were more than 1,000 radio stations and about 11,000 television sta-tions. Russia has about 24 million telephone lines.

In 1995 there were 339 daily newspapers with a total circulation of almost 57.4 million. In 1999, Russia's major newspapers, all published in Moscow, were (with circulation figures): *Trud* (1.5 million); *Krasnaya Zvezda* (100,600); *Moskovski Komsomolyets* (1.05 million); and *Rossiiskaya Gazeta* (531,200).

33 TOURISM AND RECREATION

In September 1992, Russia lifted its travel restrictions on foreigners, opening the entire country to visitors and tourists. In 1997, there were 17.4 million visitors, more than 80% from Europe; receipts

Photo credit: International Labour Office.

Russian kindergarten children go for a walk with their teacher.

totaled $6.9 billion. Tourist attractions in Moscow include the Kremlin, monasteries and churches, museums, and other cultural attractions, including opera and ballet at the world-famous Bolshoi Theater. Nearby tourist destinations include St. Petersburg (formerly Leningrad) and Kiev.

34 FAMOUS RUSSIANS

Notable among the rulers of prerevolutionary Russia were Ivan III (the Great, 1440–1505), who established Moscow as a sovereign state; Peter I (the Great, 1672–1725), a key figure in the modernization of Russia; and Alexander II (1818–81), a social reformer who freed the serfs. The founder of the Soviet state was Lenin (Vladimir Illyich Ulyanov, 1870–1924). Mikhail Gorbachev (b.1931) was the Soviet Union's leader from 1985 until its breakup in 1991. Boris Yeltsin (b.1931) had been the president of the Russian Federation until his resignation in 1999.

Russia's greatest poet Aleksandr Pushkin (1799–1837) also was a brilliant writer of prose. Ivan Turgenev (1818–83) is noted for his sketches, short stories, and the novel *Fathers and Sons*. Fyodor Dostoyevsky (1821–81) wrote outstanding psychological novels (*Crime and Punishment*, *The Brothers Karamazov*). Leo (Lev) Tolstoy (1828–1910), perhaps the greatest Russian novelist (*War and Peace*, *Anna Karenina*), also wrote plays, essays, and short stories. The playwright and short-story writer Anton Chekhov (1860–1904) was the greatest Russian writer of the late 19th century. The novels, stories, and plays of Maxim Gorky (Aleksey Peshkov, 1868–1936) bridged the tsarist and Soviet periods.

Great Russian composers include Modest Mussorgsky (1839–81), Pyotr Ilyich Tchaikovsky (1840–93), Nikolay Rimsky-Korsakov (1844–1908), Sergei Rachmaninov (1873–1943), Igor Stravinsky (1882–1971), Sergei Prokofiev (1891–1953), and Dmitry Shostakovich (1906–75).

Outstanding figures in the ballet are the impresario Sergey Diaghilev (1872–1929) and the ballet dancers Vaslav Nijinsky (1890–1950) and Anna Pavlova (1881–1931). Famous figures in the theater include Konstantin Stanislavsky (Alekseyev, 1863–1938), director and actor. The most famous film director is Sergey Eisenstein (1898–1948).

Varfolomey (Bartolomeo Francesco) Rastrelli (1700–71) designed many of the most beautiful buildings in St. Petersburg. Modern Russian artists whose work is internationally important include the Suprematist painters Kasimir Malevich (1878–1935) and El (Lazar) Lissitzky (1890–1941). Famous Russian-born artists who left their native country to work abroad include the painters Vasily Kandinsky (1866–1944) and Marc Chagall (1897–1985).

Prominent Russian scientists of the 19th and 20th centuries included the chemist Dmitry Ivanovich Mendeleyev (1834–1907), inventor of the periodic table; Ivan Petrovich Pavlov (1849–1936), expert on the human and animal nervous systems, who received the Nobel Prize in 1904; and Konstantin Eduardovich Tsiolkovsky (1857–1935), scientist and inventor in the fields of rocket engines, interplanetary travel, and aerodynamics.

35 BIBLIOGRAPHY

Belt, Don. "The World's Great Lake." *National Geographic,* June 1992, 2–39.

Bickman, Connie. *Russia.* Edina, Minn.: Abdo & Daughters, 1994.

Carrisn, Esther. *The Empire of the Czars.* Chicago: Children's Press, 1994.

Clark, Miles. "A Russian Voyage." *National Geographic,* June 1994, 114–138.

Conboy, Fiona. *Welcome to Russia.* Milwaukee, WI: Gareth Stevens, 2000.

Cumming, David. *Russia.* New York: Thompson Learning, 1995.

Edwards, Mike. "A Broken Empire." *National Geographic,* March 1993, 4–53.

Edwards, Mike. "Siberia: In from the Cold." *National Geographic,* March 1990, 2–39.

Gresko, Marcia S. *Russia.* Woodbridge, CT: Blackbirch Press, 2000.

Hoobler, Dorothy. *Russian Portraits.* Austin, Tex.: Raintree Steck-Vaughn, 1994.

Jacobsen, Karen. *The Russian Federation.* Chicago: Children's Press, 1994.

King, David C. *Russia.* Vero Beach, Fla.: Rourke Book Company, 1995.

Lye, Keith. *Passport to Russia.* New York: Franklin Watts, 1996.

Murrell, Kathleen Berton. *Russia.* New York: Alfred A. Knopf, 1998.

Perrin, Penelope. *Russia.* New York: Crestwood House, 1994.

Quigley, Howard B. "Saving Siberia's Tigers." *National Geographic,* July 1993, 38–47.

Schomp, Virginia. *Russia: New Freedoms, New Challenges.* Tarrytown, N.Y.: Benchmark Books, 1996.

Streissguth, Thomas. *A Ticket to Russia.* Minneapolis: CarolRhoda Books, 1997.

Torchinsky, Oleg. *Russia.* New York: Marshall Cavendish, 1994.

Yeltsin, Boris Nikolayevich. *The Struggle for Russia.* New York: Times Books, 1994.

RWANDA

Republic of Rwanda
Republika y'u Rwanda

CAPITAL: Kigali.

FLAG: The national flag is a tricolor of red, yellow, and green vertical stripes. The letter "R" in black, appears in the center of the yellow stripe.

ANTHEM: Rwanda Rwacu (Our Rwanda).

MONETARY UNIT: The Rwanda franc (RFr) is a paper currency. There are coins of 1, 5, 10, 20, and 50 francs and notes of 100, 500, 1,000, and 5,000 francs. RFr1 = $0.00286 (or $1 = RFr349.53).

WEIGHTS AND MEASURES: The metric system is the legal standard.

HOLIDAYS: New Year's Day, 1 January; Democracy Day, 28 January; Labor Day, 1 May; Independence Day, 1 July; Peace and National Unity Day, 5 July; Assumption, 15 August; Anniversary of 1961 Referendum, 25 September; Armed Forces' Day, 26 October; All Saints' Day, 1 November; Christmas, 25 December. Movable religious holidays include Easter Monday, Ascension, and Pentecost Monday.

TIME: 2 PM = noon GMT.

1 LOCATION AND SIZE

Rwanda, a landlocked country in east-central Africa, has an area of 26,340 square kilometers (10,170 square miles), slightly smaller than the state of Maryland. It has a total boundary length of 893 kilometers (555 miles). Rwanda's capital city, Kigali, is located near the center of the country.

2 TOPOGRAPHY

Rwanda lies on the great East African plateau. To the west, the land drops sharply to Lake Kivu in the Great Rift Valley; to the east, the land falls gradually across the central plateau to the swamps and lakes on the country's eastern border. The highest peak, Mt. Karisimbi at 4,507 meters (14,787 feet), is snowcapped. The Kagera River forms much of Rwanda's eastern border.

3 CLIMATE

The high altitude of Rwanda provides the country with a pleasant tropical highland climate. At Kigali, on the central plateau, the average temperature is 19°C (66°F). A long rainy season lasts from February to May and a short one from November through December. Annual rainfall averages as much as 160 centimeters (63 inches) in the west.

4 PLANTS AND ANIMALS

Rwanda is one of the most eroded and deforested countries in all of tropical Africa; there is little forest left. The most common trees are eucalyptus, acacia, and oil palm. Wildlife includes elephants, hippopotamuses, buffalo, cheetahs, lions, zebras, leopards, monkeys, gorillas, hyena,

Geographic Profile

Geographic Features

Size ranking: 144 of 192
Highest elevation: 4,507 meters (14,787 feet) at
  Mount Karisimbi
Lowest elevation: 950 meters (3,117 feet) at the Rusizi
  River

Land Use†

Arable land:	35%
Permanent crops:	13%
Permanent pastures:	18%
Forests:	22%
Other:	12%

Weather††

Average annual precipitation: 98.6 centimeters (38.8
  inches)
Average temperature in January: 30°C (86°F)
Average temperature in July: 30°C (86°F)

†*Arable land:* Land used for temporary crops, like
meadows for mowing or pasture, gardens, and greenhouses. *Permanent crops:* Land cultivated with crops
that occupy its use for long periods, such as cocoa,
coffee, rubber, fruit and nut orchards, and vineyards.
Permanent pastures: Land used permanently for forage crops. *Forests:* Land containing stands of trees.
Other: Any land not specified, including built-on
areas, roads, and barren land.

††Although the average daily temperature is 30°C
(86°F), temperatures during the day can fluctuate by
as much as 15°C (27°F). The average temperature in
Kigali is 19°C (66°F). Regional temperatures vary considerably due to altitude.

wild boar, antelope, crocodiles, partridges,
ducks, geese, quail, and snipe.

5 ENVIRONMENT

The war in Rwanda, beginning in 1990,
has damaged the environment. Soil erosion and overgrazing also are serious
problems, and the remaining forested area
has been reduced by uncontrolled cutting
for fuel. About 16% of the nation's city
dwellers and 33% of the rural people do
not have safe water.

In northeastern Rwanda the beautiful
Kagera National Park is a game reserve,
sheltering many types of wildlife. Rwanda
is one of the last existing habitats of the
mountain gorilla, which numbered 280 in
1986, up from 250 five years earlier. As of
1994, 11 of the nation's mammal species
and seven of its bird species were threatened with extinction, including the chim-
panzee, African elephant, and the black
rhinoceros.

6 POPULATION

Rwanda is the most densely populated
country on the African continent. In 2000,
the estimated population was more than
8.3 million. The population decreased
from about 7.7 million in 1993 to 6 million in 1995 because of the mass killings
and emigration of refugees during 1994.
The estimated population density in 2000
was 337 persons per square kilometer
(873 per square mile). A population of 9.1
million is projected for 2005. Kigali, the
capital and largest city, grew rapidly from
15,000 in 1969 to 286,000 in 2000.

7 MIGRATION

The Hutu and Tutsi are ethnic groups in
Rwanda. Their political quarrels have
caused numerous Tutsi to flee their homeland, and many have gone to Burundi.

Renewed violence in 1994 spawned a
new exodus from Rwanda. About half of
Rwanda's population fled their homes. As
many as 2.4 million refugees fled the
country, many to Zaire (now called the
Democratic Republic of the Congo—
DROC). In 1996, violence in Burundi
caused 100,000 Rwandans to return.

After the 1996 civil war in the DROC, 60,000 Rwandans returned from that country. That same year, 500,000 Rwandan refugees returned from western Tanzania. As of September 1999, Rwanda was hosting more than 36,000 asylum-seekers, including Congolese, Burundi, Somalis, Ethiopians, and Sudanese.

8 ETHNIC GROUPS

The population is about 80% Hutu. The Hutu are a Bantu-speaking people who are traditionally farmers. The Tutsi, a warrior people, once made up about 19% of the total population, but many have fled into neighboring territories for refuge. There also are some Twa, a Pygmy tribe of hunters, as well as small numbers of Asians and Europeans.

9 LANGUAGES

The main language is Kinyarwanda, a member of the Bantu language family. The official languages are Kinyarwanda and French.

10 RELIGIONS

In the late 1990s, an estimated 91.6% of Rwandans were Christian, and an estimated 57.2% of those were Roman Catholic. As much as one-half the population follows traditional African religion in conjunction with Christianity or Islam. Muslims made up approximately 2%, and there also were small groups of Baha'is, Hindus, and others.

11 TRANSPORTATION

In 1999, Rwanda had 12,000 kilometers (7,457 miles) of road, but only about 8%

LOCATION: 1°4' to 2°50's; 28°51' to 30°55'E. **BOUNDARY LENGTHS:** Uganda, 169 kilometers (105 miles); Tanzania, 217 kilometers (135 miles); Burundi, 290 kilometers (180 miles); Democratic Republic of the Congo (DROC), 217 kilometers (135 miles).

were paved. Most roads are impassable during the rainy season, and there are few bridges. In 1995, there were 7,868 automobiles. Rwanda has no railroads. There is ship traffic on Lake Kivu to the Democratic Republic of the Congo from Gisenyi, Kibuye, and Cyangugu. There are international airports at Kigali and at Kamembe. In 1991, Air Rwanda flew 10,100 passengers some 900,000 kilometers (559,000 miles).

Photo credit: Cynthia Bassett.
Rwanda's mountain gorillas draw tourists, but violent conflict and difficult economic conditions in Rwanda caused tourism to decline in the 1980s and 1990s.

12 HISTORY

Stone Age habitation, as far back as 35,000 years, has been reported in the region now called Rwanda. Between the seventh and tenth centuries AD, the Bantu-speaking Hutu people, who followed a settled, agricultural way of life, arrived, probably from the region of the Congo River basin. Between the fourteenth and fifteenth centuries, the Tutsis, herdsmen of Nilotic (Nile River) origin, entered from the north.

At the end of the fifteenth century, the Tutsis formed a state, and, in the sixteenth century, began a process of expansion that continued into the late nineteenth century. The ownership of land and cattle was gradually transferred from the Hutu tribes to the Tutsis, and a feudal system was created between the two peoples. The ownership of cattle was controlled by the Tutsis, who regulated their use by the Hutu. The Hutu did the farming and grew the food, but had no part in government, while the Tutsis did no manual labor.

In 1871, explorers Sir Henry Morton Stanley and David Livingstone landed at Bujumbura (now the capital of neighboring Burundi) and explored the Ruzizi River region. After the Berlin Conference of 1884–85, the German zone of influence in East Africa was extended to include Rwanda and Burundi. The mwami (Tutsi ruler) submitted to German rule without resistance in 1899. The Germans administered the territory until their defeat in World War I (1914–18). During the war the area was occupied by Belgium. After the war, the League of Nations awarded Belgium a mandate to rule the region, and in 1946, Ruanda-Urundi (present-day Rwanda and Burundi) became a United Nations trust territory.

Ethnic Conflict and Independence

Liberation movements in other African countries after World War II (1939–45) led the Hutu to demand social and political equality with the Tutsis. In November 1959, a Hutu revolution began, continuing sporadically for the next few years. Many Tutsis either were killed or fled to neighboring territories. On 27 June 1962, the United Nations General Assembly passed a resolution providing for the independent states of Rwanda and Burundi, and on 1 July, Rwanda became an independent country. In December 1963, following an unsuccessful invasion by Tutsi refugees from Burundi, a massacre of the remaining resident Tutsi population

Rwandan people gather to watch native dances.

caused the death of an estimated 12,000 Tutsis and more fled into neighboring countries.

In January 1964, the economic union that had existed between Burundi and Rwanda was terminated. This resulted in severe economic difficulties and internal unrest. The unstable political and economic situation led the Rwandan army to overthrow the government in July 1973. Major General Juvénal Habyarimana assumed the presidency. In 1975, his military regime created a one-party state under the National Revolutionary Movement for Development (MRND). A system of ethnic quotas was introduced that for-

mally limited the Tutsi minority to 14% of the positions in the workplace and in the schools.

Popular discontent grew through the 1980s. In October 1990, more than 1,000 Tutsi refugees invaded Rwanda from Uganda; government forces retaliated by massacring Tutsis. In spite of ceasefires negotiated between the government and Tutsi rebels in 1991 and 1992, tensions remained high.

On the political front, Habyarimana liberalized his government in the early 1990s. A power-sharing agreement between Hutus and Tutsis was signed in Tanzania in January 1993 but failed to end the fighting. The United Nations Security Council authorized a peacekeeping force, but unrest continued.

In 1994, a total breakdown occurred. In February, the minister of public works was assassinated. In April, a rocket downed an airplane carrying the presidents of Rwanda and Burundi. The president was a Hutu. They were returning to Kigali from regional peace talks in Tanzania. All aboard were killed. From that point on, Rwanda was lawless, as members of the Rwandan army and other bands of armed Hutus set out to murder all the Tutsis they could find. Hundreds of thousands, mostly Tutsis, were killed.

In July 1994, Tutsi rebels gained control of the government, prompting Hutus to flee to refugee camps in Tanzania, Zaire (now the Democratic Republic of the Congo), and Burundi. After 1994, the government of Zaire began to force Rwandans to return home from the refugee camps. From April 1994 to 1997, an estimated 100,000 refugees died or disappeared.

Between the end of the genocide and 1997, almost 90,000 suspected killers had been arrested in Rwanda. In February 1995, the United Nations Security Council created the International Criminal Tribunal for Rwanda in order to bring the killers to justice. By 1997, 1,946 of the accused had been indicted.

In October 1996, Rwandan military forces began fighting in neighboring Zaire in order to get rid of that country's longtime dictator, Mobutu Sese-Seko. Rwanda stepped in when it became clear that the United Nations did not have the political motivation to close down the refugee camps in Zaire. The Tutsi-based Rwandan Patriotic Front (RPF) saw the camps as little more than training bases for Hutu rebels. Rwandan officials also believed that Mobutu might even support another Hutu militia movement in Rwanda, and so they began supporting a long-time Zairian revolutionary, Laurent Désiré Kabila. Kabila's forces managed to overthrow Mobuto's government in less than eight months. In the process, refugee camps with Hutus were destroyed and thousands of Hutus were killed. In 1997, a million refugees returned to Rwanda; many were former Hutu soldiers from the defeated army.

On 24 April 1998, the Rwandan government conducted its first public executions of people convicted in local courts of crimes from the 1994 genocide. There were concerns, however, that the trials of these first 22 people had been conducted unfairly. Trials related to crimes allegedly committed during the genocide were being held through 2001.

13 GOVERNMENT

A peace accord with the Rwandan Patriotic Front (RPF) was signed on 4 August 1993. By 1994, the RPF had established control over the country, instituting a government of national unity, headed by a Hutu president. In May 1995, the Transitional National Assembly created a new constitution. After the resignation of President Pasteur Bizimunga (a Hutu) in early 2000, Paul Kigame was inaugurated as the first Tutsi president since independence from Belgium in 1962.

14 POLITICAL PARTIES

The Tutsi-based Rwandan Patriotic Front (RPF), an army once in exile, is now firmly entrenched within Rwanda.

Although elections have not been held, the Transitional National Assembly is structured as follows: RPF, 19 seats; Democratic Republican Movement (MDR), 13; Democratic and Socialist Party (PSD), 13; Liberal Party (PL), 13; Christian Democrats (PDC), 6; Rwandan Socialist Party (PDI), 2; and others, 2.

15 JUDICIAL SYSTEM

There are district courts, provincial courts, and courts of appeal. Also functioning are a constitutional court, a court of accounts, which examines public accounts, and a court of state security for treason and national security cases. As of 1996, the judicial system was functioning on a limited basis. Rwanda has sought help from the international community to rebuild the judiciary and appoint lower court officials.

16 ARMED FORCES

Rwanda's armed forces totaled between 37,000–47,000 in 2000, of which all but 7,000 personnel were in the army. The national police numbers 7,000.

17 ECONOMY

Rwanda has an agricultural economy with relatively few mineral resources. The manufacturing base is limited to a few basic

Photo credit: AP/Jean-Marc Bouju.

Name:	Paul Kagame
Position:	President of a republic
Took office:	22 April 2000
Birthplace:	Rwanda
Birth date:	1956
Education:	Makerere University
Of interest:	Kagame lived as a refugee for 30 years in western Uganda.

products. Soil erosion has limited growth in the agricultural sector. Poor markets, lack of natural resources, and difficult transportation problems all painted a discouraging picture for the economy. However, these problems are insignificant in comparison to those brought about in 1994 by the civil war.

18 INCOME

In 1998, Rwanda's gross domestic product (GDP) was $5.5 billion, or about $690 per person. Also that year, the average infla-

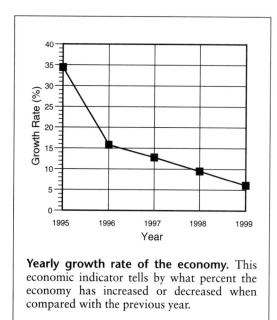

Yearly growth rate of the economy. This economic indicator tells by what percent the economy has increased or decreased when compared with the previous year.

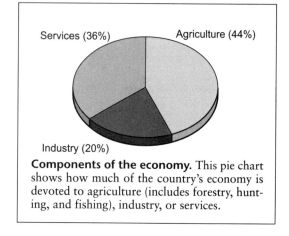

Components of the economy. This pie chart shows how much of the country's economy is devoted to agriculture (includes forestry, hunting, and fishing), industry, or services.

tion rate was 10%, resulting in an annual growth rate in GDP of 10.5%.

19 INDUSTRY

Rwanda has light industry that produces sugar, coffee, tea, flour, cigars, beer, wine, soft drinks, metal products, and assembled radios. There also are textile mills, soap factories, auto repair shops, a match factory, a pyrethrum (insecticide) refinery, and plants for producing paint, pharmaceuticals, and furniture. Industrial production includes soap, cement, radios, cigarettes, beer, soft drinks, and plastic shoes. Manufacturing contributed 10% to the average annual growth rate in 1998.

20 LABOR

According to official 1998 estimates, about 4 million people were economically active; 90% of workers were engaged in

agriculture, forestry, hunting, and fishing; and about 7% in the modern (wage) sector. The government is the largest single employer of wage laborers. About 75% of the small industrial work force is unionized as of 1999.

21 AGRICULTURE

In 1998, about 1.1 million hectares (2.8 million acres) were under cultivation. In the same year, the principal food crops (in tons) were plantains, 2.2 million; sweet potatoes, 1 million; cassava, 250,000; potatoes, 135,000; dry beans, 120,000; and sorghum, 130,000. The corn crop came to 78,000 tons and the sugarcane crop to 10,000 tons. Coffee is the chief export crop; in 1998, 13,000 tons were produced. Tea production came to about 10,000 tons in 1998. Coffee and tea together generally contribute 80% to export earnings.

22 DOMESTICATED ANIMALS

Most farmers also raise livestock. In 1998 there were 560,000 head of cattle,

Friendly Rwandan children pour out of their homes to greet the photographer.

980,000 goats, 270,000 sheep, and 80,000 pigs. There were an estimated one million chickens. Beekeeping is another important activity, with 15 tons of honey produced in 1995. About 30,000 cattle were slaughtered in 1998, providing 14,000 tons of meat.

23 FISHING

Fishing in the lakes and rivers is principally for local consumption. In 1997, Rwanda produced an estimated catch of 3,143 tons.

24 FORESTRY

In 1997, woodlands and forests covered an estimated 250,000 hectares (618,000 acres). Roundwood removals came to an estimated 5.7 million cubic meters in 1997, 95% for fuel.

25 MINING

Before the massacres of 1994, mineral commodities typically provided 10% of export earnings. In 1996, estimated mineral production included 200 tons of cassiterite (tin ore), 40 tons of tungsten ore, 10,000 tons of cement, and 100,000 kilograms of columbite and tantalite. Gold mine output was 25 kilograms (55 pounds).

26 FOREIGN TRADE

The major exports are coffee and tea, which together provide 74% of export revenue. Imports consist chiefly of food and clothing, manufactured goods, transportation equipment, machinery and tools, and petroleum products. During 1990–95, exports declined by an average of 19.9% each year, while imports grew 0.6% in value at that time. In 1996, Brazil took 45.5% of Rwanda's exports, followed at 16% by Germany.

27 ENERGY AND POWER

Rwanda imports all of its petroleum products from Kenya. Petroleum imports included, in 1994, average daily imports of 1,880 barrels of distillates, 750 barrels of gasoline, 300 barrels of jet fuel, and 190 barrels of kerosene.

Rwanda has an estimated 60 billion cubic meters (2.1 trillion cubic feet) of natural gas reserves and 6 billion cubic meters (212 billion cubic feet) of peat reserves, which could also be used as a domestic energy resource. Rwanda's electrical energy derives chiefly from hydroelectric sources. Electricity production in 1998 totaled 159 million kilowatt hours.

28 SOCIAL DEVELOPMENT

Old age pensions for workers, family allowances, and payments for those injured on the job are provided for all wage earners. In 1994, there was a total breakdown of all governmental services throughout the country.

There are government- and missionary-sponsored mutual aid societies, which increasingly supply the many social services once provided by the clan and family under Rwanda's traditional social structure.

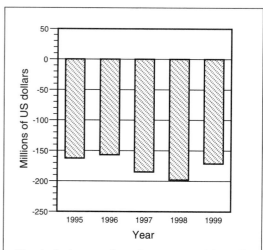

Yearly balance of trade measured in millions of US dollars. The balance of trade is the difference between what a country sells to other countries (its exports) and what it buys (its imports). If a country imports more than it exports, it has a negative balance of trade (a trade deficit). If exports exceed imports there is a positive balance of trade (a trade surplus).

29 HEALTH

In 1995, some 500,000–800,000 Rwandan refugees fled to neighboring Zaire (now the Democratic Republic of the Congo). Almost 50,000 died during the first month of the influx. In peaceful times, malnutrition is the greatest health problem in Rwanda. Kwashiorkor, a protein-calorie deficiency, is common and is increasing the severity of other prevalent diseases, among them pneumonia, tuberculosis, measles, whooping cough, and dysentery. In 1994, an estimated 7.2% of the adult population was infected with HIV (the virus that causes AIDS). There were 10,706 new AIDS cases reported in 1996. The average life expectancy was 40 years in 1999.

Selected Social Indicators

The statistics below are estimates for the period 1996 to 2000. For comparison purposes, data for the United States and averages for low-income countries and high-income countries are also given.

Indicator	Rwanda	Low-income countries	High-income countries	United States
Per capita gross national product (GNP)†	$880	$1,870	$25,690	$31,910
Population growth rate	7.9%	2.1%	0.7%	1.1%
People per square kilometer of land	337	73	29	30
Life expectancy in years	40	59	78	77
Number of physicians per 1,000 people	<0.1	1.0	2.5	2.5
Number of pupils per teacher (primary school)	n.a.	41	17	14
Illiteracy rate (15 years and older)	33%	34%	<5%	3%
Television sets per 1,000 people	0	85	693	844
Energy consumed per capita (kg of oil equivalent)	33	550	5,366	7,937

† The GNP is the total dollar value of all goods and services produced by a country in a year. The per capita GNP is calculated by dividing a country's GNP by its population and adjusting for relative purchasing power. About 15% of the world's 6.1 billion people live in high-income countries, while 40% live in low-income countries.

n.a. = data not available   > = greater than   < = less than

Sources: World Bank. World Development Indicators. Washington, D.C.: The World Bank, 2001; Central Intelligence Agency. The World Factbook. Washington, D.C.: Government Printing Office, 2000.

In 1990–97, there were 1.7 hospital beds per 1,000 inhabitants, and less than one doctor per 1,000 people. In 1993, 80% of the population had access to health care services.

30 HOUSING

The basic type of housing in the rural areas is made of mud bricks and poles, and covered with thatch. These residences are dispersed in the collines, or family farms.

31 EDUCATION

In 2000, adult illiteracy was estimated at 33% (males, 26.3%; females, 39.4%). Education is free and compulsory for all children aged 7 to 13, but the law is not widely enforced. In 1991 (the latest figures available), there were 1,710 primary schools, with 18,937 teachers and 1.1 million pupils attending. In that same year there were 94,586 pupils in secondary schools. The National University of Rwanda is located at Butare. Other known institutions are the African and Mauritian Institute of Statistics and Applied Economics in Kigali. In 1989, all higher level institutions had 3,389 pupils and 646 teaching staff.

32 MEDIA

Telephone service is limited to Kigali and a few other important centers; there were 12,593 telephones in 1991. The government-operated Radio of the Rwandan

Republic broadcasts in French, Swahili, and Kinyarwanda. In 1997 there were 102 radios per 1,000 population. There are 2 television stations in Rwanda. A French-language daily press bulletin provides news of government activities.

33 TOURISM AND RECREATION

Tourism declined in the 1990s due to war and economic factors. Tourists are drawn by Rwanda's mountain gorillas, wild game preserve, and by hiking opportunities in the Volcano National Park.

34 FAMOUS RWANDANS

Kigeri IV Rwabugiri (d.1895) was a famous ruler of precolonial Rwanda. Grégoire Kayibanda (1924–76) was the first president of independent Rwanda. Juvénal Habyarimana (1937–94) first became president in July 1973.

35 BIBLIOGRAPHY

Bodnarchuk, Kari. *Rwanda: Country Torn Apart.* Minneapolis: Lerner Publications, 2000.

Handloff, R. *Rwanda: A Country Study.* Washington, D.C.: U.S. Government Printing Office, 1990.

Pomeray, J. K. *Rwanda.* Philadelphia: Chelsea House, 2000.

Prunier, G. *The Rwanda Crisis: History of a Genocide.* New York: Columbia University Press, 1995.

Taylor, C. *Milk, Honey, and Money.* Washington, D.C.: Smithsonian Institution Press, 1992.

Twagilimana, Aimable. *Hutu and Tutsi.* Heritage Library of African Peoples. New York: Rosen Publishing Group, 1998.

ST. KITTS AND NEVIS

Federation of Saint Kitts and Nevis

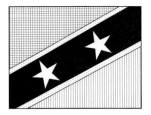

CAPITAL: Basseterre.

FLAG: Two thin diagonal yellow bands flanking a wide black diagonal band separate a green triangle at the hoist from a red triangle at the fly. On the black band are two white five-pointed stars.

ANTHEM: *National Anthem,* beginning "O land of beauty."

MONETARY UNIT: The East Caribbean dollar of 100 cents is the national currency. There are coins of 1, 2, 5, 10, and 25 cents and 1 East Caribbean dollar, and notes of 5, 10, 20, and 100 East Caribbean dollars. EC$1 = US$0.37037 (or US$1 = EC$2.70).

WEIGHTS AND MEASURES: The imperial system is used.

HOLIDAYS: New Year's Day, 1 January; Labor Day, 1st Monday in May; Bank Holiday, 1st Monday in August; Independence Day, 19 September; Prince of Wales's Birthday, 14 November; Christmas, 25 December; Boxing Day, 26 December; Carnival, 30 December. Movable religious holidays include Good Friday and Whitmonday.

TIME: 8 AM = noon GMT.

1 LOCATION AND SIZE

St. Kitts is situated in the Leeward Islands. It has a total area of 269 square kilometers (104 square miles), slightly more than 1.5 times the size of Washington, D.C. Nevis lies southeast of St. Kitts, across a channel called The Narrows; it has a land area of 93 square kilometers (36 square miles). The capital city, Basseterre, is located on St. Kitts.

2 TOPOGRAPHY

St. Kitts and Nevis are of volcanic origin. In the northwest of St. Kitts is Mount Liamuiga (Mount Misery), the island's highest peak at 1,156 meters (3,792 feet). Nevis's highest elevation is the central peak of Mt. Nevis (Nevis Pk.), at 985 meters (3,231 feet); it is usually cloud-capped. There is a black sand beach on the northwest coast.

3 CLIMATE

Temperatures range from 20°C (68°F) to 29°C (84°F) all year long. Northeast tradewinds are constant. Rain usually falls between May and November, averaging 109 centimeters (43 inches) a year.

4 PLANTS AND ANIMALS

Coconut palms, poincianas, and palmettos are abundant on the upper slopes of Mt. Nevis. Lemon trees, bougainvillea, hibiscus, and tamarind are common on both islands. There are some black-faced vervet monkeys in St. Kitts.

5 ENVIRONMENT

Deforestation has affected the nation's wildlife and contributed to soil erosion. Erosion, in turn, produces silt, which is harmful to marine life on the coral reefs. The nation's water quality is threatened by uncontrolled dumping of sewage and pollution from cruise ships.

6 POPULATION

The 2000 census counted 43,441 residents, the majority living on St. Kitts. Estimated population for 2005 is 47,000. The estimated population density in 2000 was 114 persons per square kilometer (295 per square mile), with the density of St. Kitts twice that of Nevis. Basseterre, the capital on St. Kitts, had an estimated population of 12,000 in 2000.

7 MIGRATION

Emigration has declined since the 1950s, largely because the economy enjoys almost full employment during the tourist and harvest seasons. During the off-season, some people migrate to other islands in search of work.

8 ETHNIC GROUPS

The population is mainly of African descent. Roughly 95% of the population is black, about 5% considered to be mulatto, 3% Indo-Pakistani, and 1.5% European.

9 LANGUAGES

English, sprinkled with local expressions, is the universal language.

Geographic Profile

Geographic Features

Size ranking: 185 of 192
Highest elevation: 1,156 meters (3,792 feet) at Mount Liamuiga (Mount Misery)
Lowest elevation: Sea level at the Caribbean Sea

Land Use

Arable land:	22%
Permanent crops:	17%
Permanent pastures:	3%
Forests:	17%
Other:	41%

Weather

Average annual precipitation: 109 centimeters (43 inches)
Average temperature range in January: 20–29°C (68–84°F)
Average temperature range in July: 20–29°C (68–84°F)

---

10 RELIGIONS

The Anglican Church, the largest church on the island, claims more than a third of the population. Other principal religious groups are the Church of God, the Methodist Church (33% in 1985), the Moravians, the Baptists, the Seventh-day Adventists, the Pilgrim Holiness Church, and the Roman Catholic Church (10.7% in 1985).

11 TRANSPORTATION

A light, narrow-gauge railway of 58 kilometers (36 miles) on St. Kitts is operated by the government to transport sugarcane from fields to factory, and processed sugar to coast for export. In 1998 there were 320 kilometers (199 miles) of roads on the island; the main roads circle each island. Basseterre is the principal port. A state-run motorboat service is maintained between

St. Kitts and Nevis. Golden Rock International Airport serves Basseterre; several small airlines fly to a landing strip at Newcastle, on Nevis.

12 HISTORY

Arawak Indians, followed by Caribs, were the earliest known inhabitants of the islands. Discovered by Columbus in 1493 and named St. Christopher, St. Kitts was the first of the British West Indies to be settled. Sir Thomas Warner established a settlement on St. Kitts in 1623 and led a colonial expedition to Nevis in 1628.

By the 1660s there were some 4,000 Europeans engaged in the sugar trade, based on a plantation system with slaves imported from Africa. The French gained control of the island and held it until it was retaken by the British in 1713. After another French takeover in 1782, the Treaty of Versailles (1783) again returned St. Kitts to Britain. By the late eighteenth century, the thermal baths on Nevis were attracting thousands of international tourists. Although the slaves were emancipated in 1834, many continued to work on the sugar plantations, so the sugar-based economy did not decline as rapidly as elsewhere in the West Indies.

St. Kitts, Nevis, and Anguilla (the most northerly island of the Leeward chain) were incorporated with the British Virgin Islands into a single colony in 1816. The territorial unit of St. Kitts-Nevis-Anguilla became part of the Leeward Islands Federation in 1871 and belonged to the Federation of the West Indies from 1958 to 1962. In 1967, the three islands became an associated state with full internal autonomy

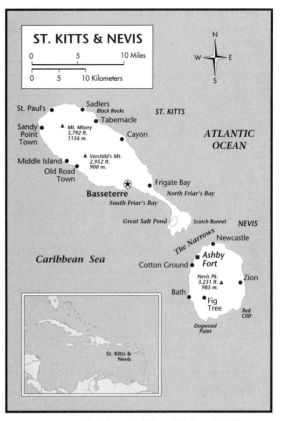

LOCATION: 17°10′ to 17°20′N; 62°24′ to 62°45′W.
TOTAL COASTLINE: 135 kilometers (84 miles).
TERRITORIAL SEA LIMIT: 12 miles.

under a new constitution. After the Anguilla islanders rebelled in 1969, British paratroopers intervened, and Anguilla was allowed to secede in 1971.

St. Kitts and Nevis became an independent federated state within the Commonwealth on 19 September 1983. Under the arrangement, Nevis was given its own legislature and the power to secede from the federation. The People's Action Movement/Nevis Reformation Party coalition won a majority of seats in the 1984 and 1989 elections, but lost to the Labour

Party in 1993. Douglas Denzil was elected prime minister in the 1995 and 2000 elections.

Beginning in June 1996, officials on Nevis announced plans to secede from the federation. On 11 August 1998, the independence referendum for Nevis received only 62% of the vote, short of the two-thirds majority needed.

The islands received attention from American law enforcement officials in August 1998 when drug trafficker Charles Miller (also known as Cecil Connor) threatened to kill American college students in St. Kitts and Nevis if the government handed him over to the United States.

13 GOVERNMENT

St. Kitts-Nevis is a federation of the two islands. Under the 1983 constitution, the British monarch is head of state and is represented by a governor-general, Dr. Cuthbert Montraville Sebastian (since 1996). The nation is governed under a parliamentary system, with legislative power vested in the single-chamber House of Assembly, consisting of the speaker, three appointed senators, and 11 elected members. Nevis also has its own legislative assembly and the right to secede under certain conditions. St. Kitts is divided into nine parishes and Nevis into five.

14 POLITICAL PARTIES

The four political parties holding seats in the House of Assembly are the Labour Party (also known as the Workers' League), the People's Action Movement,

Photo credit: EPD/Office of the Prime Minister.

Name:	Douglas Denzil
Position:	Prime minister of a constitutional monarchy with Westminster-style parliament
Took office:	6 July 1995
Birthplace:	St. Kitts-Nevis
Birth date:	14 January 1953
Education:	University of the West Indies, bachelors of science degrees in medicine and surgery
Of interest:	Douglas was once the president of the St. Kitts and Nevis Medical Association.

the Nevis Reformation Party, and the Concerned Citizen's Movement.

15 JUDICIAL SYSTEM

The Eastern Caribbean Supreme Court, established on St. Lucia, administers the judicial system. Magistrates' courts deal with petty criminal and civil cases.

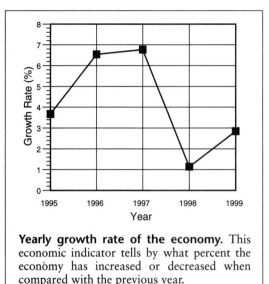

Yearly growth rate of the economy. This economic indicator tells by what percent the economy has increased or decreased when compared with the previous year.

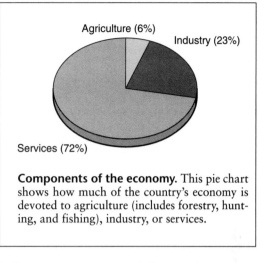

Components of the economy. This pie chart shows how much of the country's economy is devoted to agriculture (includes forestry, hunting, and fishing), industry, or services.

inflation rate was 2.9%, resulting in a growth rate in GDP of nearly 3% in 1999.

16 ARMED FORCES

Antigua and Barbuda, Dominica, Grenada, St. Kitts and Nevis, St. Lucia, and St. Vincent and the Grenadines created a Regional Security System in 1985.

17 ECONOMY

The economy is based on tourism and agriculture, particularly on sugar, which generated some 55% of export revenues in 1994. The government has been making efforts to attract foreign investment, to diversify the economy industrially, to expand tourism, and to improve local food production.

18 INCOME

In 1997, St. Kitts and Nevis's gross domestic product (GDP) was $235 million, or about $6,000 per person. The average

19 INDUSTRY

The principal manufacturing plant and largest industrial employer is the St. Kitts Sugar Manufacturing Corp., which grinds and processes sugarcane for export. St. Kitts and Nevis has transformed small electronic plants into the largest electronics assembly industry in the Eastern Caribbean. Its apparel assembly industry also has become very successful in recent years.

20 LABOR

A 1995 estimate placed the labor force at 18,172, with 69% in services and 31% in manufacturing. In 1997, the unemployment rate was 4%.

21 AGRICULTURE

The principal agricultural product of St. Kitts is sugarcane. Sugar production increased to 244,000 tons in 1998. Peanut production now ranks second. On Nevis,

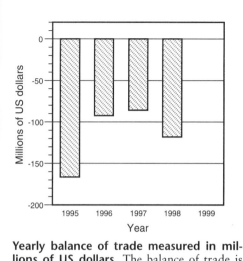

Yearly balance of trade measured in millions of US dollars. The balance of trade is the difference between what a country sells to other countries (its exports) and what it buys (its imports). If a country imports more than it exports, it has a negative balance of trade (a trade deficit). If exports exceed imports there is a positive balance of trade (a trade surplus).

sea island cotton and coconuts are the major commodities.

22 DOMESTICATED ANIMALS

Pasture areas are small, covering some 3% of the islands. Estimates of livestock in 1998 were cattle, 4,000 head; sheep, 15,000; pigs, 3,000; and goats, 11,000.

23 FISHING

Fishing is a traditional occupation that has not expanded to any great extent; the catch in 1997 was 165 tons.

24 FORESTRY

Both islands have small areas of virgin tropical forest, with palms, poincianas, and palmettos.

25 MINING

Local quarrying of some materials is used to supplement the construction industry.

26 FOREIGN TRADE

Exports of sugar, molasses, beer and ale, cotton, lobsters, machinery, food, electronics, and tobacco earned an estimated $103.5 million in 1994. Imports totaled $160 million in 1998 and included food, manufactured and consumer goods, machinery and transportation equipment, and mineral fuels. In 1998, major trade partners were the United States (69%), the Caribbean Community and Common Market (CARICOM) states (17%), the United Kingdom (11%), Canada, and Japan.

27 ENERGY AND POWER

In 1998, 85 million kilowatt hours of electricity were produced, entirely from conventional sources. St. Kitts and Nevis has no fossil fuels, and all petroleum products must be imported.

28 SOCIAL DEVELOPMENT

Effective 1978, a social security system replaced the existing fund as the provider of old age, disability, survivor, sickness, and maternity benefits. The Ministry of Women's Affairs promotes women's rights and provides counseling for abused women.

29 HEALTH

The average life expectancy was 71 years in 2000. There was less than 1 doctor available per 1,000 inhabitants in 2000.

A house by the ocean.

30 HOUSING

The Housing Authority began a program of low-cost home construction in 1977. In 1996, the National Housing Corporation and the Social Security Board signed a $30.6 million loan for the construction of new housing.

31 EDUCATION

The literacy rate is about 97%. Education is free and compulsory for 12 years. In 1998, there were a total of 21,946 students enrolled at 68 primary and secondary-level schools. At the post-secondary level, there were 51 teachers and 394 students enrolled in 1993.

32 MEDIA

In 1997 there were some 575 radios and 257 television sets per 1,000 population. There are two newspapers: the *Labour Spokesman,* published twice weekly with a 1999 circulation of 6,000; and the *Democrat*, a weekly with a 1999 circulation of 3,500.

33 TOURISM AND RECREATION

The chief historic attraction on St. Kitts is Brimstone Hill fortress, which towers 230

Selected Social Indicators

The statistics below are estimates for the period 1996 to 2000. For comparison purposes, data for the United States and averages for low-income countries and high-income countries are also given.

Indicator	St. Kitts and Nevis	Low-income countries	High-income countries	United States
Per capita gross national product (GNP)†	**$10,400**	$1,870	$25,690	$31,910
Population growth rate	**–0.2%**	2.1%	0.7%	1.1%
People per square kilometer of land	**114**	73	29	30
Life expectancy in years	**71**	59	78	77
Number of physicians per 1,000 people	**<0.5**	1.0	2.5	2.5
Number of pupils per teacher (primary school)	**n.a.**	41	17	14
Illiteracy rate (15 years and older)	**3%**	34%	<5%	3%
Television sets per 1,000 people	**257**	85	693	844
Energy consumed per capita (kg of oil equivalent)	**512**	550	5,366	7,937

† The GNP is the total dollar value of all goods and services produced by a country in a year. The per capita GNP is calculated by dividing a country's GNP by its population and adjusting for relative purchasing power. About 15% of the world's 6.1 billion people live in high-income countries, while 40% live in low-income countries.

n.a. = data not available   > = greater than   < = less than

Sources: World Bank. *World Development Indicators.* Washington, D.C.: The World Bank, 2001; Central Intelligence Agency. *The World Factbook.* Washington, D.C.: Government Printing Office, 2000.

meters (750 feet) above the Caribbean. Nevis has many beaches and historic plantations. In 1997, 88,000 stayover tourists arrived on the islands with a revenue of $72 million, a majority from the Americas.

34 FAMOUS KITTSIANS AND NEVISIANS

Sir Thomas Warner (d.1649) established the first colony on each island. US statesman Alexander Hamilton (1757–1804) was born in Charlestown. Sir Joseph Nathaniel France (1907–97) had the longest political career in the English-speaking Caribbean, serving from 1946 until his retirement in 1989.

35 BIBLIOGRAPHY

Gordon, Joyce. *Nevis: Queen of the Caribees.* London: Macmillan Caribbean, 1990.

Lowenthal, David. *West Indian Societies.* London: Oxford University Press, 1972.

Morgan, Nina. *The Caribbean and the Gulf of Mexico.* Austin, Tex.: Raintree Steck-Vaughn, 1997.

Walker, Cas. *Focus on the Caribbean.* London: Evans Brothers, 1992.

Walton, Chelle Koster. *Caribbean Ways: A Cultural Guide.* Westwood, Mass.: Riverdale, 1993.

Williams, Eric Eustace. *From Columbus to Castro: The History of the Caribbean, 1492–1969.* London: Deutsch, 1970.

ST. LUCIA

CAPITAL: Castries.

FLAG: On a blue background is a yellow triangle surmounted by a black arrowhead whose outer edges are bordered in white.

ANTHEM: *Sons and Daughters of St. Lucia.*

MONETARY UNIT: The East Caribbean dollar (EC$) of 100 cents is the national currency. There are coins of 1, 2, 5, 10, and 25 cents and 1 dollar, and notes of 5, 10, 20, and 100 East Caribbean dollars. EC$1 = US$0.37037 (or US$1 = EC$2.70).

WEIGHTS AND MEASURES: The metric system has been introduced, but imperial measures are still commonly employed.

HOLIDAYS: New Year's Day, 1 January; Carnival, 8–9 February; Independence Day, 22 February; Labor Day, 1 May; Queen's Official Birthday, 5 June; Bank Holiday, 1st Monday in August; Thanksgiving Day, 1st Monday in October; St. Lucia Day, 13 December; Christmas Day, 25 December; Boxing Day, 26 December. Movable religious holidays include Good Friday, Easter Monday, Whitmonday, and Corpus Christi.

TIME: 8 AM = noon GMT.

1 LOCATION AND SIZE

The Caribbean island of St. Lucia, part of the Windward Islands group of the Lesser Antilles, has a total area of 620 square kilometers (239 square miles), slightly less than 3.5 times the size of Washington, D.C. The capital city, Castries, is located on St. Lucia's northwest coast.

2 TOPOGRAPHY

St. Lucia is a volcanic island, with a mountainous southern half and a hilly northern half. The highest mountain, Mt. Gimie, rises 950 meters (3,116 feet) above sea level. Peaks on the southern coast, including Grand Piton (Gros Piton) at 798 meters (2,618 feet) are among the scenic highlights of the West Indies. The island has beautiful beaches, some with black volcanic sand.

3 CLIMATE

The average yearly temperature on St. Lucia is 26°C (79°F). The average rainfall at sea level is 231 centimeters (91 inches) a year. Like the rest of the West Indies, St. Lucia is vulnerable to hurricanes.

4 PLANTS AND ANIMALS

Abundant tropical plants include hibiscus, orchids, jasmine, and bougainvillea. There are no large mammals on St. Lucia. Bats are common, and there are several species of small snakes. About a hundred species of birds are found, including flycatchers, hummingbirds, and pigeons. The

Geographic Profile

Geographic Features

Size ranking: 174 of 192
Highest elevation: 950 meters (3,116 feet) at Mount Gimie
Lowest elevation: Sea level at the Caribbean Sea

Land Use

Arable land:	8%
Permanent crops:	21%
Permanent pastures:	5%
Forests:	13%
Other:	53%

Weather

Average annual precipitation: 231–380 centimeters (91–150 inches)
Average temperature in January: 26°C (79°F)
Average temperature in July: 26°C (79°F)

surrounding sea contains lobster, turtle, and conch, as well as many types of fish.

5 ENVIRONMENT

St. Lucia's forests are gradually being depleted by agricultural and commercial interests, and the loss of forest cover contributes to soil erosion. The water supply has been polluted by agricultural chemicals and sewage, and the nation does not have adequate financial resources to address the problem. Two small areas have been set aside as nature preserves. Endangered or threatened species include the St. Lucia parrot and St. Lucia white-breasted thrasher.

6 POPULATION

In 2000, the population of St. Lucia was estimated at 155,678. Some 53,000 persons lived in Castries, the capital, in 2000, about 34% of the population. The nation's population density in 2000 was 253 persons per square kilometer (655 per square mile).

7 MIGRATION

Overcrowding has resulted in emigration to neighboring countries, including Trinidad, Guyana, and the French Caribbean islands, with lesser numbers going to the United Kingdom, Canada, and the United States. In 1999, the net emigration rate was -5.19 emigres per 1,000 population.

8 ETHNIC GROUPS

Reliable statistics on ethnic groups are unavailable. It is estimated, however, that 90% of the population consists of descendants of slaves brought from Africa in the seventeenth and eighteenth centuries. Some 6% is mulatto and 3% East Indian. Approximately 1% of the population is of European descent.

9 LANGUAGES

English is the official language of St. Lucia. Nearly 20% of the population cannot speak it, however. Almost all the islanders also speak a French patois (dialect) based on a mixture of African and French grammar and a vocabulary of mostly French with some English and Spanish words.

10 RELIGIONS

The vast majority of the population (about 90%) was Roman Catholic at last estimate. There also are Anglican, Methodist, Baptist, and Seventh-day Adventist churches. The small East Indian community is divided between Hindus and Muslims.

11 TRANSPORTATION

Hewanorra International Airport is located on the southern tip of the island. The smaller Vigie Airport, located near Castries, is used for flights to and from neighboring Caribbean islands. St. Lucia has two important ports: Castries, in the north, and Vieux Fort, to the south, from which ferries link St. Lucia with St. Vincent and the Grenadines. All of the island's towns, villages, and main residential areas are linked by 1,147 kilometers (713 miles) of all-purpose roads. Motor vehicles numbered 12,157 in 1995.

12 HISTORY

Arawak and Carib Amerindians were the earliest known inhabitants of what is now St. Lucia. According to tradition, Columbus sighted St. Lucia on St. Lucy's Day (December 13) in 1498. It was not settled until the mid-seventeenth century because the Caribs defended the islands successfully for years. The French first settled the island, but it changed hands between the British and the French no fewer than 14 times, until in 1814, the British took permanent possession. In 1838, St. Lucia came under the administration of the Windward Islands government set up by Great Britain.

Unlike other islands in the area, sugar did not monopolize commerce on St. Lucia. Instead, it was one product among many others including tobacco, ginger, and cotton. Small farms rather than large plantations continued to dominate agricultural production into the twentieth century. After slavery was abolished in 1834, East Indian indentured workers were

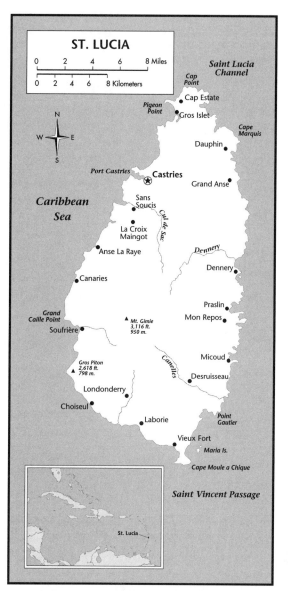

LOCATION: 13°53′N; 60°58′W. **TOTAL COASTLINE:** 158 kilometers (98 miles). **TERRITORIAL SEA LIMIT:** 12 miles.

brought to the island during the late 1800s.

St. Lucia established full internal self-government in 1967 and on 22 February

Photo credit: Susan D. Rock.

An aerial view of the town and harbor of Soufrière.

1979 became an independent member of the Commonwealth of Nations.

The first three years of independence were marked by political turmoil and civil strife, as leaders of rival parties fought bitterly. In 1982, the conservative United Workers' Party (UWP) won 14 of 17 seats in the House of Assembly. Party leader and prime minister John Compton became prime minister at independence and has governed ever since. In 1992, the UWP controlled 11 parliamentary seats. After 15 years out of office, the St. Lucia Labour Party won control in 1997.

St. Lucia suffered back-to-back tropical storms in 1994 and 1995 that caused losses of 65% and 20% of each of those years' banana crops, respectively.

13 GOVERNMENT

Under the 1979 constitution, the British monarch, as official head of government, is represented by a governor-general, Dr. Cuthbert Montraville Sebastian (since 1996). Executive power is exercised by the prime minister (Dr. Kenny Davis Anthony, since 1997) and cabinet. There is a two-chamber parliament consisting of a Senate with 11 members and a House of Assembly with 17 representatives.

14 POLITICAL PARTIES

One of the majority parties is the left-of-center St. Lucia Labor Party, led by Kenny

Anthony, which gained 16 of 17 seats in the 1997 elections, ending the dominance of the United Workers' Party (UWP). Led by John Compton, the UWP became the opposition party; it is by reputation the more conservative party. At that time, the Progressive Labour Party (PLP), led by Jon Odlum, had no representation.

15 JUDICIAL SYSTEM

The lowest court is the district or magistrate's court, above which is the Court of Summary Jurisdiction. The Eastern Caribbean Supreme Court, with international jurisdiction, is seated in Castries.

16 ARMED FORCES

There are no armed forces other than the police department and coast guard. A regional defense pact provides for joint defense and disaster contingency plans.

17 ECONOMY

Agriculture has traditionally been the main economic activity on St. Lucia, which is the leading producer of bananas in the Windward Islands group. Tourism has recently become an equally important economic activity.

18 INCOME

In 1997, the gross domestic product (GDP) was $625 million, or about $4,100 per person. The average inflation rate was 2.5%, resulting in a growth rate in GDP of more than 3% in 1999.

19 INDUSTRY

St. Lucia's manufacturing industry is the largest in the Windward Islands, with

Photo credit: EPD/Embassy of Saint Lucia.

Name:	Kenny Davis Anthony
Position:	Prime minister of a Westminster-style parliamentary democracy
Took office:	24 May 1997
Birthplace:	St. Lucia
Birth date:	8 January 1951
Education:	Vieux Fort Senior Secondary School; St. Lucia Teachers' College; University of the West Indies, bachelor's degree in government and history, LLB and master's degree in law; University of Birmingham, doctorate in law.

many assembly plants producing apparel, electronic components, plastic products, and paper and cardboard boxes. In 1998, the country experienced a decline of 9% in its industrial production growth rate, in part because of drought. Capital projects

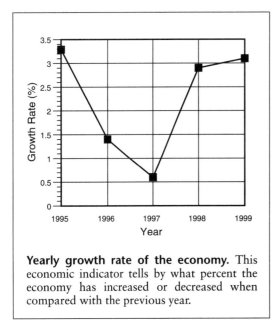

Yearly growth rate of the economy. This economic indicator tells by what percent the economy has increased or decreased when compared with the previous year.

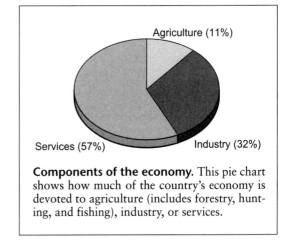

Components of the economy. This pie chart shows how much of the country's economy is devoted to agriculture (includes forestry, hunting, and fishing), industry, or services.

in construction during the fiscal year 1999/2000 stimulated growth.

20 LABOR

In 1998, the labor force was estimated at 73,660: some 13% engaged in commerce, 7.5% in tourism, 23% in agriculture, and 9% in manufacturing. Unemployment was unofficially estimated at 22% in 1998. As of 1999, there were seven labor unions representing 20% of the work force.

21 AGRICULTURE

Agriculture accounts for about 11% of GDP. The production of bananas, St. Lucia's most important crop, totaled 77,000 tons in 1998, almost all is exported. The second most important crop is coconuts, exported as oil and copra; about 12,000 tons were produced in 1998. In 1997, the value of exported

agricultural products amounted to $33.6 million.

22 DOMESTICATED ANIMALS

Production of almost every category of domesticated animals is insufficient to satisfy local demand. There are only 12,000 head of cattle on the island; milk production covers only about 25% of local demand.

23 FISHING

St. Lucia meets its own fresh fish needs. In 1997, the total catch was 1,313 tons.

24 FORESTRY

A small timber industry processes mahogany, pine, and blue mahoe. About 13% of total available land consists of forest and woodlands.

25 MINING

There is no regular commercial mining in St. Lucia, but there is some quarrying for gravel and sand.

26 FOREIGN TRADE

At 1998's year end, exports totaling $75 million included bananas, clothing, cardboard boxes, and coconut products. Imports were valued at $290 million and consisted mainly of manufactured goods, foodstuffs, machinery, fuels, and chemicals. In 1998, St. Lucia's major trade partners were the United Kingdom (50%), the United States (24%), Caribbean Community and Common Market (CARICOM) (16%), and Japan (5%). The economy of St. Lucia is highly dependent upon foreign trade.

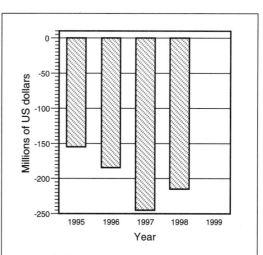

Yearly balance of trade measured in millions of US dollars. The balance of trade is the difference between what a country sells to other countries (its exports) and what it buys (its imports). If a country imports more than it exports, it has a negative balance of trade (a trade deficit). If exports exceed imports there is a positive balance of trade (a trade surplus).

27 ENERGY AND POWER

Electric power production, totaling 110 million kilowatt hours in 1998, is provided by two main diesel generating centers.

28 SOCIAL DEVELOPMENT

The National Insurance Scheme provides all workers from age 16 to 60 with old age, disability, survivor, sickness, and maternity coverage, as well as workers' compensation. Efforts have been made to improve the status of women, especially in employment.

29 HEALTH

There were five hospitals on St. Lucia in 1998. In 1995, there were 71 doctors, 401 nurses, and seven dentists. Malnutrition and intestinal disorders are the main health problems. The average life expectancy was 72 years in 2000.

30 HOUSING

The demand for private ownership of homes far exceeds the supply. In 1980, the majority of housing (74%) was built of wood.

31 EDUCATION

In 2000, the literacy rate was estimated at about 67%, remaining unchanged from the period from 1988–93. In 1997 there were 89 primary schools with 1,214 teaching staff and 31,615 students. There were 682 secondary teachers and 11,753 students. Institutions of higher learning include a branch of the University of the West Indies and the Sir Arthur Lewis Community College.

Selected Social Indicators

The statistics below are estimates for the period 1996 to 2000. For comparison purposes, data for the United States and averages for low-income countries and high-income countries are also given.

Indicator	St. Lucia	Low-income countries	High-income countries	United States
Per capita gross national product (GNP)†	$5,200	$1,870	$25,690	$31,910
Population growth rate	1.2%	2.1%	0.7%	1.1%
People per square kilometer of land	253	73	29	30
Life expectancy in years	72	59	78	77
Number of physicians per 1,000 people	<0.5	1.0	2.5	2.5
Number of pupils per teacher (primary school)	27	41	17	14
Illiteracy rate (15 years and older)	33%	34%	<5%	3%
Television sets per 1,000 people	205	85	693	844
Energy consumed per capita (kg of oil equivalent)	346	550	5,366	7,937

† The GNP is the total dollar value of all goods and services produced by a country in a year. The per capita GNP is calculated by dividing a country's GNP by its population and adjusting for relative purchasing power. About 15% of the world's 6.1 billion people live in high-income countries, while 40% live in low-income countries.

n.a. = data not available   > = greater than   < = less than

Sources: World Bank. *World Development Indicators*. Washington, D.C.: The World Bank, 2001; Central Intelligence Agency. *The World Factbook*. Washington, D.C.: Government Printing Office, 2000.

32 MEDIA

Three newspapers are published in St. Lucia: The *Voice of St. Lucia* (1999 circulation 15,000), the *Crusader* (4,000), and the *Star* (6,000). There were an estimated 26,000 telephones in service in 1995; there also were 4 AM and 1 FM radio stations and 1 TV station in the same year. In 1998 there were 668 radios and 205 TV sets per 1,000 population.

33 TOURISM AND RECREATION

Dramatic tropical scenery, beautiful beaches, and excellent water-sports facilities are St. Lucia's principal tourist attractions. Of special interest are the Sulphur Springs (the world's only drive-in volcano). Some 248,406 tourists visited St. Lucia in 1997, with receipts totaling $282 million.

34 FAMOUS ST. LUCIANS

John G.M. Compton (b.1926), trained as a barrister and one of the founders of the United Workers' Party, was prime minister from 1982 until 1996. The writer Derek Walcott (b.1930) is best known for his epic autobiographical poem *Another Life*.

35 BIBLIOGRAPHY

Breen, Henry Hegart. *St. Lucia: Historical, Statistical, and Descriptive*. London: F. Cass, 1970.

Eggleston, Hazel. *Saint Lucia Diary*. Greenwich, Conn.: Devin-Adair, 1977.

Martinique, Guadeloupe, Dominica & St. Lucia Alive! Edison, N.J.: Hunter, 2000.

Philpott, Don. *St. Lucia*. Lincolnwood, Ill.: Passport Books, 1996.

ST. VINCENT AND THE GRENADINES

CAPITAL: Kingstown.

FLAG: Three vertical bands of blue, yellow, and green; centered on the yellow band are three green diamonds arranged in a v-pattern.

ANTHEM: *National Anthem,* beginning "St. Vincent! Land so beautiful."

MONETARY UNIT: The East Caribbean dollar (EC$) of 100 cents is the national currency. There are coins of 1, 2, 5, 10, and 25 cents and 1 dollar, and notes of 5, 10, 20, and 100 East Caribbean dollars. EC$1 = US$0.3704 (or US$1 = EC$2.70).

WEIGHTS AND MEASURES: The imperial measures are used.

HOLIDAYS: New Year's Day, 1 January; Labor Day, 1 May; CARICOM Day, 5 July; Carnival, 6 July; Bank Holiday, 1st Monday in August; Independence Day, 27 October; Christmas Day, 25 December; Boxing Day, 26 December. Movable religious holidays include Good Friday, Easter Monday, and Whitmonday.

TIME: 8 AM = noon GMT.

1 LOCATION AND SIZE

St. Vincent is located in the Windward Islands group of the Lesser Antilles. Scattered between St. Vincent and Grenada are more than 100 small islands called the Grenadines, half of which belong to St. Vincent and the other half to Grenada. The total land area of the country is 340 square kilometers (131 square miles), slightly less than twice the size of Washington, D.C. The capital city, Kingstown, is located on the southeast coast of the island of St. Vincent.

2 TOPOGRAPHY

St. Vincent is a rugged island of volcanic formation, and the Grenadines are formed by a volcanic ridge running north-south between St. Vincent and Grenada, its neighbor to the southwest. The highest peak on St. Vincent is Soufrière, an active volcano with an altitude of 1,234 meters (4,048 feet). The low-lying Grenadines have wide beaches and shallow bays and harbors, but most have no source of fresh water except rainfall.

3 CLIMATE

The islands enjoy a pleasant tropical climate all year round, with a yearly average temperature of 26°C (79°F). The warmest month is September, with an average temperature of 27°C (81°F); the coolest is January, with an average temperature of 25°C (77°F). The average yearly rainfall on St. Vincent is 231 centimeters (91 inches).

4 PLANTS AND ANIMALS

The shallow waters of the Grenadines abound with marine life. Lobsters, conch, fish of all varieties, and turtles can be found. Whales are frequently sighted, and

Geographic Profile

Geographic Features

Size ranking: 182 of 192
Highest elevation: 1,234 meters (4,048 feet) at
 Soufrière
Lowest elevation: Sea level at the Caribbean Sea

Land Use

Arable land:	10%
Permanent crops:	18%
Permanent pastures:	5%
Forests:	36%
Other:	31%

Weather

Average temperature: 26°C (79°F)
Average temperature in January: 25°C (77°F)
Average temperature in September: 27°C (81°F)
Average annual precipitation: 231–380 centimeters
 (91–150 inches)

large iguana can be found on some of the waterless rocks and cays. In Kingstown, on St. Vincent, there is a famous botanical garden. Some of the many birds found in St. Vincent are the trembler, the bananaquit, and the Antillean crested hummingbird.

5 ENVIRONMENT

The principal recurring threat to the environment comes from the Soufrière volcano. In April 1979, the volcano was active for weeks, covering mountains, forests, and plantation fields with volcanic ash. Pollution from pleasure yachts has seriously affected the eastern shorelines of all the major islands of the Grenadines; even swimming has become dangerous. The central highlands of St. Vincent have been set aside as a natural preservation area for the St. Vincent parrot, wren, and solitaire. In the Grenadines, the hawksbill, green sea, and leatherback turtles are endangered.

6 POPULATION

As of 2000, St. Vincent and the Grenadines had a population of 121,188, of whom the majority lived on St. Vincent. The projected population for 2005 is 126,000. The population of Kingstown, the capital, was 27,000 in 2000, including suburbs. Overall, the islands' population density in 2000 was 293 persons per square kilometer (759 per square mile).

7 MIGRATION

Although no reliable statistics are available, emigration is known to take place to Trinidad, Guyana, Guadeloupe, and Martinique. In 1999, the net migration rate was -7.43 emigres per 1,000 population.

8 ETHNIC GROUPS

About 65% of the islanders are descendants of slaves brought from Africa. About 20% of the population is of mixed origin; roughly 5.5% are East Indians, of Asian descent; 3.5% are of European descent; and about 2% of the people are Amerindians. Of the mixed group, about 1,000 persons, identified as Black Caribs, descend from the intermarriage of runaway or shipwrecked slaves and Amerindians.

9 LANGUAGES

English is the official language of St. Vincent and the Grenadines. Some islanders speak a French patois (dialect), representing a mixture of African and French grammar, with a mostly French vocabulary and some English and Spanish words. A few islanders speak French as their first language.

10 RELIGIONS

The majority of the population is Protestant, with about 36% Anglican and 40% members of other Protestant churches; but there is a significant Roman Catholic minority (10%). Members of the East Indian community are either Hindus or Muslims.

11 TRANSPORTATION

St. Vincent is on the main air routes of the Caribbean, with direct flights to Trinidad and Barbados as well as the other islands to the north. The international airport is located on the southern tip of the island, near Kingstown. Small airports are located on Union, Canouan, and Mustique islands.

All of the Grenadines have excellent harbors served by a ferry service operating out of Kingstown. Many foreign-owned merchant ships register with St. Vincent and the Grenadines because it is cheaper than registering in their own country. In 1998, the merchant fleet had 814 ships totaling 7.7 million gross registered tons. The main road of St. Vincent connects all the main towns with the capital. As of 1998, the islands had about 1,040 kilometers (646 miles) roads, of which 30% were paved. About 8,110 vehicles were registered in 1995, including 4,935 passenger cars.

12 HISTORY

The Arawak Amerindians, who migrated from South America, are the earliest known inhabitants of St. Vincent and the Grenadines. The Caribs inhabited the

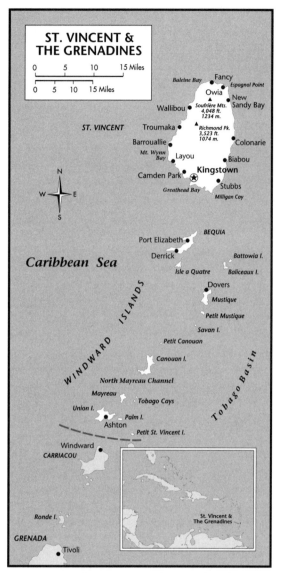

LOCATION: St. Vincent—13°6' to 14°35' N; 61°6' to 61°20' W. **TOTAL COASTLINE:** 84 kilometers (52 miles). **TERRITORIAL SEA LIMIT:** 12 miles.

islands when Christopher Columbus reached St. Vincent on 22 January 1498.

St. Vincent was left to the Carib Amerindians by British and French agreement in 1660 and continued to have a sizable

Amerindian population until the early eighteenth century. The island was taken formally by the British in 1763, who ruled from then on, except for a period of French rule from 1779 to 1783.

The island changed its ethnic character during the next century. When the remaining Amerindian and mixed-blood population rebelled against the British in 1795, most were expelled from the island. Those who remained were decimated by an eruption of the Soufrière volcano in 1812. They were replaced by African slaves, who were freed in 1834; Madeiran Portuguese, who immigrated in 1848 because of a labor shortage; and Asian indentured laborers, who arrived later in the nineteenth century.

St. Vincent was administered as a crown colony within the Windward Islands group from 1833 until 1960, when it joined the Federation of the West Indies. The federation fell apart in 1962, and St. Vincent became a self-governing state in association with the United Kingdom seven years later. On 27 October 1979, St. Vincent and the Grenadines achieved full independence as a member of the Commonwealth of Nations.

During the first months of independence, the young nation faced a rebellion by a group of Rastafarians (semi-political, semi-religious cult based in Jamaica) attempting to secede. The revolt was put down with help from neighboring Barbados. Otherwise, the political system has had few disruptions. The government at independence under the St. Vincent Labor Party gave way to the New Democratic

Photo credit: AP/Ricardo Figueroa.

Name:	Ralph Gonsalves
Position:	Prime minister of a parliamentary democracy
Took office:	2001
Birthplace:	Colonaire, St. Vincent and the Grenadines
Birth date:	8 August 1946
Religion:	Roman Catholic
Education:	University of the West Indies; obtained economic and government degrees in Jamaica; University of Manchester, England; Makerere University, Uganda; Gray's Inn, London, professional law qualification
Spouse:	Eloise Harris Gonsalves
Children:	Camillo, Adam, Isis, Storm, and Soleil
Of interest:	In college, Gonsalves participated in a variety of activities, including writing for the school newspaper, playing cricket, and being a member in a steelband. He also is a champion debater.

Party (NDP) in 1984, with the NDP renewing its electoral majority in 1989 and again in 1994 and 1998.

13 GOVERNMENT

The British monarch, represented by a governor-general (Sir Charles Antrobus), is formally head of the government. Executive power is in the hands of the prime minister (Ralph Gonsalves) and cabinet, who are members of the majority party in the legislature. The single-chamber legislature is a 21-seat House of Assembly consisting of 15 elected representatives and six appointed senators. The nation is divided into eight local districts, two of which cover the Grenadines.

14 POLITICAL PARTIES

There are two major parties and three minor parties on the islands. The majority party is the New Democratic Party (NDP), led by Prime Minister Ralph Gonsalves. The St. Vincent Labour Party (SVLP) was in power at independence and governed until the 1984 elections.

15 JUDICIAL SYSTEM

The islands are divided into three judicial districts, each with its own magistrate's court. Appeals may be carried to the East Caribbean Supreme Court, based in St. Lucia.

16 ARMED FORCES

There are no armed forces except those of the police department. A regional defense pact provides for joint coast-guard operations, military exercises, and disaster contingency plans.

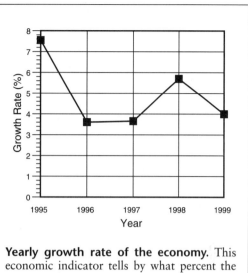

Yearly growth rate of the economy. This economic indicator tells by what percent the economy has increased or decreased when compared with the previous year.

17 ECONOMY

In recent years, tourism and manufacturing have been expanding steadily. However, St. Vincent and the Grenadines continues to rely heavily on agriculture for its economic progress.

18 INCOME

In 1998, the gross domestic product (GDP) was $289 million, or about $2,400 per person. The average inflation rate was 2.5%, resulting in an annual growth rate in GDP of 4%.

19 INDUSTRY

A large amount of industrial activity centers on the processing of agricultural products. Nonagricultural industries include several garment factories, a furniture factory, an electronics plant, and a corrugated cardboard box plant.

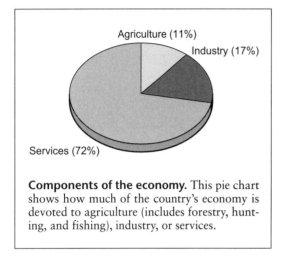

Components of the economy. This pie chart shows how much of the country's economy is devoted to agriculture (includes forestry, hunting, and fishing), industry, or services.

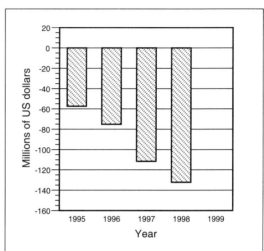

Yearly balance of trade measured in millions of US dollars. The balance of trade is the difference between what a country sells to other countries (its exports) and what it buys (its imports). If a country imports more than it exports, it has a negative balance of trade (a trade deficit). If exports exceed imports there is a positive balance of trade (a trade surplus).

20 LABOR

Some 37,800 persons make up the work force. Unemployment was 35–40% in the late 1990s. One of the first authentic labor unions in the West Indies was formed in St. Vincent in 1935, during the Great Depression.

21 AGRICULTURE

About half of St. Vincent is devoted to crop growing. Bananas constitute the main crop; vegetables, coconut, spices, and sugarcane also are important. In 1998, 55,000 tons of bananas were produced. Other crops in 1998 included coconuts, 23,000 tons; sugarcane, 20,000 tons; sweet potatoes, 2,000 tons; and plantains, 1,000 tons.

22 DOMESTICATED ANIMALS

Rough estimates of the livestock population in 1998 include 6,000 head of cattle, 9,000 hogs, 13,000 sheep, 6,000 goats, and 100,000 poultry of all types.

23 FISHING

At one time, St. Vincent and Bequia were the centers for a thriving whaling industry, but only six humpback whales were captured from 1982 to 1991. In 1997, the total fish catch amounted to 1,410 tons. Technical assistance and training to fishermen and fisheries staff is being sponsored by the Canadian Fisheries Development Project.

24 FORESTRY

There is practically no commercial forestry. Some local timber is used for residential and boat construction.

ST. VINCENT AND THE GRENADINES

Selected Social Indicators

The statistics below are estimates for the period 1996 to 2000. For comparison purposes, data for the United States and averages for low-income countries and high-income countries are also given.

Indicator	St. Vincent and the Grenadines	Low-income countries	High-income countries	United States
Per capita gross national product (GNP)†	$4,990	$1,870	$25,690	$31,910
Population growth rate	0.4%	2.1%	0.7%	1.1%
People per square kilometer of land	293	73	29	30
Life expectancy in years	73	59	78	77
Number of physicians per 1,000 people	<0.5	1.0	2.5	2.5
Number of pupils per teacher (primary school)	20	41	17	14
Illiteracy rate (15 years and older)	4%	34%	<5%	3%
Television sets per 1,000 people	156	85	693	844
Energy consumed per capita (kg of oil equivalent)	207	550	5,366	7,937

† The GNP is the total dollar value of all goods and services produced by a country in a year. The per capita GNP is calculated by dividing a country's GNP by its population and adjusting for relative purchasing power. About 15% of the world's 6.1 billion people live in high-income countries, while 40% live in low-income countries.

n.a. = data not available   > = greater than   < = less than

Sources: World Bank. *World Development Indicators.* Washington, D.C.: The World Bank, 2001; Central Intelligence Agency. *The World Factbook.* Washington, D.C.: Government Printing Office, 2000.

25 MINING

There is no commercial mining. Some sand is extracted for local construction projects.

26 FOREIGN TRADE

Exports include bananas, eddoes, flour, sweet potatoes, arrowroot starch, and tennis racquets. Imports are composed of food, beverages, tobacco, machinery and equipment, and manufactured goods. Exports in 1998 went primarily to other CARICOM countries (50%), with the remainder going primarily to the United Kingdom, and the US. Imports came from the United States, the United Kingdom, Italy, Japan, and Canada.

27 ENERGY AND POWER

Two hydroelectric plants provide 34% of the electricity generated. In 1998, total power generation amounted to 64 million kilowatt hours.

28 SOCIAL DEVELOPMENT

The social security system provides benefits for old age, disability, death, sickness, and maternity. Employers fund a compulsory workers' compensation program. St. Vincent has an extensive program of community development, and a national family planning program. A new law requiring that women receive equal pay for equal work went into effect in 1990. In 1995, a domestic violence law was passed that established a family court to handle cases of spousal abuse.

29 HEALTH

As of 1998, Kingstown had a general hospital with 209 beds, and there were five rural hospitals. Approximately 38 outpatient clinics provide medical care throughout the nation. In 1990 there were an estimated 2.7 hospital beds per 1,000 inhabitants. In 1995 there were 53 doctors. Gastrointestinal diseases continue to be a problem, although they are less so than in the past. Life expectancy was 73 years in 2000.

30 HOUSING

The government has undertaken housing renewal projects in both rural and urban areas and has sought to provide housing for workers on industrial estates. Another government program supplies building materials at low cost to working people.

31 EDUCATION

Primary education, which lasts for seven years, is free but not compulsory. There were 65 primary schools in 1994, with enrollment at 21,386 and 1,080 teaching staff. In secondary schools the same year, there were 9,870 students and 395 teachers. The government-assisted School for Children with Special Needs serves handicapped students. At the postsecondary level there are a teachers' training college, affiliated with the University of the West Indies, and a technical college; nearly 68% of students are women. Adult education classes are offered by the Ministry of Education. Literacy is estimated at 96%.

32 MEDIA

There is one main newspaper, the *Voice of St. Vincent,* appearing three times a week, with a circulation of 9,000. There are two radio stations and one television station. In 1997 there were 627 radios and 156 television sets per 1,000 population.

33 TOURISM AND RECREATION

Tourism is oriented toward yachting, with havens located on most of the Grenadines. Posh resorts have been created on many of the smaller Grenadines, with villas and cottages built alongside small private beaches. There were a total of 1,272 hotel rooms in 1997. The number of tourist arrivals totaled 65,143 that year, of whom the majority were from the Americas; total expenditures were $70 million.

34 FAMOUS ST. VINCENTIANS

Robert Milton Cato (b.1915) was prime minister from independence until 1984; James FitzAllen Mitchell (b.1931) followed from 1984 until 2001, when he was succeeded by Ralph Gonsalves (b.1946). Sir Fred Albert Phillips (b.1918) is a specialist on international law.

35 BIBLIOGRAPHY

Bobrow, Jill, and Dana Jinkins. *St. Vincent and the Grenadines*. Waitsfield, Vt.: Concepts Publishing, 1993.

Morgan, Nina. *The Caribbean and the Gulf of Mexico*. Austin, Tex.: Raintree Steck-Vaughn, 1997.

Potter, Robert B. *St. Vincent and the Grenadines*. Santa Barbara, Calif.: Clio, 1992.

Walton, Chelle Koster. *Caribbean Ways: A Cultural Guide*. Westwood, Mass.: Riverdale, 1993.

Young, Virginia Heyer. *Becoming West Indian: Culture, Self, and Nation in St. Vincent*. Washington, D.C.: Smithsonian Institution Press, 1993.

SAMOA

Independent State of Samoa

Malo Sa'oloto Tuto'atasi o Samoa i Sisifo

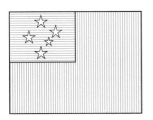

CAPITAL: Apia.

FLAG: The upper left quarter of the flag is blue and bears five white, five-rayed stars representing the Southern Cross; the remainder of the flag is red.

ANTHEM: *The Flag of Freedom.*

MONETARY UNIT: The Samoan tala (ws$) is a paper currency of 100 sene. There are coins of 1, 2, 5, 10, 20, and 50 sene and 1 tala, and notes of 2, 5, 10, 20, and 100 talas. ws$1 = us$0.3283 (or us$1 = s$3.046).

WEIGHTS AND MEASURES: British weights and measures are used.

HOLIDAYS: New Year's, 1–2 January; Independence Holidays (first three workdays of June), Anzac Day, 25 April; Christmas Day, 25 December; Boxing Day, 26 December. Movable religious holidays are Good Friday, Easter Monday, and Whitmonday.

TIME: 1 AM = noon GMT.

1 LOCATION AND SIZE

Samoa consists of the islands of Savai'i and Upolu and several smaller islands, of which only two are inhabited. The group, situated in the Pacific Ocean among the South Sea islands, has a total land area of 2,860 square kilometers (1,104 square miles), slightly smaller than the state of Rhode Island. Its total boundary length is 371 kilometers (231 miles).

2 TOPOGRAPHY

The islands are volcanic, with coral reefs surrounding most of them. Rugged ranges rise to 1,100 meters (3,609 feet) on Upolu and 1,858 meters (6,096 feet) on Savai'i.

3 CLIMATE

The mean daily temperature is about 27°C (81°F). Rainfall averages 287 centimeters (113 inches) annually, and the average yearly relative humidity is 83%.

4 PLANTS AND ANIMALS

Along the coast there are mangrove forests, pandanus, hibiscus, and beach vegetation. Inland, the rainforests contain many kinds of trees. The higher elevations of Savai'i contain moss forest and mountain scrub (low-growing shrubs).

The 16 native species of birds include small doves, parrots, pigeons, and wild ducks. The only mammals native to Samoa are the rat and the flying fox.

5 ENVIRONMENT

According to United Nation's sources, the forests are eliminated at a rate of 4,000–8,000 hectares (9,800–21,600 acres) per year due to the expansion of farmland. A lack of adequate sewage disposal and other forms of pollution are a threat to both the reefs and the marine life which inhabit them.

6 POPULATION

The population of Samoa in 2000 was estimated at 235,302. The population density was 61 persons per square kilometer (158 per square mile) in 1998. During the 1990s, the population increased by an average of 2.3% a year. The population projection for 2005 was 262,000. Apia, the capital and only major town, had a population of 33,000 in 2000.

7 MIGRATION

Emigration (estimated at 5,278 in 1988) consists mainly of students going to New Zealand to continue their education and Samoans seeking work there. In addition, several thousand Samoans live in American Samoa and other parts of the United States. The total number of Samoans living abroad in these countries and Australia was estimated at 76,200 in 1989.

8 ETHNIC GROUPS

Samoans comprise more than 90% of the total population. The Samoans are the second-largest branch of the Polynesians, a people occupying the scattered islands of the Pacific from Hawaii to New Zealand and from eastern Fiji to Easter Island.

Geographic Profile

Geographic Features

Size ranking: 164 of 192
Highest elevation: 1,858 meters (6,096 feet) at Mount Silisili
Lowest elevation: Sea level at the Pacific Ocean

Land Use†

Arable land:	19%
Permanent crops:	24%
Permanent pastures:	0%
Forests:	47%
Other:	10%

Weather

Average annual precipitation: 287 centimeters (113 inches)
Mean daily temperature: 27°C (81°F)

†*Arable land:* Land used for temporary crops, like meadows for mowing or pasture, gardens, and greenhouses. *Permanent crops:* Land cultivated with crops that occupy its use for long periods, such as cocoa, coffee, rubber, fruit and nut orchards, and vineyards. *Permanent pastures:* Land used permanently for forage crops. *Forests:* Land containing stands of trees. *Other:* Any land not specified, including built-on areas, roads, and barren land.

Most of the remaining Samoans are of mixed Samoan and European or Asian descent. Europeans, other Pacific islanders, and Asians make up less than 1% of the total.

9 LANGUAGES

Samoan is the universal language, but both Samoan and English are official. Some Chinese also is spoken. Most of the part-Samoans and many others speak English, and it is taught in the schools.

10 RELIGIONS

More than 99% of Samoans profess some form of Christianity. The Congregational Christian Church of Samoa is the largest religious body in the 43% of the population in 1999. The Roman Catholic (21%) and Methodist (17%) churches had large followings in 1999. Mormon and Seventh-Day Adventist churches, the Baha'is, and a number of other denominations have smaller congregations.

11 TRANSPORTATION

The road system in 1996 totaled 790 kilometers (491 miles). In 1995 there were 1,068 passenger cars and 1,169 commercial vehicles. Diesel-powered launches carry passengers and freight around the islands, and small motor vessels maintain services between Apia and Pago Pago in American Samoa.

Apia is the principal port. Polynesian Airlines provides daily air connections with Pago Pago and regularly scheduled flights to other Pacific destinations. Faleolo Airport, 35 kilometers (22 miles) west of Apia, is the principal air terminal.

12 HISTORY

The western world knew little about Samoa until after the arrival of the missionary John Williams in 1830. Representatives of Great Britain and the United States were soon stationed in Apia. Between 1847 and 1861, the United States appointed a commercial agent, and Britain and the city of Hamburg appointed consuls.

British, American, and German consular agents aligned themselves with various feuding tribal chiefs until the resulting tension and intrigues led to civil war in 1889. Britain, the United States, and Germany set up a neutral government under King

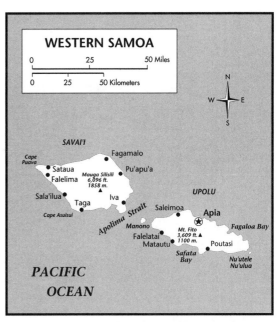

LOCATION: 13° to 15°s; 171° to 173°w. **BOUNDARY LENGTHS:** Savai'i 188 kilometers (117 miles); Upolu coastline, 183 kilometers (114 miles). **TERRITORIAL SEA LIMIT:** 12 miles.

Malietoa Laupepea, but after the king's death in 1898 the three powers intervened once again and abolished the kingship. In 1900, Samoa became a German protectorate. With the outbreak of World War I (1914–18), New Zealand military forces occupied Samoa, and from 1919 to 1946, New Zealand administered the islands under a mandate of the League of Nations.

Between 1927 and 1936, a nationalistic organization known as the Mau embarked on a program of civil disobedience. In 1946, the Untied Nations General Assembly and New Zealand began a process leading toward ultimate self-government of Samoa. On 1 January 1962, Samoa became an independent nation under the

Photo credit: Susan D. Rock.

One of Apia's 72 churches.

name of Western Samoa. Upon independence, Fiame Faumuina Mataafa was Western Samoa's first prime minister (1962–70) and served again in that post from 1973 until his death in 1975.

During the late 1970s and early 1980s, Western Samoa suffered from a worsening economy and growing political and social unrest. A divisive public-sector strike from 6 April to 2 July 1981 cut many essential services to a critical level. Controversy erupted in 1982 over the signing by the HRPP (Human Rights Protection Party) government in August of a protocol with New Zealand that reduced the right of Samoans to New Zealand citizenship. Va'ai Kolone became prime minister in January 1986 as head of a new coalition

government. In 1991, Western Samoa held its first elections where all adult citizens were permitted to vote. The HRPP kept the majority.

In July 1997, the country officially changed its name from Western Samoa to Samoa following a June vote by the legislative assembly. Tofilau Eti resigned due to poor health in November 1998 and died in March 1999 at the age of 74. He was succeeded by deputy prime minister Tuilaepa Sailele Malielegaoi, who began his second term in 2001.

13 GOVERNMENT

The powers and functions of the head of state are far-reaching. All legislation must have his assent before it becomes law. He also has power to grant pardons and reprieves and to suspend or commute any sentence by any court. The parliament consists of the head of state and the Fono, which is made up of one elected member from each of 45 Samoan constituencies. Local government is carried out by the village *fono*, or council.

14 POLITICAL PARTIES

Political parties are becoming increasingly important. In a general election held in April 1991, the ruling HRPP (Human Rights Protection Party) won 28 of 47 seats in the Parliament (Fono) and made Tofilau Eti prime minister again.

15 JUDICIAL SYSTEM

The Supreme Court has full civil and criminal jurisdiction for the administration of justice in Samoa. The Court of Appeal consists of three judges who may be judges of the Supreme Court. Magistrates' courts are subordinate courts with varying degrees of authority.

The Land and Titles Court has jurisdiction in disputes over Samoan land and succession to Samoan titles. Some civil and criminal matters are handled by village traditional courts which apply a very different procedure than that used in the official western-style courts.

16 ARMED FORCES

Samoa has no armed forces.

Prime Minister

Name:	Tuilaepa Sailele Malielegaoi
Position:	Prime minister of a constitutional monarchy under native chief
Took office:	24 November 1998
Birthplace:	Lepa Village, Samoa
Birth date:	1946
Education:	Marist Brothers' St. Joseph's College, Samoa; St. Paul's College, Auckland, New Zealand; University of Auckland, bachelor and master of commerce degrees, specialization in accounting and economics
Children:	Several children
Of interest:	When Malielegaoi became prime minister, media attention focused on the sacrifices his family made for his education.

---

17 ECONOMY

The economy is based largely on agriculture. Tourist revenues and earnings by overseas workers are important sources of foreign exchange. Economic performance has suffered since 1990 due to the devastation to crops and tourism caused by two cyclones, Ofa and Val. In 1994, a fungus destroyed 97% of the taro crop and set the economy back. Samoa has the highest unemployment rate and the lowest wages in Oceania, the south Pacific region.

18 INCOME

In 1997, Samoa's gross domestic product (GDP) was US$470 million, or about US$2,100 per person. The average inflation rate was 2.2%, resulting in a growth in GDP of 3.4%.

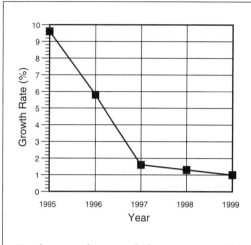

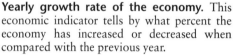

Yearly growth rate of the economy. This economic indicator tells by what percent the economy has increased or decreased when compared with the previous year.

an estimated 65% of the labor force worked in agriculture, 30% in services, and 5% in industry.

21 AGRICULTURE

Most Samoans grow food crops for home consumption and cash crops for export. In 1998, coconut production was 130,000 tons, and taro (coco yam) production amounted to 37,000 tons. Exports of cocoa have fallen in recent years, thereby discouraging production. Since 1991, production has been under 1,000 tons. Exports of food products in 1997 amounted to US$8.1 million.

22 DOMESTICATED ANIMALS

Pigs and cattle form the bulk of the livestock. In 1998, pigs, which are common in the villages, were estimated to number 179,000 and cattle, 26,000.

23 FISHING

The local fish catch has steadily fallen from 4,020 tons in 1982 to 565 tons in 1991; by 1997, the catch rebounded to 4,590 tons, with tuna comprising about 30%.

19 INDUSTRY

Industries include food- and timber-processing facilities, a brewery, cigarette and match factories, and small individual enterprises for processing coffee and for manufacturing curios, soap, carbonated drinks, light metal products, garments, footwear, and other consumer products.

20 LABOR

No Samoan is entirely dependent on wages for sustenance; all share in the products of their family lands and can always return to them. Agriculture, forestry, and fishing account for half of wage employment. Over the years, thousands of skilled and semiskilled Samoans have left the islands, mainly drawn away by better economic opportunities in New Zealand, Australia, and the United States. In 1995,

24 FORESTRY

The nation's forest area is estimated at 136,000 hectares (336,000 acres). Timber imports were estimated at US$741,000 in 1997.

25 MINING

No minerals of commercial value are known to exist in Samoa.

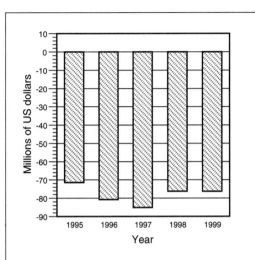

Yearly balance of trade measured in millions of US dollars. The balance of trade is the difference between what a country sells to other countries (its exports) and what it buys (its imports). If a country imports more than it exports, it has a negative balance of trade (a trade deficit). If exports exceed imports there is a positive balance of trade (a trade surplus).

26 FOREIGN TRADE

Imports consist chiefly of food, fuels and chemicals, machinery, transportation equipment, and other manufactured articles. The principal exports are taro, coconut cream, and automotive seat belts. Also exported are coconut oil, coconuts, copra (dried coconut meat), cocoa, timber, and clothing. Samoa imports more than it exports. Samoa's leading trade partners are Australia, New Zealand, Germany, the United States, Japan, and other Pacific islands.

27 ENERGY AND POWER

Samoa has depended heavily on imported energy, but hydroelectric power accounted for nearly 40% of electrical generation in 1996. Electricity production totaled 65 million kilowatt hours in 1998.

28 SOCIAL DEVELOPMENT

A social security system provides for employee retirement pensions, disability benefits, and death benefits. Workers' compensation is compulsory.

In Samoan society, obligations to the *aiga*, or extended family, are often given precedence over individual rights. While there is some discrimination against women, they can play an important role in society, especially female *matai*, or heads of families.

29 HEALTH

In 1990, there were 50 physicians in Samoa. District nurses are stationed at strategic points throughout the islands. Child health clinics are a regular feature of their work. Life expectancy was 69.8 years in 1999.

30 HOUSING

Many Samoans live in traditional houses called *fales*. A fale is usually round or oval, with pebble floors and a thatch roof. It has no walls, being supported on the sides by posts. Coconut-leaf blinds can be lowered to keep out wind and rain. A popular Samoan-European type of dwelling is an oblong concrete house with some walls, often with separate rooms in each corner; like the fale it is open at the sides.

Photo credit: Susan D. Rock.

Vendors selling their goods at a new market in Apia.

31 EDUCATION

The adult literacy rate is estimated to be more than 97%. In 1991 there were 30 primary schools with 7,884 pupils and 524 teachers. At the secondary level, there were 3,643 pupils and 266 teachers.

The University of the South Pacific School of Agriculture maintains a campus at Alafua. The University of Samoa offers courses in both arts and sciences.

32 MEDIA

In 1995 there were 8,000 telephones in use. The Samoan Broadcasting Service transmits radio programs on two stations in Samoan and English and provides direct broadcasts from the Fono. In 1997 there were an estimated 323 radios and 25 television sets in use per 1,000 population.

There are several bilingual weeklies, including the *Samoa Weekly* (1995 circulation 4,500), *Samoa Observer* (3,500), *Samoa Times* (3,000), and *South Sea Star* (2,000).

33 TOURISM AND RECREATION

Since 1966, the government has encouraged tourism. The major tourist attractions are the beaches and traditional villages. In 1997, there were 68,000 tourist arrivals.

The head of state lives on the island of Apia, which also was once the home of author Robert Louis Stevenson; Stevenson's grave is there. Pastimes include swimming, water skiing, and fishing. Soccer and cricket are popular local sports.

34 FAMOUS SAMOANS

The Scottish author Robert Louis Stevenson (1850–94) lived principally on one of the tiny islands of Samoa, and on Apia, from 1889 until his death. Samoans famous since independence include Malietoa Tanumafili II (b.1913), who was named head of state in 1962, and Fiame Faumuina Mataafa (d.1975), who served as prime minister from 1962 to 1970 and again from 1973 until his death. Tofilau Eti (b.American Samoa, 1925?–99) was prime minister from 1982 to 1985, when he resigned and was succeeded by Va'ai Kolone, who held the office until 1991. That year, Eti again assumed the prime minster post. In 1998, he was succeeded by Tuilaepa Sailele Malielegaoi (b.1946).

35 BIBLIOGRAPHY

Henderson, Faye. *Western Samoa*, a country profile. 2d ed. Washington, D.C.: Library of Congress, 1980.

Lockwood, Victoria S., Thomas G. Harding, and Ben J. Wallace, ed. *Contemporary Pacific Societies: Studies in Development and Change*. Englewood Cliffs, N.J.: Prentice Hall, 1993.

Mead, Margaret. *Coming of Age in Samoa*. London: Penguin, 1961 (orig. 1928).

Talbot, Dorinda. *Samoa*. Hawthorn, Vic.: Lonely Planet, 1998.

SAN MARINO

The Most Serene Republic of San Marino

La Serenissima Repubblica di San Marino

CAPITAL: San Marino.

FLAG: The flag is divided horizontally into two equal bands, sky blue below and white above, with the national coat of arms superimposed in the center.

ANTHEM: *Onore a te, onore, o antica repubblica (Honor to You, O Ancient Republic).*

MONETARY UNIT: San Marino principally uses the Italian lira (L) as currency; Vatican City State currency also is honored. The country issues its own coins in standard Italian denominations in limited numbers as well. Coins of San Marino may circulate in both the republic and in Italy. L1 = $0.00059 (or $1 = L1,668.7).

WEIGHTS AND MEASURES: The metric system is the legal standard.

HOLIDAYS: New Year's Day, 1 January; Epiphany, 6 January; Anniversary of St. Agatha, second patron saint of the republic, and of the liberation of San Marino (1740), 5 February; Anniversary of the Arengo, 25 March; Investiture of the Captains-Regent, 1 April and 1 October; Labor Day, 1 May; Fall of Fascism, 28 July; Assumption and August Bank Holiday, 14–16 August; Anniversary of the Foundation of San Marino, 3 September; All Saint's Day, 1 November; Commemoration of the Dead, 2 November; Immaculate Conception, 8 December; Christmas, 24–26 December; New Year's Eve, 31 December. Movable religious holidays include Easter Monday and Ascension.

TIME: 1 PM = noon GMT.

1 LOCATION AND SIZE

San Marino is the third-smallest country in Europe, with an area of 60 square kilometers (23.2 square miles), about one-third the size of Washington, D.C. It is a landlocked state completely surrounded by Italy, with a total boundary length of 39 kilometers (24 miles).

2 TOPOGRAPHY

The town of San Marino is on the slopes and at the summit of Mount Titano (Monte Titano) at 739 meters (2,425 feet), which has three peaks. Level areas around the base of Mt. Titano provide land for agricultural use.

3 CLIMATE

The climate is that of northeastern Italy: rather mild in winter, but with temperatures frequently below freezing, and warm and pleasant in the summer, reaching a maximum of 26°C (79°F). Annual rainfall averages about 89 centimeters (35 inches).

Geographic Profile

Geographic Features

Size ranking: 188 of 192
Highest elevation: 739 meters (2,425 feet) at Monte Titano
Lowest elevation: 55 meters (180 feet) at Fiume Ausa

Land Use

Arable land:	17%
Permanent crops:	0%
Permanent pastures:	0%
Forests:	0%
Other:	83%

Weather

Maximum annual temperature: 26°C (79°F)
Average annual precipitation: 89 centimeters (35 inches)

4 PLANTS AND ANIMALS

The republic has the same native plants and animals as northeastern Italy.

5 ENVIRONMENT

Information on the environment is not available.

6 POPULATION

The resident population was estimated at 25,215 in 2000. Population density that year was 433 persons per square kilometer (1,121 per square mile). In 2000, about 5,000 people lived in the capital, also called San Marino.

7 MIGRATION

Immigrants come chiefly from Italy; emigration is mainly to Italy, the United States, France, and Belgium.

8 ETHNIC GROUPS

The native population is mostly of Italian origin.

9 LANGUAGES

Italian is the official language.

10 RELIGIONS

With few exceptions, the population is Roman Catholic, and Roman Catholicism is the official religion.

11 TRANSPORTATION

Streets and roads within the republic total about 220 kilometers (140 miles), and there is regular bus service between San Marino and the Italian city of Rimini. Motor vehicle registrations in 1995 included 22,945 passenger cars and 3,546 commercial vehicles.

12 HISTORY

San Marino is the oldest republic in the world. It is the sole survivor of the independent states that existed in Italy at various times, from the downfall of the western Roman Empire to the proclamation of the Kingdom of Italy in 1861.

According to tradition, the republic was founded in the fourth century AD by Marinus, a Christian stonecutter who fled from Dalmatia (across the Adriatic Sea from Italy in present-day Croatia) to avoid religious persecution. Later canonized (declared a saint), St. Marinus is known in Italian as San Marino. There was a monastery in San Marino in existence at least as early as 885.

Because of the poverty of the region and the mountainous terrain, San Marino was rarely disturbed by outside powers. It was briefly held by Cesare Borgia (an Italina military and church leader) in 1503, but in 1549 its sovereignty (independence) was confirmed by Pope Paul III. In 1739, a military force under Cardinal Giulio Alberoni occupied San Marino. In the following year, Pope Clement II terminated the occupation and signed a treaty of friendship with the tiny republic. Napoleon allowed San Marino to retain its liberty.

In 1849, Giuseppe Garibaldi, the liberator of Italy, took refuge from the Austrians in San Marino. San Marino and Italy entered into a treaty of friendship in 1862, which is still in effect. In 1922–43, during the period of Benito Mussolini's rule in Italy, San Marino adopted a Fascist (dictatorial) type of government. Despite its neutrality in World War II (1939–45), San Marino was bombed by Allied (United Kingdom, United States, and their allies) planes on 26 June 1944. The raid caused heavy damage, especially to the railway line, and killed a number of persons.

Since 1945, government control has shifted between parties of the right and left, often in coalitions. In 1986, a Communist–Christian Democratic coalition came to power.

LOCATION: 12°27′E and 43°56′N.

13 GOVERNMENT

Legislative power is exercised by the Grand and General Council of 60 members, regularly elected every five years by universal vote at age 18. The council elects from among its members a State Congress of ten members, which makes and carries out most administrative decisions. Two members of the council are named every six months to head the executive branch of the government; one represents the town of San Marino and the other the countryside.

14 POLITICAL PARTIES

The political parties in San Marino have close ties with the corresponding parties in Italy. In 1998, party representation after elections was as follows: Christian Democratic Party, 25; San Marino Socialist Party, 14; Democratic Progressive Party (formerly the San Marino Communist Party), 11; Popular Alliance, 6; Socialists for Reform, 2; and Communist Renewal, 2.

15 JUDICIAL SYSTEM

There is a civil court, a criminal court, and a superior court. Most criminal cases are tried before Italian magistrates because, with the exception of minor civil suits, the judges in cases in San Marino are not allowed to be citizens of San Marino. The highest appellate court is the Council of Twelve.

16 ARMED FORCES

The San Marino militia officially consists of all able-bodied citizens between the ages of 16 and 55, but the armed forces are principally for purposes of ceremonial display.

17 ECONOMY

Farming was formerly the principal occupation, but it has been replaced in importance by light manufacturing. However, the main sources of income are tourism and payments by citizens of San Marino (Sanmarinese) living abroad. Some government revenue comes from the sale of postage stamps and coins and from a subsidy by Italy.

18 INCOME

In 1997, San Marino's gross domestic product (GDP) was $500 million, or $20,000 per person. In 1995, the average inflation rate was 5.3%.

19 INDUSTRY

Manufacturing is limited to light industries such as textiles, bricks and tiles, leather goods, clothing, and metalwork. Cotton textiles are woven at Serravalle; bricks and tiles are made in La Dogana, which also has a dyeing plant; and cement factories and a tannery are located in Acquaviva, as well as a paper-making plant. Synthetic rubber also is produced. The pottery of Borgo Maggiore is well known. Gold and silver souvenirs are made for the tourist trade. Other products are Moscato wine, olive oil, and baked goods.

20 LABOR

Most of the inhabitants are farmers or stock raisers. The labor force in 1999 totaled about 14,300 persons, most of whom worked in manufacturing or service occupations. There is little unemployment (553 persons in 1998).

21 AGRICULTURE

About 17% of the land is arable. Annual crop production includes wheat and grapes, as well as other grains, vegetables, fruits, and livestock feed.

22 DOMESTICATED ANIMALS

Livestock raising uses some 1,400 hectares (3,500 acres), or about 23% of the total area. Cattle, hogs, sheep, and horses are raised.

23 FISHING

There is no significant fishing.

Selected Social Indicators

The statistics below are estimates for the period 1996 to 2000. For comparison purposes, data for the United States and averages for low-income countries and high-income countries are also given.

Indicator	San Marina	Low-income countries	High-income countries	United States
Per capita gross national product (GNP)†	$20,000	$1,870	$25,690	$31,910
Population growth rate	1.4%	2.1%	0.7%	1.1%
People per square kilometer of land	433	73	29	30
Life expectancy in years	81	59	78	77
Number of physicians per 1,000 people	n.a.	1.0	2.5	2.5
Number of pupils per teacher (primary school)	n.a.	41	17	14
Illiteracy rate (15 years and older)	4%	34%	<5%	3%
Television sets per 1,000 people	334	85	693	844
Energy consumed per capita (kg of oil equivalent)	n.a.	550	5,366	7,937

† The GNP is the total dollar value of all goods and services produced by a country in a year. The per capita GNP is calculated by dividing a country's GNP by its population and adjusting for relative purchasing power. About 15% of the world's 6.1 billion people live in high-income countries, while 40% live in low-income countries.

n.a. = data not available   > = greater than   < = less than

Sources: World Bank. *World Development Indicators*. Washington, D.C.: The World Bank, 2001; Central Intelligence Agency. *The World Factbook*. Washington, D.C.: Government Printing Office, 2000.

24 FORESTRY

Small quantities of wood are cut for local use.

25 MINING

San Marino has no commercial mineral resources.

26 FOREIGN TRADE

Principal exports are wine, textiles, furniture, quarried stone, ceramics, and handicrafts. The chief imports are raw materials and a wide variety of consumer goods. San Marino has a customs union (agreement allowing for import and export) with Italy.

27 ENERGY AND POWER

Electric power is imported from Italy.

28 SOCIAL DEVELOPMENT

The government maintains a comprehensive social insurance program, including disability, family supplement payments, and old-age pensions. In 1982, Sanmarinese women who married foreign citizens were given the right to keep their citizenships.

29 HEALTH

Public health institutions include the State Hospital, a dispensary for the poor, and a laboratory of hygiene and prophylaxis. All citizens receive free, comprehensive medical care. Estimated average life expectancy in 2000 was 81 years.

30 HOUSING

In 1986, San Marino had 7,926 dwellings, nearly all with electricity and piped-in water. Most new construction is financed privately.

31 EDUCATION

Primary education is compulsory for all children between the ages of 6 and 14; the adult literacy rate is about 96%. The program of instruction is patterned after Italy's.

In 1997, there were 14 elementary schools, with 1,170 students and 221 teachers; middle and upper-secondary schools enrolled 1,192 pupils during the same year. San Marino students (Sanmarinese) are able to enroll at Italian universities.

32 MEDIA

There are no local radio stations, but there is one television station that receives mostly foreign broadcasts. In 1997 there were 595 radios and 334 television sets per 1,000 population. A telephone system integrated into Italy's system served 14,100 telephones in 1995.

There were several daily newspapers in 1999, including *Il Nuovo Titano* and *San Marino Italia*. There also are a number of government bulletins.

33 TOURISM AND RECREATION

The government has promoted tourism so successfully that during summer months, the number of San Marino residents is often exceeded by the number of visitors. Growth in the tourist industry has increased the demand for San Marino's stamps and coins, gold and silver souvenirs, handicrafts, and pottery.

Principal attractions are the three medieval fortresses at the summit of Mt. Titano (Monte Titano), the magnificent view of the Italian city of Rimini, and the Italian coast of the Adriatic Sea.

34 FAMOUS SANMARINESE

Well-known Italians associated with San Marino include Cardinal Giulio Alberoni (1664–1752), who attempted to subject the republic to papal domination in 1739–40; and Giuseppe Garibaldi (1807–82), the great Italian patriot, who obtained refuge from the Austrians in San Marino in 1849.

35 BIBLIOGRAPHY

Bent, James Theodore. *A Freak of Freedom; or, The Republic of San Marino.* Port Washington, N.Y.: Kennikat Press, 1970 (orig. 1879).

Catling, Christopher. *Umbria, the Marches, and San Marino.* Lincolnwood, Ill.: Passport Books, 1994.

Carrick, Noel. *San Marino.* New York: Chelsea House, 1988.

SÃO TOMÉ AND PRÍNCIPE

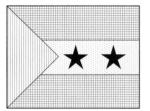

Democratic Republic of São Tomé and Príncipe
República Democrática de São Tomé e Príncipe

CAPITAL: São Tomé.

FLAG: The flag consists of three unequal horizontal stripes of green, yellow, and green; there is a red triangle at the hoist, and two black stars on the yellow stripe.

ANTHEM: *Independéncia Total (Total Independence).*

MONETARY UNIT: The dobra (Db) is equal to 100 centimos. There are coins of 50 centimos and 1, 2, 5, 10, and 20 dobras, and notes of 50, 100, 500, and 1,000 dobras. Db 1 = $0.00013 (or $1 = Db7,200.00)

WEIGHTS AND MEASURES: The metric system is used.

HOLIDAYS: New Year's Day, 1 January; Martyrs' Day, 4 February; Labor Day, 1 May; Independence Day, 12 July; Armed Forces Day, first week in September; Farmers' Day, 30 September. The principal Christian holidays also are observed.

TIME: GMT.

1 LOCATION AND SIZE

São Tomé and Príncipe, the smallest country in Africa, lies in the Gulf of Guinea off the west coast of Gabon.

The nation has an area of 960 square kilometers (371 square miles), of which São Tomé comprises 855 square kilometers (330 square miles), and Príncipe 109 square kilometers (42 square miles). Comparatively, the nation's combined area is slightly less than 5.5 times the size of Washington, D.C.

São Tomé has a coastline of 141 kilometers (88 miles); Príncipe's shoreline is 209 kilometers (130 miles). The capital city, São Tomé, is located on the northeast coast of the island of São Tomé.

2 TOPOGRAPHY

The islands form part of a chain of extinct volcanoes and are both quite mountainous. Pico de São Tomé, at 2,024 meters (6,640 feet) is the highest peak on São Tomé; Pico de Príncipe is Príncipe's tallest mountain.

3 CLIMATE

Coastal temperatures average 27°C (81°F), but the mountain regions average only 20°C (68°F). From October to May, São Tomé and Príncipe receive between 380 and 510 centimeters (150–200 inches) of rain.

4 PLANTS AND ANIMALS

Except for the coastal flatlands, where cocoa and coffee plantations predominate,

Geographic Profile

Geographic Features

Size ranking: 168 of 192
Highest elevation: 2,024 meters (6,640 feet) at Pico de São Tomé
Lowest elevation: Sea level at the Atlantic Ocean

Land Use†

Arable land:	2%
Permanent crops:	36%
Permanent pastures:	1%
Forests:	29%
Other:	32%

Weather††

Average annual precipitation: 87.2 centimeters (34.3 inches)
Average temperature in January: 27°C (81°F)
Average temperature in July: 23.8°C (74.8°F)

†*Arable land:* Land used for temporary crops, like meadows for mowing or pasture, gardens, and greenhouses. *Permanent crops:* Land cultivated with crops that occupy its use for long periods, such as cocoa, coffee, rubber, fruit and nut orchards, and vineyards. *Permanent pastures:* Land used permanently for forage crops. *Forests:* Land containing stands of trees. *Other:* Any land not specified, including built-on areas, roads, and barren land.

††The measurements for precipitation and average temperature were taken at weather stations closest to the country's largest city. Precipitation and average temperature can vary significantly within a country, due to factors such as latitude, altitude, coastal proximity, and wind patterns.

São Tomé and Príncipe are dominated by forestland. There is little livestock, but domestic fowl are abundant.

5 ENVIRONMENT

The nation lacks an adequate water treatment system, and its forests are threatened by overuse. The cities have inadequate sewage treatment. Soil erosion and exhaustion are other major environmental problems.

6 POPULATION

In 2000, the estimated population of São Tomé and Príncipe was 159,832, the minority living on São Tomé. The estimated population density was 151 persons per square kilometer (391 persons per square mile). During the 1990s, the population increased by an average of 2.9% a year. The projected population for 2005 was 187,000. The capital city, São Tomé, had an estimated 57,000 inhabitants in 2000.

7 MIGRATION

After independence in 1975, almost all the 3,000–4,000 European settlers, and most Cape Verdeans, left the islands.

8 ETHNIC GROUPS

Most of the islands' permanent residents are Fôrros, descendants of the Portuguese colonists and their African slaves. The Angolares, descendants of shipwrecked Angolan slaves, live along the southeast coast of São Tomé.

9 LANGUAGES

Portuguese, the official language, is spoken in a Creole dialect that reveals the heavy influence of African Bantu languages.

10 RELIGIONS

Roman Catholicism is the dominant religion, with professing Catholics estimated at 90% in 1998. Traditional African religions also are practiced, and there is a small Protestant minority.

11 TRANSPORTATION

There are about 320 kilometers (199 miles) of surfaced roads. São Tomé and Santo António are the main ports. In 1997, 25,000 passengers were carried on scheduled domestic and international flights.

12 HISTORY

São Tomé and Príncipe were probably uninhabited volcanic islands when the Portuguese landed there in 1471. They were declared a concession (a grant of land in exchange for services) of Portugal in 1485. The islands were completely taken over by the Portuguese crown in 1522 and 1573. By the mid-sixteenth century, the islands were Africa's leading exporter of sugar. By 1908 São Tomé had become the world's largest producer of cocoa. Plantation slavery or slavelike contract labor remained the basis of island labor for hundreds of years, even after slavery formally ended.

The Committee for the Liberation of São Tomé and Príncipe (later renamed the Movement for the Liberation of São Tomé and Príncipe—MLSTP) was formed in 1960 and recognized by Portugal in 1974 as the sole legitimate representative of the people of São Tomé and Príncipe. On 12 July 1975, the islands achieved full independence. On the same day, Manuel Pinto da Costa, the secretary-general of the MLSTP, became the country's first president. In 1979, Prime Minister Miguel dos Anjos da Cunha Lisboa Trovoada was arrested and charged with attempting to seize power. By 1985, São Tomé and

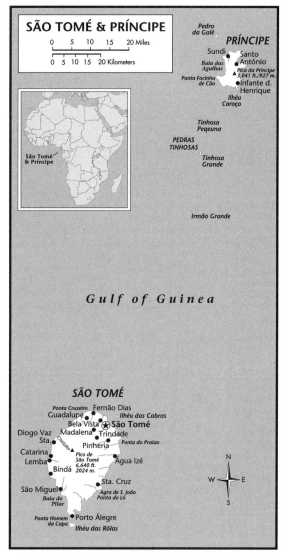

LOCATION: São Tomé: 0°13′N and 6°37′E. Príncipe: 1°37′N and 7°24′E. **TERRITORIAL SEA LIMIT:** 12 miles.

Príncipe had begun to establish closer ties with the West.

In 1990, a new policy of *abertura,* or political and economic "opening," led to the legalization of opposition parties and direct elections with secret balloting. A number of groups united as the Party of Democratic Convergence-Group of Reflection (PDC-GR), led by former prime minister Miguel Trovoada, who was elected president on 3 March 1991 (and again in 1996). In 1992, the government began a strict program to strengthen the economy. Gasoline prices increased, and the currency was devalued by 40%. The measures prompted massive demonstrations and calls for the dissolution of the government. The parliament then appointed Norberto Alegre prime minister, who then formed a new government.

The PDC-GR continued to dominate the central government in 1993, but opposition grew as the PDC-GR was increasingly seen as corrupt and complacent. In August 1995, five army officers led a bloodless coup, but the elected government was put back into power with the promise to institute reforms and bring opposition members into the government.

The MLSTP won the November 1998 election, taking 31 of the 55 parliamentary seats. The new Prime Minister, Guilherme Posser da Costa, announced an austerity program to help relaunch the economy and vowed to fight corruption.

13 GOVERNMENT

A new constitution was adopted by the People's Assembly in April 1990. The president is chosen for a maximum of two five-year terms. The People's Assembly, now composed of 55 members, is elected to four-year terms. Voting is universal at age 18.

14 POLITICAL PARTIES

On 15 October 1974, the government of Portugal recognized the Movement for the Liberation of São Tomé and Príncipe (Movimento de Libertação de São Tomé e Príncipe—MLSTP) as the sole legitimate representative for the islands. After independence, the MLSTP became the only political party. With the legalization of opposition party activity, Miguel Trovoada, an MLSTP founder who had been exiled, formed the Democratic Convergence Party-Group of Reflection (PDC-GR). Other parties include The Democratic Opposition Coalition (CODO) and the Christian Democratic Front (FDC).

15 JUDICIAL SYSTEM

The highest court is the Supreme Tribunal, which is named by and responsible to the People's Assembly. The constitution affords parties in civil cases the right to a fair public trial and a right to appeal. The constitution also affords criminal defendants a public trial before a judge as well as legal representation.

16 ARMED FORCES

A small citizen's army was formed in 1975 by the Movement for the Liberation of São Tomé and Príncipe (MLSTP) government after Portuguese troops were withdrawn.

17 ECONOMY

São Tomé and Príncipe is one of the poorest countries in the world. The economy is based on cocoa-producing plantation agriculture, but the fall of cocoa prices since

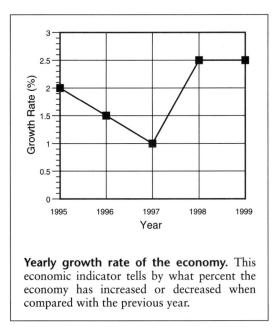

Yearly growth rate of the economy. This economic indicator tells by what percent the economy has increased or decreased when compared with the previous year.

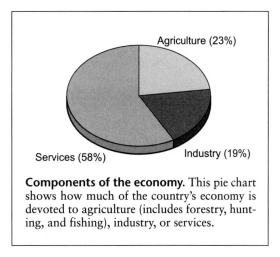

Components of the economy. This pie chart shows how much of the country's economy is devoted to agriculture (includes forestry, hunting, and fishing), industry, or services.

the early 1980s has created serious problems for the government, which abandoned socialist-style economic policies in favor of market-style policies.

Offshore oil production and the diversification of agriculture were the government's goals for economic growth in 1999.

18 INCOME

In 1998, gross domestic product (GDP) was estimated at $164 million, per capita being estimated at $1,100. In 1999, the average annual growth of GDP was 2.5%, and the average annual inflation rate was 21%.

19 INDUSTRY

São Tomé has very little industry. Soap, beverages, finished wood and furniture, bread, textiles, bricks and ceramics, gar-

ments, and palm oil are produced on the islands.

20 LABOR

Agriculture and fishing supported more than half of the population. Laborers for the plantation sector come from mainland Africa and Cape Verde on a contract basis. Workers may organize and bargain collectively. Unemployment can reach upwards of 50% because of the unpopularity of plantation work. There is no minimum wage in any sector of the economy.

21 AGRICULTURE

About half of all cultivated land is used for cocoa production, which is the major export crop. Production of cocoa was believed to be about 3,000 tons in 1998. Cocoa exports account for 80% of export earnings. Copra (dried coconut meat used to produce coconut oil) is the second most important crop; production in 1998 totaled about 1,000 tons. Other agricultural products in 1998 were palm kernels,

2,000 tons; bananas, 16,000 tons; cassava, 3,000 tons; and coconuts, 29,000 tons.

22 DOMESTICATED ANIMALS

The livestock sector, largely pigs, was plagued by African swine fever in 1992, necessitating the destruction of the entire herd of some 30,000 animals. In 1998 there were an estimated 4,000 head of cattle, 3,000 sheep, 5,000 goats, and 2,000 pigs.

23 FISHING

The Angolare (descendants of shipwrecked slaves) community of São Tomé supplies fish to the domestic market. In 1997, the catch was 3,338 tons.

24 FORESTRY

Wood is used on the plantations for fuel to dry cocoa beans and elsewhere as a building material. Roundwood removals are estimated at 9,000 cubic meters (12,000 cubic yards) a year. Much of the forestland is inaccessible.

25 MINING

Mineral wealth remains largely unexplored, although lime deposits are exploited for the local market.

26 FOREIGN TRADE

São Tomé and Príncipe's trade balance depends on price levels for cocoa, which accounts for about 90% of export earnings. Copra (dried coconut meat used to produce coconut oil) also is exported. The leading imports are foodstuffs, fuels, textiles, and machinery. The leading purchasers of exports are the Netherlands and Germany. In 1999, exports were estimated at $4.9 million and imports at $19.5 million.

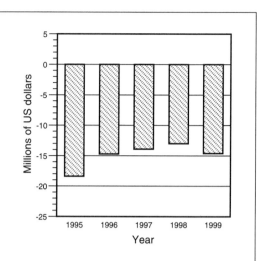

Yearly balance of trade measured in millions of US dollars. The balance of trade is the difference between what a country sells to other countries (its exports) and what it buys (its imports). If a country imports more than it exports, it has a negative balance of trade (a trade deficit). If exports exceed imports, there is a positive balance of trade (a trade surplus).

27 ENERGY AND POWER

About half of São Tomé's 15 million kilowatt hours of electric power in 1998 were produced by hydroelectricity; the rest was thermal. Only a quarter of the nation's households have electricity.

28 SOCIAL DEVELOPMENT

Before independence in 1975, social welfare was handled largely by the plantation corporations, missionaries, and private agencies. After independence, the govern-

Selected Social Indicators

The statistics below are estimates for the period 1996 to 2000. For comparison purposes, data for the United States and averages for low-income countries and high-income countries are also given.

Indicator	São Tomé and Príncipe	Low-income countries	High-income countries	United States
Per capita gross national product (GNP)†	$1,100	$1,870	$25,690	$31,910
Population growth rate	3.2%	2.1%	0.7%	1.1%
People per square kilometer of land	151	73	29	30
Life expectancy in years	65	59	78	77
Number of physicians per 1,000 people	n.a.	1.0	2.5	2.5
Number of pupils per teacher (primary school)	n.a.	41	17	14
Illiteracy rate (15 years and older)	27%	34%	<5%	3%
Television sets per 1,000 people	144	85	693	844
Energy consumed per capita (kg of oil equivalent)	182	550	5,366	7,937

† The GNP is the total dollar value of all goods and services produced by a country in a year. The per capita GNP is calculated by dividing a country's GNP by its population and adjusting for relative purchasing power. About 15% of the world's 6.1 billion people live in high-income countries, while 40% live in low-income countries.

n.a. = data not available   > = greater than   < = less than

Sources: World Bank. *World Development Indicators*. Washington, D.C.: The World Bank, 2001; Central Intelligence Agency. *The World Factbook*. Washington, D.C.: Government Printing Office, 2000.

ment assumed responsibility for fostering community well-being.

29 HEALTH

Malnutrition continues to plague the country. There were an estimated 220 cases of tuberculosis per 100,000 people reported in 1990. Life expectancy was 65 years in 1999. In 1983 there were 16 hospitals and dispensaries, and, by 1989, 61 doctors.

30 HOUSING

Housing on the islands varies greatly, from the estate houses of the plantation headquarters to the thatch huts of the plantation laborers. Some town buildings are wooden; others are mud block with timber, as are plantation-labor dormitories.

31 EDUCATION

Schooling is compulsory for three years only. Primary education is for four years and secondary has two stages: the first four years are followed by three years.

In 1989 there were 19,822 pupils in 64 primary schools with 559 teachers; in general secondary schools, there were 318 teachers and 7,446 pupils. In 2000, adult literacy was estimated at 73%.

32 MEDIA

The *Diario da Republica* (1995 circulation was 500) is published weekly by the government. *Noticias São Tomé e Príncipe* is a quarterly, with a 1995 circulation of 900.

The national radio station broadcasts in Portuguese; there were an estimated 206 radios and 144 television sets per 1,000 population in 2000. A television station broadcasts two days a week. In 1995 there were 2,400 telephones in use.

33 TOURISM AND RECREATION

São Tomé and Príncipe's scenic beauty, wildlife, and unique historic architecture have the potential to attract tourists, but tourist facilities are minimal. The first tourist hotel opened in 1986.

34 FAMOUS SÃO TOMÉANS

Rei Amador (d.1596), who rebelled against the Portuguese, is a national hero. Alda de Espírito Santo (b.1926) is a poet and nationalist leader. Manuel Pinto da Costa (b.1937) became the country's first president on 12 July 1975.

35 BIBLIOGRAPHY

Hodges, Tony. *Sao Tome and Principe: from Plantation Colony to Microstate.* Boulder, Colo.: Westview Press, 1988.

Nevinson, Henry Wood. *A Modern Slavery.* With an introduction by Basil Davidson. London: Daimon Press, 1963 (orig. 1906).

Sao Tome and Principe, Background Notes. Washington, D.C.: U.S. Government Printing Office, 1997.

Shaw, Caroline S. *Sao Tome and Principe.* Santa Barbara, Calif.: Clio Press, 1994.

SA'UDI ARABIA

Kingdom of Sa'udi Arabia

Al-Mamlakah al-'Arabiyah as-Sa'udiyah

CAPITAL: Riyadh (Ar-Riyad).

FLAG: The national flag bears in white on a green field the inscription, in Arabic, "There is no god but Allah, and Mohammad is the messenger of Allah." There is a long white sword beneath the inscription; the sword handle is toward the fly.

ANTHEM: The National Anthem is a short instrumental selection.

MONETARY UNIT: The Sa'udi riyal (SR) is divided into 20 qursh (piasters), in turn divided into 5 halalah. There are coins of 1, 5, 10, 25, 50, and 100 halalah and notes of 1, 5, 10, 50, 100, and 500 riyals. SR1 = $0.2670 (or $1 = SR3.7450).

WEIGHTS AND MEASURES: The metric system has been officially adopted.

HOLIDAYS: Muslim religious holidays include 1st of Muharram (Muslim New Year), 'Id al-Fitr, and 'Id al-'Adha'.

TIME: 3 PM = noon GMT.

1 LOCATION AND SIZE

Sa'udi Arabia, the third-largest country in Asia, constitutes about four-fifths of the Arabian Peninsula in Southwest Asia. Its precise area is difficult to specify because several of its borders are incompletely marked out. According to United Nations estimates, the nation has an area of 1,960,582 square kilometers (756,985 square miles), slightly less than one-fourth the size of the United States, with a total estimated boundary length of 7,055 kilometers (4,384 miles).

Sa'udi Arabia's capital city, Riyadh, is located in the east central part of the country.

2 TOPOGRAPHY

A narrow plain, the Tihamat ash Sham, parallels the Red Sea coast, as do the Hijaz Mountains (Al Hijaz), which rise sharply from the sea. The highest mountains are in the south. East of the Hijaz, the mountains give way to the central uplands. The Dahna (Ad Dahna), a desert region, separates the uplands from the low plateau to the east, which, in turn, gives way to the low-lying Persian Gulf region.

At least one-third of the total area is sandy desert. There are no lakes, and except for artesian wells (wells where water flows to the surface naturally) in the eastern oases, there is no constant flowing water.

3 CLIMATE

From May to September, the hottest period, daytime temperatures reach 54°C (129°F) in the interior and are among the highest recorded anywhere in the world.

Geographic Profile

Geographic Features

Size ranking: 13 of 192
Highest elevation: 3,133 meters (10,279 feet) at Jabal Sawda'
Lowest elevation: Sea level at the Persian Gulf

Land Use†

Arable land:	2%
Permanent crops:	0%
Permanent pastures:	56%
Forests:	1%
Other:	41%

Weather††

Average annual precipitation: 9 centimeters (3.5 inches)
Average temperature in January: 16.1°C (61.0°F)
Average temperature in July: 40.1°C (104.2°F)

†*Arable land:* Land used for temporary crops, like meadows for mowing or pasture, gardens, and greenhouses. *Permanent crops:* Land cultivated with crops that occupy its use for long periods, such as cocoa, coffee, rubber, fruit and nut orchards, and vineyards. *Permanent pastures:* Land used permanently for forage crops. *Forests:* Land containing stands of trees. *Other:* Any land not specified, including built-on areas, roads, and barren land.

††The measurements for precipitation and average temperature were taken at weather stations closest to the country's largest city. Precipitation and average temperature can vary significantly within a country, due to factors such as latitude, altitude, coastal proximity, and wind patterns.

From October through April, the climate is more moderate, with evening temperatures between 16° and 21°C (61° and 70°F). Average annual rainfall is 9 centimeters (3.5 inches).

4 PLANTS AND ANIMALS

The date palm, mangrove, tamarisk, and acacia are common. Wild mammals include the oryx, jerboa, fox, lynx, wildcat, monkey, panther, and jackal. The favorite game bird is the bustard. The country is renowned for its camels and Arabian horses. Fish abound in the coastal waters, and insects, scorpions, lizards, and snakes are numerous.

5 ENVIRONMENT

The dumping of up to six million barrels of oil in the surrounding waters and the destruction of Kuwait's oil wells by fire during the Persian Gulf War (1991) polluted Sa'udi Arabia's air and water. Sa'udi Arabia uses 47% of its water for farming and 8% for industrial purposes.

In 1994, nine of the nation's mammal species and 12 types of birds were endangered. Two type of plants were threatened with extinction.

6 POPULATION

A 2000 census recorded the population as 22.2 million. There is much debate as to the reliability of official census figures, however. The population was estimated by the US Census Bureau at 20.8 million in mid-1998. During the 1990s, the population grew by an annual average of 2.2%. A population of 26.3 million is projected for 2005.

The estimated population density in 2000 was nine persons per square kilometer (23 per square mile). Riyadh, the capital, had a metropolitan population of 3.3 million in 2000; Jiddah, 1.8 million; and Mecca, 920,000.

Sa'udi Arabia's population is overwhelmingly male—the United Nations estimated that there were 124 men for every 100 women in 1998.

SA'UDI ARABIA

| 0 | 100 | 200 Miles |
| 0 | 100 | 200 Kilometers |

LOCATION: 16°23′ to 32°14′N; 34°30′ to 56°22′W. **BOUNDARY LENGTHS:** Jordan, 728 kilometers (455 miles); Iraq, 814 kilometers (505 miles); Kuwait, 222 kilometers (138 miles); Persian Gulf coastline, 751 kilometers (468 miles); Qatar, 60 kilometers (37 miles); UAE, 457 kilometers (285 miles); Oman, 676 kilometers (420 miles); Yemen 1,458 kilometers (906 miles); Red Sea coastline, 1,889 kilometers (1,170 miles). **TERRITORIAL SEA LIMIT:** 12 miles.

General view of the city of Ha'il.

7 MIGRATION

Palestinian Arabs, displaced by the establishment of the state of Israel, are the chief immigrant group. In the early 1990s there were significant numbers of foreign workers from the United States, European countries, Turkey, Jordan, Syria, Jordan, Kuwait, Yemen, the Republic of Korea (ROK), Pakistan, India, Sri Lanka, and the Philippines. In 1990 when Iraq invaded Kuwait, Sa'udi Arabia reacted by expelling Palestinians, as well as workers from Jordan and Yemen, for their countries' support of Iraq. The foreign population was 4.6 million in 1992 (27% of the total population). After the Gulf War (1991), 93,000 Iraqis were granted temporary asylum (political protection). Since then, 60,000 have returned to Iraq.

8 ETHNIC GROUPS

The great majority of the Sa'udis have a common Arabian ancestry (90%). Traces of descent from Turks, Iranians, Indonesians, Pakistanis, Indians, various African groups, and other non-Arab Muslim peoples appear in the Hijaz mountains.

9 LANGUAGES

Arabic, the native language of the native population, is a Semitic language related to Hebrew and Aramaic. The language is written in a cursive script from right to left. Most business people and merchants in oil-producing areas and commercial centers understand English. Government correspondence must be written in Arabic.

10 RELIGIONS

About 85% of the people of Sa'udi Arabia are Sunni Muslims. Most other Sa'udis are Shi'ite Muslims. The holy city of Mecca (Makkah) is the center of Islam and the site of the sacred Ka'bah sanctuary, toward which all Muslims face at prayer. There are several thousand foreign Christian workers—mostly Arab, American, and European.

11 TRANSPORTATION

In 1996 there were 162,000 kilometers (100,667 miles) of highways. In 1995, motor passenger car registrations totaled 1.7 million, and there were 1.1 million commercial vehicles. Railroad lines totaled 1,390 kilometers (864 miles) of track at last estimate.

Jiddah (Jeddah), on the Red Sea, is the chief port of entry for Muslim pilgrims going to Mecca; other ports include Ad-Dammam, Yanbu 'al Bahr, and Jizan. The government-owned Sa'udi Arabian Airlines (Saudia) operates regular domestic and foreign flights to major cities. There are major airports at Jiddah, Riyadh, and 20 other cities.

12 HISTORY

For several thousand years, Arabia has been inhabited by nomadic Semitic tribes. Towns were established at various oases and along caravan routes. During the seventh century AD, followers of Mohammad expanded beyond the Mecca-Medina region and within a century conquered most of the Mediterranean region between Persia (present-day Iran) in the east and Spain in the west.

Although Arabs were dominant in many parts of the Muslim world and there was a great medieval flowering of Arab civilization, the Arabian Peninsula itself (except for the holy cities of Mecca and Medina [Al Madinah]) declined in importance and remained virtually isolated for almost a thousand years. Throughout this period, Arabia was little less than a province of successive Islamic kingdoms (caliphates) that established their capitals in Damascus, Baghdad, Cairo, and Constantinople (now Istanbul).

The Birth of the Sa'udi Kingdom

The foundations of the kingdom of Sa'udi Arabia were laid in the eighteenth century in a program of religious reform and territorial expansion by the Sa'ud family and Mohammad bin 'Abd al-Wahhab, who preached a return to the fundamentals of Islam. First the central uplands, and then the Hijaz mountains were brought under Sa'udi control, as well as the holy city of Mecca. A long struggle with the Ottoman Turks (1811–18) finally resulted in Sa'udi defeat.

Under Faisal (Faysal, r.1843–67), the Sa'udis regained control of the region. They lost it to the Ibn-Rashids in 1891, but succeeded in breaking the Rashidi power in 1906. In December 1915, the Sa'udi leader Ibn-Sa'ud signed a treaty with the British

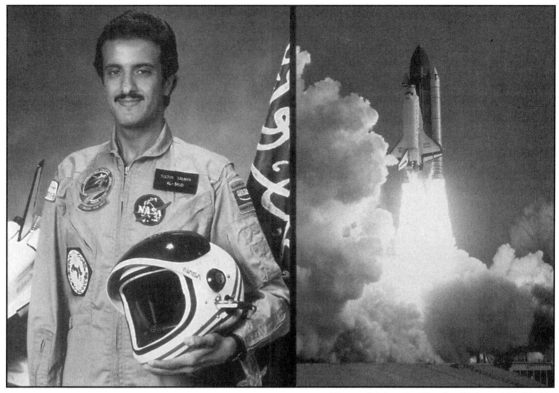

Sa'udi payload specialist Prince Sultan bin Salman Al-Saud flew aboard the U.S. space shuttle, making him the first Arab and Muslim in space.

that placed Sa'udi foreign relations under British control in return for a sizable subsidy.

In the 1920s, Ibn-Sa'ud consolidated his power, defeating challenges by Hussein ibn-'Ali (Husayn ibn-'Ali), the sharif (of noble ancestry in an Islamic country) of Mecca, and capturing At Ta'if, Mecca, and Medina, as well as Jiddah. On 22 September 1932, the various parts of the realm were combined into the Kingdom of Sa'udi Arabia, with much the same boundaries that exist today.

Oil and the Modern Sa'udi State

With the discovery of oil in the 1930s, the history of Sa'udi Arabia was changed forever. Reserves have proved vast—about one-fourth of the world's total—and production, begun in earnest after World War II (1939–45), has provided a huge income, much of it expended on construction and social services. Sa'udi Arabia's petroleum-derived wealth has considerably enhanced the country's influence in world economic and political forums.

Since the 1980s, the government has regulated its petroleum production to stabilize the international oil market and has used its influence as the most powerful moderate member of the Organization of Petroleum Exporting Countries (OPEC) to restrain the more radical members.

Political life in Sa'udi Arabia has remained basically stable in recent decades, despite several abrupt changes of leadership. Crown Prince Fahd Bin Abdul Aziz al-Saud ascended the throne in 1982 after his half-brother, King Khaled, died of a heart attack. King Fahd has encouraged continuing modernization while seeking to preserve the nation's social stability and Islamic heritage.

Sa'udi Arabia's wealth and selective generosity have given it great political influence throughout the world and especially in the Middle East. It suspended aid to Egypt after that country's peace talks with Israel at Camp David, Maryland, but renewed relations in 1987. It secretly contributed substantial funds to United States president Ronald Reagan's administration for combating communist regimes in Central America. It actively supported Iraq during the war with Iran and tried, in vain, to prevent Iraq's conflict with Kuwait.

When Iraq invaded Kuwait in 1990, Sa'udi Arabia, fearing Iraqi aggression, radically altered its traditional policy to permit the stationing of foreign troops on its soil. Riyadh made substantial contributions of arms, oil, and funds to the Allied victory, cutting off subsidies to and expelling Palestinians and workers from Jordan, Yemen, and other countries that had supported Iraq in the period after the invasion.

Sa'udi Arabia and the United States consult closely on political, economic, commercial, and security matters. These supports became more visible following the Gulf War (1991), and continued Iraqi resistance to disarm. Some Sa'udis became annoyed with the US military presence in Sa'udi Arabia in 1993–94 and considered it offensive to Islam. In 1995, seven people, including five Americans, were killed by a terrorist attack on a military training center in Riyadh. In June 1996, a car bomb exploded in front of a housing complex for US military personnel, killing 19 servicemen.

In 1990, 1994, 1997, and 1998, tragic accidents occurred during the *hajj,* the traditional Muslim pilgrimage to Mecca which attracts millions. More than 2,000 pilgrims have been killed in stampedes or fires since 1990.

13 GOVERNMENT

Sa'udi Arabia is a religiously based monarchy in which the sovereign's dominant powers are regulated according to Muslim law (*Shari'ah*), tribal law, and custom. There is no written constitution; laws must be compatible with Islamic law. The Council of Ministers is appointed by the king to advise on policy, originate legislation, and supervise the growing bureaucracy. In 1992, King Fahd announced the creation of the *Majlis al Shura,* an advisory body that would provide a forum for public debate.

Photo credit: EPD/Government of Saudi Arabia.

Name:	Fahd Bin Abdul Aziz al-Saud
Position:	King and Prime Minister of a monarchy
Took office:	13 June 1982
Birthplace:	Riyadh, Sa'udi Arabia
Birth date:	1923
Education:	Received practical training at his father's court
Of interest:	In 1953, al-Saud became the first minister of education in the country's history. Since about 1999, Crown Prince Abdullah has been considered king in all but name, due to the failing health of al-Saud.

With the deterioration of King Fahd's health in 1997, his half-brother, Crown Prince Abdullah, took over the reins of government.

The kingdom is divided into 14 emirates (state in an Islamic nation), each headed by a crown-appointed governor.

14 POLITICAL PARTIES

There are no political parties in Sa'udi Arabia.

15 JUDICIAL SYSTEM

The king acts as the highest court of appeal and has the power of pardon. The judiciary consists of lower courts that handle misdemeanors and minor civil cases; high courts of Islamic law (Shari'ah); and courts of appeal. An 11-member Supreme Council of Justice reviews all sentences of execution, cutting, or stoning.

16 ARMED FORCES

Sa'udi Arabia's armed forces totaled 105,500 personnel in 2000, having doubled in size to meet the Iraqi threat. The army had 70,000 personnel, 1,055 main battle tanks, 570 armored fighting vehicles, and 33 batteries of surface-to-air missiles. The navy's strength was about 13,500 personnel (3,000 marines), who manned 8 frigates and 26 other combatants. The air force had 18,000 personnel and 432 combat aircraft. In 1997 Sa'udi Arabia spent $18.1 billion on its own forces.

17 ECONOMY

The economy is heavily dependent on oil production. Oil provided more than 90% of export value and 75% of government revenues in 1999.

The government has tried to diversify the economy by developing industries using petroleum, including steel and petrochemical manufacture. The economy is open to private investors, but the govern-

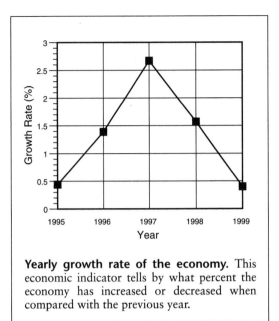

Yearly growth rate of the economy. This economic indicator tells by what percent the economy has increased or decreased when compared with the previous year.

ment plays a significant role in the economy.

18 INCOME

Sa'udi Arabia's gross domestic product (GDP) in 1998 was $186 billion, or about $9,000 per person. In 1999, the average inflation rate was 1.4%, resulting in a growth in GDP of just under 0.5%.

19 INDUSTRY

The country is attempting to diversify its manufacturing. Industrial products include cement, steel, glass, metal manufactures, automotive parts, building materials, and other industrial products, along with petroleum refinery products and petrochemicals. Total refinery capacity in 1995 was 1.6 million barrels per day. Sa'udi Arabia produced 588 million barrels of refined petroleum products that year.

20 LABOR

In 1991, about three million foreigners worked in Sa'udi Arabia, mostly in the oil and construction sector. The total labor force in 1998 stood at seven million, with 40% in government, 25% in industry and oil (comprising 47% of the economy), 30% in services (47% of economy), and 5% in agriculture (6% of economy). No labor unions exist (they are illegal), but there are professional and trade guilds.

21 AGRICULTURE

Agriculture engaged about 5% of the labor force, and contributed about 6% to the gross domestic product (GDP) in 1998. Only about 1.1% of Sa'udi Arabia's land area is cultivated, although 40% is suitable for grazing. Agricultural irrigation accounts for 90% of total water needs, with wheat production alone using about one-third of the country's annual water supply.

Although Sa'udi Arabia has more than seven million date palms and provides about 12% of the world's supply of dates (an estimated 600,000 tons in 1998), the growing of dates has declined in recent decades in favor of wheat, corn, sorghum, tomatoes, onions, grapes, and a variety of other fruits and vegetables. Wheat output was 1.8 million tons in 1998.

22 DOMESTICATED ANIMALS

As of 1998, Sa'udi Arabia had an estimated eight million sheep, 4.4 million goats, 422,000 camels, 200,000 head of cattle, 97,000 donkeys, and 3,000 horses. Donkeys and mules are still valued as pack

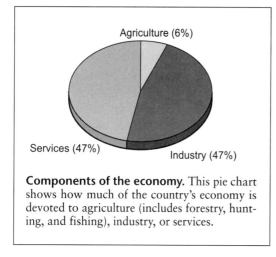

Agriculture (6%)

Services (47%)

Industry (47%)

Components of the economy. This pie chart shows how much of the country's economy is devoted to agriculture (includes forestry, hunting, and fishing), industry, or services.

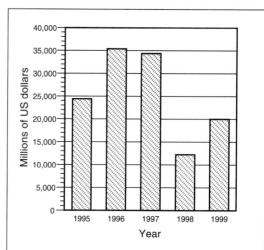

Yearly balance of trade measured in millions of US dollars. The balance of trade is the difference between what a country sells to other countries (its exports) and what it buys (its imports). If a country imports more than it exports, it has a negative balance of trade (a trade deficit). If exports exceed imports there is a positive balance of trade (a trade surplus).

animals, and the northern Persian Gulf coast area is well known for its white donkeys. Goats are kept for milk; their hair is used in rugs and tents, and the skins serve as water bags. In 1998, Sa'udi Arabia had an estimated 95 million poultry. Domestic production of chickens met 56% of the country's consumption in 1996.

Pork products, for raising or by import, are banned because of Islamic law.

23 FISHING

Fishing provides employment and self-sufficiency to communities on both Sa'udi coasts, although cash earnings are negligible. The fish catch was estimated at 54,085 tons in 1997.

24 FORESTRY

Only 0.6% of Sa'udi Arabia is forested. The principal varieties of forest growth—acacia, date, juniper, wild olive, sidr, tamarind, and tamarisk—are generally not useful for timber, but some wood from date palms is used for construction.

25 MINING

Mining experts suspect that Sa'udi Arabia has substantial national reserves of gold, iron ore, silver, copper, zinc, lead, pyrites, phosphate, magnesite, barite, marble, and gypsum. An intensive search for these deposits is being carried on by Sa'udi and foreign companies. Production of metal concentrate and bullion in 1996 included copper, 834 tons; gold (crude bullion), 8,300 kilograms; and silver, 16,608 kilograms.

26 FOREIGN TRADE

Total exports were valued at $48 billion in 1999, and imports were estimated at $28 billion that year. Oil accounted for more than 90% of export earnings that year.

Selected Social Indicators

The statistics below are estimates for the period 1996 to 2000. For comparison purposes, data for the United States and averages for low-income countries and high-income countries are also given.

Indicator	Sa'udi Arabia	Low-income countries	High-income countries	United States
Per capita gross national product (GNP)†	**$11,050**	$1,870	$25,690	$31,910
Population growth rate	**3.4%**	2.1%	0.7%	1.1%
People per square kilometer of land	**9**	73	29	30
Life expectancy in years	**72**	59	78	77
Number of physicians per 1,000 people	**1.3**	1.0	2.5	2.5
Number of pupils per teacher (primary school)	**14**	41	17	14
Illiteracy rate (15 years and older)	**23%**	34%	<5%	3%
Television sets per 1,000 people	**263**	85	693	844
Energy consumed per capita (kg of oil equivalent)	**5,244**	550	5,366	7,937

† The GNP is the total dollar value of all goods and services produced by a country in a year. The per capita GNP is calculated by dividing a country's GNP by its population and adjusting for relative purchasing power. About 15% of the world's 6.1 billion people live in high-income countries, while 40% live in low-income countries.

n.a. = data not available   > = greater than   < = less than

Sources: World Bank. *World Development Indicators.* Washington, D.C.: The World Bank, 2001; Central Intelligence Agency. *The World Factbook.* Washington, D.C.: Government Printing Office, 2000.

Non-oil exports included dates, pearls, jewelry, mineral products, and hides and skins. The major categories of imports included machinery and electrical appliances, grains and other food imports, transportation equipment, and consumer goods. European Union countries account for almost 20% of Sa'udi Arabia's exports and supply over 30% of imports. Japan takes about 17% of exports and supplies over 7% of imports. The United States accounts for over 15% of exports and 21% of imports.

27 ENERGY AND POWER

With the dissolution of the former Soviet Union in December 1991, Sa'udi Arabia became the world's largest oil producer. Proven reserves of crude oil were estimated at 263.5 billion barrels, or about 25% of the world's known deposits, in 2000. In 1998, an estimated 8.5 million barrels of oil were produced per day.

Natural gas production was 46.7 billion cubic meters (1,650 billion cubic feet) in 1998. Reserves of natural gas were estimated at 5.8 trillion cubic meters (204.5 trillion cubic feet) in 2000, or the world's fifth largest reserves.

Sa'udi Arabia has limited waterpower resources, and oil-powered diesel engines generate most of its electric power. Electrical service reached 92% of the population by 1992. Electric power production in 1998 amounted to 110.1 billion kilowatt hours. Solar energy is becoming increasingly important as an alternative to diesel power.

28 SOCIAL DEVELOPMENT

Social welfare in Sa'udi Arabia is traditionally provided through the family or tribe. Those with no family or tribal ties have recourse to the traditional Islamic religious foundations or may request government relief. Social insurance provides health care, disability, death, old age pension, and survivor benefits for workers and their families. A large company with many employees in Sa'udi Arabia, ARAMCO, has a welfare plan for its employees that includes pension funds, accident compensation, and free medical care.

In 1999, only 5% of the labor force was female, because they are limited by law in their contact with men. Extreme modesty of dress is required, and women are not permitted to drive motor vehicles.

Sa'udi Arabia does not recognize international standards on human rights. Privacy, speech, assembly, association, movement, and religious choice are not protected.

29 HEALTH

In 1990–97, hospital beds per 1,000 people equaled 2.5. Health personnel in 1990 included 21,110 physicians, 1,967 dentists, and 48,066 nurses (about 3.8 per 1,000).

The public health care system is supplemented by a small but generally excellent private health sector. In 1992, 97% of the population had access to health care services. Total health care expenditures in 1990 were $4.8 billion.

Sa'udi Arabia still suffers from severe health problems. A major cause of disease is malnutrition, leading to widespread scurvy, rickets, night blindness, and anemia, as well as low resistance to tuberculosis. Dysentery attacks all ages and classes, and trachoma is common.

A government campaign was successful in eradicating malaria; typhoid is widespread, but acquired immunity prevents serious outbreaks of this disease.

In 1995, 95% of the population had access to safe water and 86% had adequate sanitation. In 1960, life expectancy at birth was 43 years; it averaged 72 years in 1999.

30 HOUSING

The continuing inflow of rural people to towns and cities, coupled with the rise in levels of expectation among the urban population, has created a serious housing problem; improvement in urban housing is one of Sa'udi Arabia's foremost economic needs. Some 506,800 dwelling units were built during 1974–85. In 1984, 78,884 building permits were issued, 84% of these for concrete dwellings and 8% for housing units of blocks and bricks.

31 EDUCATION

The literacy rate was 77% in 2000. In 1997 there were 11,506 primary schools, with 2.2 million pupils and 175,458 teachers. Secondary schools had 1.5 million students and 119,881 teachers. Higher

Schoolboys answering their teacher.

education was pursued in 90 institutions, with 273,992 students and 15,868 instructors in 1997. Principal universities are King Sa'ud University (formerly Riyadh University) and King Abdul Aziz University of Jiddah.

32 MEDIA

The telephone system was greatly expanded in the late 1970s, and in 1995 some 1.6 million telephones were in use. The number of radios was estimated at 319, and the number of television sets at 263 per 1,000 population in 2000.

Newspapers are privately owned; criticism of the fundamental principles of Islam and of basic national institutions, including the royal family, is not permitted. The largest Arabic daily papers (with 1999 circulations) are *Al–Asharq Al-Awsat* (224,900); *Al-Jazirah* (90,000); and *Al-Riyadh* (150,000). Leading English-language dailies are the *Arab News* (110,000) and *Saudi Gazette* (22,000).

33 TOURISM AND RECREATION

Sa'udi Arabia is one of the hardest places in the world to visit. Tourist visas are not issued, and foreign visitors must show letters of invitation from Sa'udi employers or sponsors to enter the country. Every year, however, there is a great influx of pilgrims to Mecca (Mekkah) and Medina (Al Madinah), cities that non-Muslims are forbidden to enter. In 1998 the number of pilgrims totaled more than 2 million. Total visitor arrivals totaled 3.7 million.

Traditional sports include hunting with salukis (tall, swift, slender hunting dogs), falconry, and horse and camel racing. Modern sports facilities include the Riyadh Stadium, complete with Olympic-standard running tracks and soccer fields.

34 FAMOUS SA'UDIS

Sa'udi Arabia is heir to an Islamic civilization that developed from the teachings of Muhammad (570–632), founder of Islam, born of the tribe of Quraysh in Mecca. The branch of Islam which claims most contemporary Sa'udis is that preached by Mohammad bin 'Abd al-Wahhab (1703?–91), a fundamentalist reformer.

The Sa'udi who has gained greatest renown outside the modern kingdom of Sa'udi Arabia is 'Abd al-'Aziz ibn 'Abd ar-Rahman al-Faysal as-Sa'ud, better known as Ibn-Sa'ud (1880–1953), considered the father of his country. In 1964, Faisal (Fay-sal ibn-'Abd al-'Aziz as-Sa'ud, 1906–75) was proclaimed king. Upon his assassination in March 1975, he was succeeded as king and prime minister by Khaled (Khalid ibn-'Abd al-'Aziz, 1913–82). Ahmad Zaki Yamani (b.1930), a former minister of petroleum and mineral resources, gained an international reputation as a spokesman for the oil-exporting countries.

35 BIBLIOGRAPHY

Anderson, Laurie Halse. *Saudi Arabia*. Minneapolis: Carolrhoda Books, 2001.

Alireza, Marianne. "Women of Arabia." *National Geographic,* October 1987, 423–453.

Fazio, Wende. *Saudi Arabia*. New York: Children's Press, 1999.

Goodwin, William. *Saudi Arabia*. San Diego, Calif.: Lucent Books, 2001.

Honeyman, Susannah. *Saudi Arabia*. Austin, Tex.: Raintree Steck-Vaughn, 1995.

Kostiner, Joseph. *The Making of Sa'udi Arabia, 1916–1936: from Chieftancy to Monarchical State*. New York: Oxford University Press, 1993.

Lawrence, T. E. *Seven Pillars of Wisdom*. New York: Penguin, 1976 (orig. 1926).

McCarthy, Kevin. *Saudi Arabia*. Parsippany, N.J.: Dillon Press, 1997.

Metz, Helen Chapin, ed. *Sa'udi Arabia: A Country Study*. 5th ed. Washington, D.C.: Library of Congress, 1993.

Mulloy, Martin. *Saudi Arabia*. Philadelphia: Chelsea House, 1999.

Nagel, Rob, and Anne Commire. "Muhammad." In *World Leaders, People Who Shaped the World*. Volume I: Africa and Asia. Detroit: U*X*L, 1994.

SENEGAL

Republic of Senegal
République du Sénégal

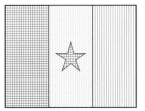

CAPITAL: Dakar.

FLAG: The flag is a tricolor of green, yellow, and red vertical stripes; at the center of the yellow stripe is a green star.

ANTHEM: Begins "Pincez, tous, vos koras, frappez les balafons" ("Pluck your koras, strike the balafons").

MONETARY UNIT: The Communauté Financière Africaine franc (CFA Fr) is the national currency. There are coins of 1, 2, 5, 10, 25, 50, 100, and 500 CFA francs, and notes of 50, 100, 500, 1,000, 5,000, and 10,000 CFA francs. CFA Fr1 = $0.00154 (or $1 = CFA Fr647.25).

WEIGHTS AND MEASURES: The metric system is the legal standard.

HOLIDAYS: New Year's Day, 1 January; Independence Day, 4 April; Labor Day, 1 May; Day of Association, 14 July; Assumption, 15 August; All Saints' Day, 1 November; Christmas, 25 December. Movable religious holidays include 'Id al-Fitr, 'Id al-'Adha', Milad an-Nabi, Good Friday, Easter Monday, Ascension, and Pentecost Monday.

TIME: GMT.

1 LOCATION AND SIZE

Situated on the western bulge of Africa, Senegal has a land area of 196,190 square kilometers (75,749 square miles), slightly smaller than the state of South Dakota. The total boundary length of Senegal is 3,171 kilometers (1,970 miles). Senegal's capital city, Dakar, is located on the Atlantic coast.

2 TOPOGRAPHY

There are dunes in the northern part of the Senegal coast. Behind the coast is a sandy plain. The Casamance River region in the south is low but more varied, while to the southeast lie the Tamgué foothills. Much of the northwest of Senegal (known as the Ferlo) is desert-like, but the center and most of the south are open savanna, or tropical grasslands. The major rivers are the Senegal, Saloum, Gambia, and Casamance.

3 CLIMATE

The average annual rainfall ranges from 34 centimeters (13 inches) in the extreme north to 155 centimeters (61 inches) in the southwest. Temperatures vary according to the season. At Dakar, during the cool season (December–April), the average daily maximum is 26°C (79°F) and the average minimum is 17°C (63°F). During the hot season (May–November), the averages are 30°C (86°F) and 20°C (68°F).

4 PLANTS AND ANIMALS

The most tropical part of southern Senegal has mangrove swamps and remnants of

Geographic Profile

Geographic Features

Size ranking: 85 of 192
Highest elevation: 581 meters (1,906 feet) at an
  unnamed location in the Futa Jaldon foothills
Lowest elevation: Sea level at the Atlantic Ocean

Land Use

Arable land: 12%
Permanent crops: 0%
Permanent pastures: 16%
Forests: 54%
Other: 18%

Weather

Average annual precipitation: 57.8 centimeters (22.8
  inches)
Average temperature in January: 21.1°C (70.0°F)
Average temperature in July: 27.3°C (81.1°F)

high forest, including oil palms, bamboo, African teak, and the silk-cotton tree. The dry thornland of the northeast has spiny shrubs, especially acacia, including the gum-bearing species. Most of Senegal is savanna, or tropical grassland. The lion and leopard are occasionally found in the northeast, as are chimpanzees, elephants, hippopotamuses, and buffalo. The wild pig, hare, guinea fowl, quail, and bustard are widely distributed. Insects and birds are abundant, and there are numerous lizards, snakes, and other reptiles.

5 ENVIRONMENT

In much of Senegal, increasing amounts of land are turning to desert (in a process called desertification) because of overgrazing, inadequately controlled cutting of forests for fuel, and soil erosion from overcultivation. Dakar, the capital, suffers from such typical urban problems as improper sanitation (especially during the rainy season, when sewers overflow) and

air pollution from motor vehicles. Some 16% of the nation's city dwellers and 72% of the people living in rural areas do not have pure water. Senegal's cities produce 0.6 million tons of solid waste per year. Senegal has six national parks. In 1994, 11 mammal species and five bird species were endangered, and 32 types of plants were threatened with extinction.

6 POPULATION

The United Nations estimated Senegal's 2000 population at 10.4 million. A population of 12.2 million is projected by the US Census Bureau for 2005. It was estimated that 47% of the population lived in urban areas in 2000. The average estimated population density was 48 persons per square kilometer (124 per square mile) in 2000. Dakar, the capital and principal city, had a population of about 2 million in 2000.

7 MIGRATION

There is seasonal migration between The Gambia and Senegal in connection with cultivation and harvesting of peanuts. There are perhaps 20,000 French and more than 18,000 Lebanese in the country, about a third of whom have Senegalese nationality. Senegal was home to 64,000 Mauritanian refugees in mid-1997.

8 ETHNIC GROUPS

The largest ethnic group is the Wolof, who made up 44% of the total population in 1998. Closely related are the Sérer (15%), in west-central Senegal, and the Lebu, concentrated in the Dakar area. Other important groups are the Tukulor, the Fulani

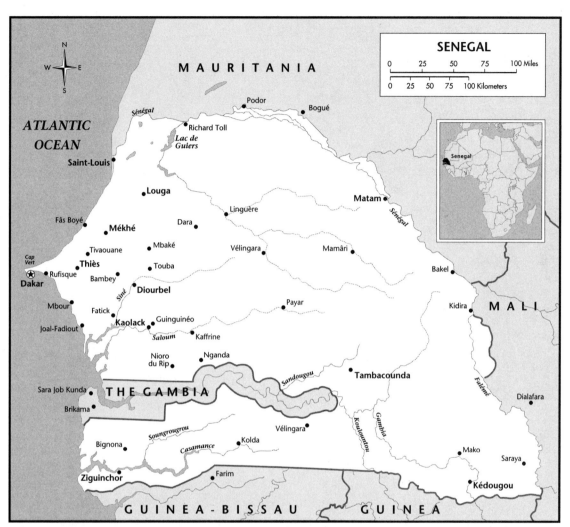

LOCATION: 11°30′ to 17°30′w; 12° to 17°N. **BOUNDARY LENGTHS:** Mauritania, 813 kilometers (505 miles); Mali, 419 kilometers (260 miles); Guinea, 330 kilometers (205 miles); Guinea-Bissau, 338 kilometers (210 miles); Atlantic coastline, 531 kilometers (330 miles); the Gambia, 740 kilometers (460 miles). **TERRITORIAL SEA LIMIT:** 12 miles.

(Peul) and Bambara, the Maelinkó or Mandingo, and the Diola.

Sérer, 14%; Mandingue, 6%; Diola, 6%; and Sarakhole/Sohinke, 1.4%.

9 LANGUAGES

French, the official language, is the language of administration and of the schools. Wolof was spoken by 71% of the people in Senegal in 1988; Poular, 21%;

10 RELIGIONS

The constitution provides for religious freedom. In 1998, 94% of the people professed Islam. About 4% of Senegalese are Christians, mainly Roman Catholics, with

great ports of Africa. The port can accommodate ships of up to 100,000 tons. Gross capacity of the single merchant vessel in 1998 came to 1,995 tons. The Senegal, Saloum, and Casamance rivers are all navigable, to varying degrees. Dakar's Yoff International Airport, a West African air center, is served by many foreign airlines.

12 HISTORY

Between the tenth and fifteenth centuries AD, the Wolof and Sérer peoples entered Senegal from the northeast. The fourteenth century saw the emergence of the Jolof empire, controlling the six Wolof states of Jolof, Kayor, Baol, Walo, Sine, and Salum. Toward the end of the seventeenth century Jolof power declined, due, at least partly, to struggles between the states. European activities in Senegal began with the Portuguese arrival at the Cap Vert Peninsula and the mouth of the Senegal River in 1444–45.

The Portuguese enjoyed a monopoly on trade in slaves and gold until the seventeenth century, when they were succeeded by the Dutch, who virtually dominated all trade by 1650. The later seventeenth century brought the beginnings of the rivalry between the English and the French, which dominated the eighteenth century in Senegal and elsewhere in Africa.

Peanut cultivation, the foundation of Senegal's modern economy, began around 1850. Between 1895 and 1904, a series of decrees consolidated eight territories into a French West Africa federation, of which Dakar became the capital. In 1920, a Colonial Council, partly elected by the citizens of the towns and partly consisting of

Photo credit: Cynthia Bassett.

Senegalese boy dressed in a typical Senegalese cotton garment.

the rest (2%) observing African traditional religions.

11 TRANSPORTATION

Senegal has 904 kilometers (562 miles) of railroads, all owned by the government. Of Senegal's 14,576 kilometers (9,058 miles) of classified roads in 1999, some 4,271 kilometers (2,654 miles) were tarred. There were 106,000 passenger cars and 48,000 commercial vehicles in 1995.

Favorably located at the westernmost point of the continent and possessing up-to-date equipment, Dakar is one of the

chiefs from the rest of Senegal, was established. All the elected bodies were suppressed in 1940 but restored at the end of World War II (1939–45). Under the constitution of 1946, Senegal was given two deputies in the French parliament, and a Territorial Assembly was established. The following year, Senegal accepted the new French constitution and became a self-governing republic within the French Community.

In June 1960 Senegal joined the Mali Federation together with Mali and French Sudan, but conflicting views soon led to its breakup; a month later the Legislative Assembly of Senegal proclaimed Senegal's national independence. A new constitution was adopted, and on 5 September 1960, Léopold-Sédar Senghor was elected president and Mamadou Dia became prime minister, retaining the position he had held since 1957 as head of the government. In 1962, the legislature overthrew Dia's government, and Senghor was elected by unanimous vote as head of government. Less than three months later, the electorate approved a new constitution that abolished the post of prime minister and made the president both chief of state and head of the executive branch.

Having been reelected in 1968, 1973, and 1978, Senghor resigned as president at the end of 1980 and was succeeded by Abdou Diouf. In February 1982, Senegal and The Gambia formed the Confederation of Senegambia with Diouf as president. The two countries pledged to integrate their armed and security forces, form an economic and monetary union, and coordinate foreign policy and communications.

Diouf was elected to a full term as president of Senegal on 27 February 1983. He reformed the government, making it less corrupt and more efficient. In the 1988 national elections, Diouf carried 77% of the vote. In April 1989, a nationwide state of emergency was declared and a curfew imposed in Dakar after rioters, enraged by reports of the killing of hundreds of Senegalese in Mauritania, killed dozens of Mauritanians. Relations with Mauritania were broken and armed clashes along the border and internal rioting led to the expulsion of most Mauritanians residing in Senegal. Diplomatic relations were reestablished in April 1992 and the northern border along the Senegal River was reopened.

In the southernmost province of Casamance, a separatist group, the Movement of Democratic Forces of the Casamance (MFDC), has challenged the armed forces for years. A July 1993 ceasefire agreement appears to be holding, although there are numerous charges of human rights abuses by both sides, and hundreds have been killed. From 1990 to 1993, Senegalese armed forces played a major role in the peacekeeping effort in Liberia.

Diouf again won reelection in February 1993. Diouf's principal opponent, Maitre Abdoulaye Wade of the Democratic Party, won the presidency in 2000, securing the growth of democracy in Senegal.

Photo credit: EPD/Government of Senegal.

Name:	Abdoulaye Wade
Position:	President of a republic under multiparty democratic rule
Took office:	2000
Birthplace:	Kebemer, Senegal
Birth date:	29 May 1926
Education:	Besancon, doctorate in law and economics
Spouse:	Viviane Vert (college sweetheart)
Children:	One son, Karim; one daughter, Sindjeli
Of interest:	Wade once played the violin and guitar. He is fluent in French, English, and Wolof. Wade's known trademark is his shaved head.

13 GOVERNMENT

Legislative power is exercised by a 120-member National Assembly, elected for five years simultaneously with the president. Under the 1963 constitution, as amended, the president of the republic determines national policy and has the power to dissolve the National Assembly. If the president asks the assembly to reconsider a measure it has enacted, the bill must be passed again by a three-fifths majority before it becomes law. The assembly elects the 16 members of the High Court of Justice from among its ranks.

14 POLITICAL PARTIES

Since independence in 1960, the UPS (Union Progressiste Sénégalaise—UPS) has been the dominant political party. In 1976, the UPS changed its name to the Senegalese Socialist Party (Parti Socialiste Sénégalais—PS), after joining the Socialist International. There was no legal opposition party from 1966 until 1974, when the Senegalese Democratic Party (Parti Démocratique Sénégalais—PDS) was formed in order to meet the constitutional requirement for a responsible opposition. In 1981, the constitution, which had restricted the number of political parties to four, was amended to end all restrictions. Seven parties contested the National Assembly elections of 9 May 1993, including the Jappoo Leggeeyal ("Let Us Unite") Party, the Democratic League, the Independence and Labor Party (PIT), and the Senegalese Democratic Union/ Renewal Party. Since the 1980s, there has been a steady increase in PDS representation and decline in PS support.

15 JUDICIAL SYSTEM

The High Council of the Magistrature, founded in 1960 and headed by the president, determines the constitutionality of laws and international commitments and decides when members of the legislature and the executive have exceeded their authority. A 16-member High Court of Justice, founded in 1962 and elected by the National Assembly from among its own members, presides over impeachment proceedings. The Supreme Court, founded in 1960, is made up of members appointed by the president of the republic on the advice of the High Council of the Magistrature.

16 ARMED FORCES

Senegal's armed forces totaled about 11,000 men in 2000. The army of 10,000 men included 10 infantry or armored battalions, one artillery battalion, and one engineering battalion. The navy of 600 had 10 patrol craft and small landing craft, and the air force of 400 had eight aircraft. Military outlays in 1997 were about $68 million. Senegal supplied a battalion for service in Liberia and United Nations observers in three other nations. France maintains a reinforced marine regiment of 1,200 in Senegal.

17 ECONOMY

Senegal's economy is based on its agricultural sector, primarily peanut production, and a modest industrial sector. Agriculture is highly vulnerable to declining rainfall, expansion of the desert onto farm land, and changes in world food prices. When the first of a series of droughts struck in the latter part of the 1960s, the economy deteriorated rapidly. Today, 35 years after achieving independence, Senegal's resource-poor economy remains fragile and dependent upon foreign donors.

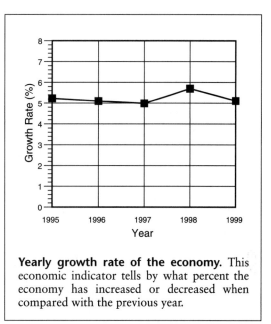

Yearly growth rate of the economy. This economic indicator tells by what percent the economy has increased or decreased when compared with the previous year.

In 1994, France suddenly devalued the CFA franc, causing its value to drop in half overnight. Prices for imported goods soared and the inflation rate hit 32%. The devaluation was designed to encourage new investment and discourage importing goods that could be made in Senegal. After the initial shock, the government was able to reschedule its debt, and foreign assistance increased. The inflation rate was just 1.8% in 1998.

18 INCOME

In 1998, Senegal's gross domestic product (GDP) was $15.6 billion, or about $1,600 per person. In 1999, the average inflation rate was 1.8%, resulting in a growth in GDP of roughly 5%.

19 INDUSTRY

In French-speaking West Africa, Senegal's manufacturing sector is second only to

Fish products have surpassed peanuts as Senegal's number-one export.

that of the Côte d'Ivoire (Ivory Coast). Processing of agricultural products (oil mills, sugar refineries, fish canneries, flour mills, bakeries, beverage and dairy processing, and tobacco manufacturing) plays a key role. Especially important are the four groundnut-processing mills, which produced 55,951 tons of groundnut oil for export in 1994.

Textiles, leather goods, chemicals, paper, wood products, and building materials also are important manufactures. The textile industry includes four cotton-ginning mills; factories for weaving, dyeing, and printing cloth; and plants that produce mattresses, thread, and hats. Other industrial products include plywood, boats, bicycles, soap, paints, acetylene, sulfuric acid, phosphoric acid, phosphate fertilizer, and cigarettes.

20 LABOR

The total work force was about 4 million in 1999, with 70% in agriculture (19% of the GDP). Senegal's fundamental labor legislation provides for collective agreements between employers and trade unions, for the fixing of basic minimum wages by the government on recommendation of advisory committees, and for a 40- to 48-hour workweek. The right to strike is recognized by law, and there are special labor courts.

21 AGRICULTURE

Only about 11% of Senegal's total land area is cultivated. Millet occupied 36% of the cultivated land in 1998; and peanuts, 32%. Production of unshelled peanuts varies widely because of periodic drought, and it is frequently underreported because of unauthorized sales to processors in neighboring countries. In 1998, the reported production was 728,000 tons (95% for oil). Cotton is Senegal's other major export crop. Seed cotton production was 52,000 tons in 1998.

Production of food crops, some of which are grown in rotation with peanuts, does not meet Senegal's needs. Production in 1998 included (in thousands of tons): millet, 426; sorghum, 118; rice, 174; corn, 60; and cassava, 47. About 8,000 hectares (19,700 acres) yielded 883,000 tons of sugarcane in 1998.

22 DOMESTICATED ANIMALS

Raising livestock is a primary activity in the northern section of Senegal and a secondary one for farmers in the southern and central regions. In 1998, the estimated livestock population included 3 million head of cattle, 4.2 million sheep, 3.6 million goats, 506,000 horses, 376,000 donkeys, 320,000 hogs, 8,000 camels, and 44 million poultry. The slaughter in 1998 yielded an estimated 47,000 tons of beef and veal and 29,000 tons of sheep and goat meat. Hides are exported or used in local shoe production and handicrafts.

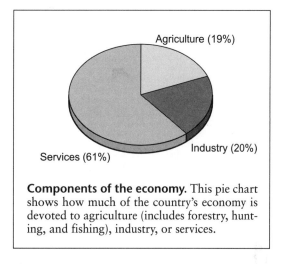

Components of the economy. This pie chart shows how much of the country's economy is devoted to agriculture (includes forestry, hunting, and fishing), industry, or services.

23 FISHING

Senegal has a flourishing fishing industry, and Dakar is one of the most important Atlantic tuna ports. In 1997, fish exports amounted to only $286.7 million, up from $218 million in 1991. The total catch in 1997 was 507,140 tons, 53% of which was sardines.

24 FORESTRY

Senegal has about 7.6 million hectares (18.8 million acres) of classified woodland and forest, most of it in the southern Casamance region. Timber production is small, with firewood and charcoal being the most important forest products. About 5.3 million cubic meters of roundwood were cut in 1997, of which about 86% went for fuel.

25 MINING

Minerals accounted for almost 20% of export earnings in 1996. Mining, especially of phosphates at a deposit some 80

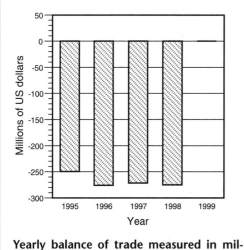

Yearly balance of trade measured in millions of US dollars. The balance of trade is the difference between what a country sells to other countries (its exports) and what it buys (its imports). If a country imports more than it exports, it has a negative balance of trade (a trade deficit). If exports exceed imports there is a positive balance of trade (a trade surplus).

kilometers (50 miles) northeast of Dakar, has taken on added importance for Senegal's economy in the postindependence era. Production of aluminum phosphate stood at 40,000 tons in 1996. Calcium phosphate output reached 1.6 million tons in 1995, and mining of sea salt rose to about 120,000 tons in 1996.

26 FOREIGN TRADE

Food products, petroleum refinery products, phosphates, chemicals, and cotton are the leading exports. In 1996, fish products accounted for 26.6% of exports; peanut products, 10%; and phosphates, 3.3%. The leading imports are industrial products, machinery and transport equipment, and food products. France is Senegal's principal trading partner, accounting

for 22% of exports and 36% of imports in 1999. Senegal sent about 12.8% of its exports to Italy and 7.3% to Mali in 1995. Its imports came primarily from the United States, Thailand, Spain, Italy, and France.

27 ENERGY AND POWER

Electric power generation is almost entirely thermal. Production in 1998 totaled 1.2 billion kilowatt hours, 98% of it in public plants. There are extensive reserves of peat along the coast between Dakar and Saint-Louis. An oil refinery near Dakar, with an annual capacity of 1.2 million tons, produces petroleum products from imported crude oil. Natural gas production in 1994 totaled 39 million cubic meters (1.4 billion cubic feet).

28 SOCIAL DEVELOPMENT

Since 1956, a system of family allowances for wage earners has provided small maternity and child benefits. Shared equally by employer and employee is a 6% contribution to a fund for general medical and hospital expenses. In addition, employees contribute 4.8% of gross salary to a retirement fund and employers 7.2%; the retirement age is 55.

Discrimination against women is widespread in education and employment. Non-Muslims also may face discrimination in civil, political, or economic matters, even though minority religions are protected under the law.

29 HEALTH

In 2000, there was less than 1 doctor per 1,000 people, and about 1 hospital bed

Selected Social Indicators

The statistics below are estimates for the period 1996 to 2000. For comparison purposes, data for the United States and averages for low-income countries and high-income countries are also given.

Indicator	Senegal	Low-income countries	High-income countries	United States
Per capita gross national product (GNP)†	$1,400	$1,870	$25,690	$31,910
Population growth rate	2.7%	2.1%	0.7%	1.1%
People per square kilometer of land	48	73	29	30
Life expectancy in years	52	59	78	77
Number of physicians per 1,000 people	<0.5	1.0	2.5	2.5
Number of pupils per teacher (primary school)	54	41	17	14
Illiteracy rate (15 years and older)	62%	34%	<5%	3%
Television sets per 1,000 people	41	85	693	844
Energy consumed per capita (kg of oil equivalent)	312	550	5,366	7,937

† The GNP is the total dollar value of all goods and services produced by a country in a year. The per capita GNP is calculated by dividing a country's GNP by its population and adjusting for relative purchasing power. About 15% of the world's 6.1 billion people live in high-income countries, while 40% live in low-income countries.

n.a. = data not available   > = greater than   < = less than

Sources: World Bank. World Development Indicators. Washington, D.C.: The World Bank, 2001; Central Intelligence Agency. The World Factbook. Washington, D.C.: Government Printing Office, 2000.

per 1,000 people. In 1993, only 40% of the population had access to health care services.

Major health problems include measles and, to a lesser extent, meningitis, along with water-related diseases such as malaria and schistosomiasis. In 1996, only 90% of the urban and 44% of the rural population had access to safe water and only 12% of rural dwellers had adequate sanitation. Life expectancy was about 52 years in 2000.

30 HOUSING

Most housing in Dakar is like that of a European city. Elsewhere, housing ranges from European-type structures to the circular mud huts with thatched roofs common in villages. Since World War II (1939–45), the growth of Dakar and other towns has been rapid, with government activity largely concentrated on improvement of urban housing and sanitation.

31 EDUCATION

Education is compulsory at the primary level between ages 7 and 13; however, because of a lack of facilities, just more than half the children in this age group attend school. In 1998, there were 3,884 primary schools in which more than one million students were enrolled. At the secondary level, 215,988 students were attending schools the same year. The University of Dakar has two graduate schools and numerous research centers. For more than 30 years, the University of Dakar offered free tuition and generous subsidies to students. In 1994, however, it began a program aimed at reducing enrollment, raising academic standards, and getting students to pay for more of the cost. A polytechnic college opened at Thiès in 1973. Other colleges include a national school of administration at Dakar and a school of sciences and veterinary medicine for French-speaking Africa. Universities and equivalent institutions had 24,081 students in 1995. Illiteracy rates are high: in 2000, some 62% of adults were illiterate.

32 MEDIA

Telephone and telegraph services, publicly owned and operated, are highly efficient by African standards, particularly in the coastal area and in the main centers of peanut production.

The two national radio networks based in Dakar broadcast mostly in French, while the regional stations in Rufisque, Saint-Louis, Tambacounda, Kaolack, and Ziguinchor, which originate their own programs, broadcast primarily in six local languages. There were 890,000 radios in 1995. Transmission of educational television programs began in 1973, and by 1995 there were 282,000 television sets in use. There were two daily newspapers in 1999: *Le Soleil du Sénégal,* the Senegalese Socialist Party (PS) newspaper (with an estimated 45,000 circulation), and *Sud Quotidien* (30,000).

33 TOURISM AND RECREATION

The comfortable climate, variety of cultural attractions, physical features such as the coastal beaches and the 5,996-square-kilometer (2,315-square-mile) Niokolo-Koba National Park, and the relative proximity to Europe have combined to make Senegal an increasingly popular vacation area, and international conference center. In 1997, 313,000 foreign tourists arrived at hotels and other facilities, spending an estimated $153 million.

34 FAMOUS SENEGALESE

Blaise Diagne (1872–1934) was the first African to be elected to the French parliament. Léopold-Sédar Senghor (b.1906), president of Senegal from 1960 until his retirement in 1980, is a French-language poet of distinction. Abdou Diouf (b.1935) was president of Senegal from 1981 to 2000, after serving as Senghor's prime minister from 1970 through 1980. Senegalese writers include David Diop (1927–60), an internationally known poet. Ousmane Sembene (b.1923) is a film director and writer of international repute.

35 BIBLIOGRAPHY

Beaton, Margaret. *Senegal.* New York: Children's Press, 1997.

Berg, Elizabeth. *Senegal.* New York: Marshall Cavendish, 1999.

Nagel, Rob, and Anne Commire. "Léopold Sédar Senghor." In *World Leaders, People Who Shaped the World.* Volume I: Africa and Asia. Detroit: U*X*L, 1994.

Senegal in Pictures. Minneapolis: Lerner Publications, 1988.

Vaillant, Janet G. *Black, French, and African: A Life of Leopold Sedar Senghor.* Cambridge, Mass.: Harvard University Press, 1990.

SEYCHELLES

Republic of Seychelles

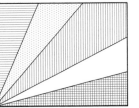

CAPITAL: Victoria.

FLAG: The flag is made up of five oblique bands of (left to right) blue, yellow, red, white, and green.

ANTHEM: Begins "Seychellois both staunch and true."

MONETARY UNIT: The Seychelles rupee (R) is a paper currency of 100 cents. There are coins of 5, 10, and 25 cents and 1, 5, 10, 20, 25, 50, 100, 1,000, and 1,500 rupees and notes of 10, 25, 50, and 100 rupees. R1 = $0.18846 (or $1 = R5.306).

WEIGHTS AND MEASURES: The metric system is the legal standard.

HOLIDAYS: New Year's, 1–2 January; Labor Day, 1 May; National Day, 5 June; Independence Day, 29 June; Assumption, 15 August; All Saints' Day, 1 November; Immaculate Conception, 8 December; Christmas, 25 December. Movable religious holidays include Good Friday, Easter Monday, Corpus Christi, and Ascension.

TIME: 4 PM = noon GMT.

1 LOCATION AND SIZE

Seychelles, an archipelago in the Indian Ocean, consists of an estimated 115 islands, most of which are not permanently inhabited. The second-smallest country in Africa, Seychelles has an area of 455 square kilometers (176 square miles), slightly more than 2.5 times the size of Washington, D.C. The capital city of Seychelles, Victoria, is located on the island of Mahé.

2 TOPOGRAPHY

One of two main clusters of islands, the granitic (made of hard rock) islands rise above the sea surface to form a peak or ridge with rugged crests, towering cliffs, boulders, and domes. The coralline Seychelles are, in contrast, low lying, rising only a few feet above the surface of the sea.

3 CLIMATE

Coastal temperatures are fairly constant at about 27°C (81°F) throughout the year. At higher altitudes, temperatures are lower, especially at night. Average annual rainfall is 236 centimeters (93 inches) at sea level, as much as 356 centimeters (140 inches) in the mountains, and much lower on the southwestern coral islands, averaging about 50 centimeters (20 inches) a year on Aldabra.

4 PLANTS AND ANIMALS

On Praslin and Curieuse islands, the native forests of coco-de-mer have been protected in small reserves. Its fruit, a huge coconut weighing up to 18 kilograms (40 pounds), is the largest seed in the

Geographic Profile

Geographic Features

Size ranking: 177 of 192
Highest elevation: 912 meters (2,992 feet) at Morne
   Seychellois
Lowest elevation: Sea level at the Indian Ocean

Land Use

Arable land:	2%
Permanent crops:	13%
Permanent pastures:	0%
Forests:	11%
Other:	74%

Weather

Average monthly precipitation (Aldabra): 50
   centimeters (20 inches)
Average temperature in January: 24–29°C (75–84°F)
Average temperature in July: 24–29°C (75–84°F)

world. Virtually all the broadleaf ever-green rainforest has been cut down. Sharks abound in the surrounding oceans; on land the most noteworthy animal is the giant tortoise, a species now sorely depleted. There is a great variety of bird life.

5 ENVIRONMENT

The monitoring of the environment is complicated by the fact that Seychelles consists of 115 islands distributed over an area of 1.3 million square kilometers (501,800 square miles). The nation has a water pollution problem due to industrial byproducts and sewage. Fires, landslides, and oil leakage also affect the environment in Seychelles. The Aldabra Island atoll (coral island) is a native wildlife preserve.

6 POPULATION

The population was estimated at 79,672 in 2000. In the same year, an estimated 40,000 people lived in Victoria, the capital and principal city. The estimated average population density in 2000 was 178 persons per square kilometer (461 persons per square mile).

7 MIGRATION

In 1999, the net emigration rate was -6.32 emigres per 1,000 population.

8 ETHNIC GROUPS

The bulk of the population is Seychellois, a mixture of African, French, and Asian strains.

9 LANGUAGES

Creole, a simplified form of French with borrowings from African languages, has been the primary language since 1981 and is the initial language in public schools. English and French also are widely used.

10 RELIGIONS

In 1998, some 88% of the population was Roman Catholic; with 8% Anglicans; and Hindus, Muslims, Baptists, Assembly of God, Pentacostals, and Seventh-day Adventists making up the remaining 4%.

11 TRANSPORTATION

The road network totaled 280 kilometers (174 miles) in 1999. There were 5,100 automobiles, and 2,000 commercial vehicles in 1995.

Until the opening of Seychelles International Airport on Mahé in 1971, the Seychelles Islands were entirely dependent on the sea for their links with the rest of the world. Air Seychelles, which also runs domestic flights, carried about 384,000 passengers in 1997.

12 HISTORY

The Seychelles Islands (then uninhabited) were discovered by the Portuguese explorer Vasco da Gama in 1502. The French began colonization of the islands in 1768, when a party of 22 Frenchmen arrived, bringing with them a number of slaves. The French and British warred for control of the islands between 1793 and 1813. Under the Treaty of Paris (1814), Seychelles, together with Mauritius, were ceded to Britain. On 31 August 1903, the islands became a British crown colony.

Seychelles achieved independence at 12:05 AM on 29 June 1976. Richard Marie Mancham, leader of the conservative Seychelles Democratic Party, became president on independence, heading a coalition government that included Seychelles People's United Party (SPUP) leader France Albert René as prime minister. Mancham was overthrown by a coup on 5 June 1977 and went into exile, and René became president. He suspended the constitution, dismissed the legislature, and ruled by decree.

The constitution of March 1979, adopted by referendum, established a one-party state. René was reelected president without opposition in June 1984. Since then, Seychelles has made progress economically and socially. Under rising pressure to democratize, in December 1991, René agreed to reform the system.

Multiparty elections were held in July 1992, and many dissidents, including

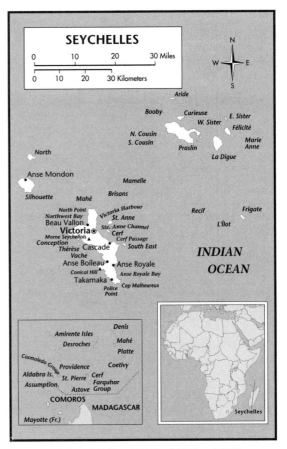

LOCATION: 3°41′ to 10°13′s; 46°12′ to 56°17′E.
TERRITORIAL SEA LIMIT: 12 miles.

Mancham, returned from exile. Finally, in June 1993, 73% of the voters approved a new constitution providing for multiparty government. In 1993 (and again in 1998) France Albert René won the presidency, and his party the great majority of the legislative seats.

13 GOVERNMENT

In June 1993, 74% of the voters approved a new constitution drafted by a bipartisan commission. It called for multiparty elec-

Photo credit: Susan D. Rock.

Boatmen in a secluded beach cove near Victoria.

tions of a president and a National Assembly of 33 members, of which 22 are directly elected and 11 allocated on a proportional basis.

14 POLITICAL PARTIES

The Seychelles People's Progressive Front (SPPF), was established in 1979 as the sole legal party, with the avowed objective of creating a socialist state. The Seychelles Democratic Party (SDP) was declared to have "disappeared," and there were at least three opposition groups in exile.

After President René's 1991 announcement of a return to multiparty democracy, many dissidents returned from exile and the Democratic Party (DP) was reestab-

lished, as well as the Seychelles Party (PS), the Seychelles Democratic Movement (MSPD), and the Seychelles Liberal Party (SLP).

15 JUDICIAL SYSTEM

Cases are first tried in Magistrates' courts. The Supreme Court hears appeals and takes original jurisdiction of some cases, and the Court of Appeal hears appeals from the Supreme Court. Appointment to the post of chief justice is made by the president of Seychelles.

16 ARMED FORCES

The Seychelles People's Liberation Army (SPLA) was merged with a People's Militia in 1981 to form the Seychelles People's

Miniature "Big Ben" in the center of the city of Victoria.

Defense Force (SPDF). There are 450 men, including an army of 200 and a national guard of 250 that are equipped with six naval craft, seven aircraft, and infantry weapons. In 1998, the SPLA spent $11 million on defense.

17 ECONOMY

With the opening of the international airport in 1971, the Seychelles economy began to move away from cash crops to the development of tourism. In 1996, tourism accounted for more than 20% of the gross domestic product (GDP), employed 30% of the labor force, and provided more than 70% of foreign exchange earnings. Seychelles is heavily dependent on imports and financial aid.

18 INCOME

In 1997, Seychelles' gross domestic product (GDP) was $550 million, or about $7,000 per person. In 1999, the average inflation rate was 1.4%, resulting in a growth rate in GDP of 1.5%.

19 INDUSTRY

Manufacturing contributes about 13% of GDP. The largest plant is the tuna cannery, opened in 1987 and privatized in 1995 with a 60% purchase by Heinz Inc. of the United States. The rest are small and process local agricultural products, including tea, copra, and vanilla. There is a plastics factory, a brewery and soft drink bottler, and a cinnamon distiller.

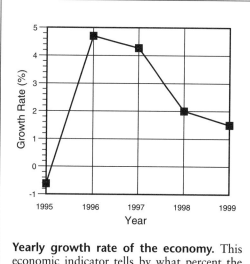

Yearly growth rate of the economy. This economic indicator tells by what percent the economy has increased or decreased when compared with the previous year.

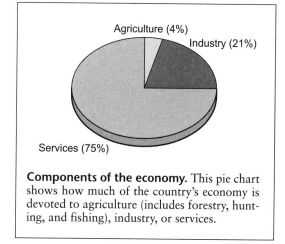

Components of the economy. This pie chart shows how much of the country's economy is devoted to agriculture (includes forestry, hunting, and fishing), industry, or services.

20 LABOR

In 1995, formal employment was 25,430. About 60% of employment is in the public sector, including state-owned companies. Agriculture accounted for 7.5% of employment in 1995 (comprising 4% of GDP); manufacturing and construction, 19.5%; hotels and restaurants, 14.2%; transportation and communications, 19%; and other services, 39.8%.

21 AGRICULTURE

Production in 1998 included 4,000 tons of coconuts and about 2,000 tons of bananas. Other crops produced for export are cinnamon bark, vanilla, and cloves. Tea planting began in the early 1960s.

22 DOMESTICATED ANIMALS

Seychelles is self-sufficient in the production of pork, poultry, and eggs. In 1998, there were about 18,000 hogs, 5,000 goats, and 1,000 head of cattle.

23 FISHING

Fish landings by the domestic fleet totaled 1,562 tons of jack and 1,114 tons of patagonian squid in 1997. The total catch that year was 5,928 tons.

24 FORESTRY

Little natural forest remains. Coconut plantations are the main source of timber, aside from imports.

25 MINING

Mineral production consists of small quantities of rock, coral, and sand for construction.

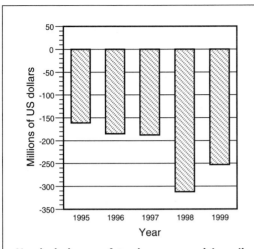

Yearly balance of trade measured in millions of US dollars. The balance of trade is the difference between what a country sells to other countries (its exports) and what it buys (its imports). If a country imports more than it exports, it has a negative balance of trade (a trade deficit). If exports exceed imports there is a positive balance of trade (a trade surplus).

26 FOREIGN TRADE

The principal exports in 1998 were fish, cinnamon, dried shark fins, and copra (dried coconut meat). Industrial supplies comprised 17.1% of total imports in 1996. Machinery followed at 15.6%; food, beverages, and tobacco at 18.9%; and transportation equipment at 33.7%.

The major export markets in 1998 (in millions of US dollars) were the United Kingdom (30), Italy (16), Netherlands (18), and France (19). The leading import suppliers were South Africa (52), Singapore (40), and the United Kingdom (36).

27 ENERGY AND POWER

Practically the whole of Mahé is now supplied with electricity produced by diesel power in Victoria. Output reached 113 million kilowatt hours in 1998.

28 SOCIAL DEVELOPMENT

The National Provident Fund makes payments for marriage, emigration, disability, survivors, and old age. There also is a workers' compensation scheme. Health services are free for all residents.

29 HEALTH

There are five hospitals, and, in 1990, there were 90 doctors. The average life expectancy was 72 years in 2000. In 1994, 3.9% of the gross domestic product (GDP) went to health expenditures.

30 HOUSING

Most homes are of wood or stone with corrugated iron roofs; many rural houses are thatched.

31 EDUCATION

Public education is free and compulsory for children between the ages of 6 and 16. In 1996, there were 9,886 students in primary schools and 9,099 students in secondary schools. Seychelles does not provide education at university level, but many students study abroad, especially in the United Kingdom. Adult literacy was estimated at 58% in 2000.

32 MEDIA

The number of telephones in use was 11,300 in 1995. Radio-Television Sey-

Selected Social Indicators

The statistics below are estimates for the period 1996 to 2000. For comparison purposes, data for the United States and averages for low-income countries and high-income countries are also given.

Indicator	Seychelles	Low-income countries	High-income countries	United States
Per capita gross national product (GNP)†	$7,500	$1,870	$25,690	$31,910
Population growth rate	0.5%	2.1%	0.7%	1.1%
People per square kilometer of land	178	73	29	30
Life expectancy in years	72	59	78	77
Number of physicians per 1,000 people	1.2	1.0	2.5	2.5
Number of pupils per teacher (primary school)	17	41	17	14
Illiteracy rate (15 years and older)	42%	34%	<5%	3%
Television sets per 1,000 people	138	85	693	844
Energy consumed per capita (kg of oil equivalent)	1,634	550	5,366	7,937

† The GNP is the total dollar value of all goods and services produced by a country in a year. The per capita GNP is calculated by dividing a country's GNP by its population and adjusting for relative purchasing power. About 15% of the world's 6.1 billion people live in high-income countries, while 40% live in low-income countries.

n.a. = data not available   > = greater than   < = less than

Sources: World Bank. World Development Indicators. Washington, D.C.: The World Bank, 2001; Central Intelligence Agency. The World Factbook. Washington, D.C.: Government Printing Office, 2000.

chelles broadcasts in English, French, and Creole. There were about 627 radios and 138 television sets per 1,000 population in 2000. Television service began in 1983. There is one daily newspaper—*Seychelles Nation* (1999 circulation about 3,500)—published in English, French, and Creole.

33 TOURISM AND RECREATION

The prosperity of Seychelles depends on tourism. Visitors can enjoy coral beaches; water sports including scuba diving, water skiing, and windsurfing; and boat or yacht tours of the islands. The archipelago's wildlife also is a popular tourist attraction.

There were 128,252 visitor arrivals in 1998, more than 85% from European countries. Income from tourism was $122 million in 1997. That year, 2,276 hotel rooms were filled to 57% of capacity.

34 FAMOUS SEYCHELLOIS

Sir James Richard Marie Mancham (b.1939), became Seychelles' first president in 1976. He was deposed in 1977 by France Albert René (b.1935).

35 BIBLIOGRAPHY

Amin, Mohamed. *Journey Through Seychelles*. Edison, NJ: Hunter, 1994.

Bennett, George. *Seychelles*. Denver, Colo.: Clio Press, 1993.

Carpin, Sarah. *Seychelles*. New York: Odyssey Publications, 1999.

Doubilet, David. "Journey to Aldabra." *National Geographic,* March 1995, 90–113.

Franda, Marcus. *The Seychelles: Unquiet Islands.* Boulder, Colo.: Westview, 1982.

SIERRA LEONE

Republic of Sierra Leone

CAPITAL: Freetown.

FLAG: The national flag is a tricolor of green, white, and blue horizontal stripes.

ANTHEM: Begins "High we exalt thee, realm of the free, Great is the love we have for thee."

MONETARY UNIT: The leone (Le) is a paper currency of 100 cents. There are coins of 1/2, 1, 5, 10, 20, and 50 cents, and notes of 1, 2, 5, 10, 20, 50, 100, and 500 leones. Le1 = $0.00043 (or $1 = Le2,324.77).

WEIGHTS AND MEASURES: The metric system is employed.

HOLIDAYS: New Year's Day, 1 January; Independence Day, 27 April; Bank Holiday, August; Christmas, 24–25 December; Boxing Day, 26 December. Movable religious holidays include Good Friday, Easter Monday, Whitmonday, 'Id al-Fitr, 'Id al-'Adha', and Milad an-Nabi.

TIME: GMT.

1 LOCATION AND SIZE

Situated on the west coast of Africa, Sierra Leone has an area of 71,740 square kilometers (27,699 square miles), slightly smaller than the state of South Carolina. It has a total boundary length of 1,364 kilometers (847 miles). In addition to the mainland proper, Sierra Leone also includes the offshore Banana and Turtle islands and Sherbro Island, and other small islands. Sierra Leone's capital city, Freetown, is located on the Atlantic Coast.

2 TOPOGRAPHY

The Sierra Leone peninsula in the extreme west is mostly mountainous, rising to about 884 meters (2,900 feet). Other areas in the west consist of coastal mangrove swamps. To the east, there are coastal plains with many navigable rivers and, far-

ther eastward, a plateau. The highest peak is Loma Mansa in the Loma Mountains, at 1,948 meters (6,390 feet).

3 CLIMATE

Temperatures and humidity are high, and rainfall is heavy. The average temperature is about 27°C (81°F) on the coast and almost as high on the eastern plateau. There are distinct wet and dry seasons, with rainfall averaging more than 315 centimeters (125 inches) a year for the country as a whole.

4 PLANTS AND ANIMALS

There are savanna, or grasslands, in the north, while low bush is found in the south-central area, and forest or high bush in the southeast. There also are swamplands, and 3–5% of the land is rainforest. Sierra Leone is West Africa's only remain-

Geographic Profile

Geographic Features

Size ranking: 116 of 192
Highest elevation: 1,948 meters (6,390 feet) at Loma Mansa (Bintimani)
Lowest elevation: Sea level at the Atlantic Ocean

Land Use†

Arable land:	7%
Permanent crops:	1%
Permanent pastures:	31%
Forests:	28%
Other:	33%

Weather††

Average annual precipitation (Freetown): 331.8 centimeters (130.6 inches)
Average temperature in January (Freetown): 26.6°C (79.9°F)
Average temperature in July (Freetown): 25.1°C (77.2°F)

†*Arable land:* Land used for temporary crops, like meadows for mowing or pasture, gardens, and greenhouses. *Permanent crops:* Land cultivated with crops that occupy its use for long periods, such as cocoa, coffee, rubber, fruit and nut orchards, and vineyards. *Permanent pastures:* Land used permanently for forage crops. *Forests:* Land containing stands of trees. *Other:* Any land not specified, including built-on areas, roads, and barren land.

††The measurements for precipitation and average temperature were taken at weather stations closest to the country's largest city. Precipitation and average temperature can vary significantly within a country, due to factors such as latitude, altitude, coastal proximity, and wind patterns.

ing habitat for the emerald cuckoo, which has been described as the most beautiful bird in Africa. Many birds that breed in Europe winter in Sierra Leone. Crocodiles and hippopotamuses are native to the coastal plain.

5 ENVIRONMENT

Water pollution is a significant problem in Sierra Leone due to mining byproducts and sewage. The nation has 38.4 cubic miles of water, of which 89% is used for farming and 4% for industrial purposes. Forty-two percent of the nation's city dwellers and 80% of those living in rural areas do not have pure water. The nation's cities produce 0.3 million tons of solid waste per year.

Forestland is being converted to agricultural land due to the need for food by a population that increased by 80% during the period between 1963 and 1990. Hunting for food has reduced the stock of wild mammals. Cutamba Killimi National Park, which has some wildlife species found only in this part of West Africa, is exploited by poachers. As of 1994, 13 of Sierra Leone's mammal species and seven bird species were endangered. Twelve of the nation's plant species also were threatened.

6 POPULATION

The population of Sierra Leone was 5.5 million, according to a 2000 estimate. The average population density was 69 persons per square kilometer (179 per square mile) in 2000. During the 1990s, the population grew by an average of 2.5% a year. A population of 6.4 million is projected for 2005. Freetown, the capital, had an estimated population of 699,000 in 2000.

7 MIGRATION

Historically, there has been considerable movement over the borders to and from Guinea and Liberia. Since the beginning of the Liberian civil war in 1991, hundreds of thousands of refugees have left Sierra Leone. Of these, 250,000 went to Guinea, 120,000 went to Liberia, and 4,000 went to the Gambia. As of September 1999, Sierra Leoneans made up the UN's largest refugee caseload. As of the end of 1999, there were 16,000 Liberian refugees in Sierra Leone.

8 ETHNIC GROUPS

The African population of Sierra Leone is composed of some 20 native ethnic groups, the two largest being the Mende (about 30% of the population) and Temne (about 30%). Other peoples are the Bullom, Fulani, Gola, Kissi, Kono, Koranko, Krim, and Kru. There also are 40,000–80,000 Creoles, descendants of settlers from Europe, the West Indies, and other regions.

9 LANGUAGES

The Mende and Temne languages are widely spoken in the south and north, respectively. The common language is Krio, the mother tongue of the Creoles. English is the official language.

10 RELIGIONS

Approximately 10% of the population followed African traditional religions in the 1990s, 60% were Muslim, and about 30% were Christian. Reliable data is not available.

11 TRANSPORTATION

In the early 1970s, following a World Bank recommendation, Sierra Leone dismantled most of its rail system and replaced it with new roadways; in the mid-1980s, only 84 kilometers (52 miles) of narrow-gauge railway remained. Sierra Leone had about 11,674 kilometers

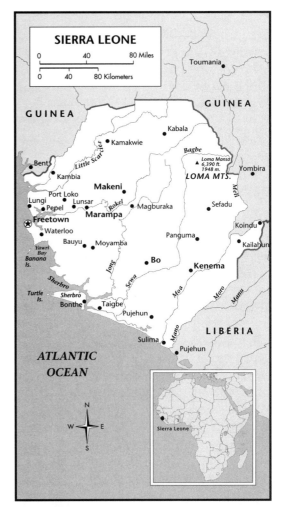

LOCATION: 6°55′ to 10°N; 10°16′ to 13°18′w. **BOUNDARY LENGTHS:** Guinea, 652 kilometers (405 miles); Liberia, 306 kilometers (190 miles); Atlantic coastline, 406 kilometers (252 miles). **TERRITORIAL SEA LIMIT:** 12 miles.

(7,253 miles) of roads, of which 9% were paved in 1999. In 1995 there were 44,317 registered motor vehicles, including 32,415 automobiles, and 11,902 commercial vehicles.

Freetown has one of the finest natural harbors in the world. Sierra Leone has

many rivers, but most are navigable only over short distances for about three months of the year, during the rainy season. An international airport at Lungi is connected by ferry to Freetown, across the bay. Domestic air service operates from Hastings Airfield, 22 kilometers (14 miles) from Freetown, linking the capital to nearly all the large provincial towns.

12 HISTORY

Archaeological research indicates that by AD 800 the use of iron had been introduced into what is now Sierra Leone and that by AD 1000 the coastal peoples were practicing agriculture. Beginning perhaps in the thirteenth century, migrants arrived from the north. European contact began in 1462 with the Portuguese explorer Pedro da Cintra, who gave the mountainous peninsula the name Sierra Leone ("Lion Mountains"). From the sixteenth to the early nineteenth century, the region was raided for slaves for the Atlantic trade, and later in the nineteenth century it was ravaged by African war leaders and slavers. The colony of Sierra Leone was founded by the British as a home for African slaves freed in England. The first settlers arrived in 1787.

The Sierra Leone Company was formed in 1791 to administer the settlement, but the burden of defense and settlement proved too heavy for the company, and Sierra Leone was transferred to the British crown in 1808. The colony received additions of land up to 1861 through various treaties from the local chiefs. After 1807, when the British Parliament passed an act making the slave trade illegal, the new colony was used as a base from which the act could be enforced. In 1896, a British protectorate was declared over the hinterland of Sierra Leone, which was separate from the colony. A 1924 constitution provided for the election of three members to a Legislative Council, and the constitution of 1951 provided for an elected majority, resulting in African rule. In 1958, Milton Margai became Sierra Leone's first prime minister; in 1960, he led a delegation to London, England, to establish conditions for full independence.

Independence

Sierra Leone became an independent country within the British Commonwealth of Nations on 27 April 1961. After the 1967 national elections, there were two successive military coups, and a state of emergency was declared in 1970. In 1971, a new constitution was adopted, and the country was declared a republic on 19 April 1971. Siaka Stevens, then prime minister, became the nation's first president. An alleged plot to overthrow Stevens failed in 1974, and in March 1976 he was elected without opposition for a second five-year term as president. In 1978, a new constitution was adopted, making the country a one-party state.

Stevens did not run for reelection as president in 1985, yielding power to his handpicked successor, Major General Joseph Saidu Momoh, the armed forces commander. By 29 April 1992, Momoh was overthrown in a military coup and fled to Guinea. A National Provisional Ruling Council (NPRC) was created but, shortly afterward, the head of the five-member junta, Lieutenant Colonel Yahya, was arrested by his colleagues and replaced by Captain Valentine Strasser, who was formally designated head of state.

The Strasser government soon limited the status of the 1991 constitution by a series of decrees and public notices. The NPRC (National Provisional Ruling Council) dissolved parliament and political parties and ruled by decree. There was fighting in the southeast, where the forces of the National Patriot Front of Liberia and Sierra Leone dissidents were fighting with Sierra Leone armed forces. Forces from the Economic Community of West African States (ECOWAS) Monitoring Group sought to create a ceasefire zone along the boundary between the two countries. In November 1993, Strasser announced a unilateral ceasefire and an amnesty for rebels. In November 1993, Strasser issued a timetable for a transition to democracy to culminate in general elections in late 1995. A month later, the NPRC released a "Working Document on the Constitution" to serve as the basis for public debates leading to a constitutional referendum in May 1995.

Strasser was overthrown in 1996 by his deputy Brigadier Julius Maada Brio and given safe passage out of the country. Presidential and parliamentary elections took place in February 1996 and were met with violent opposition by rebel forces resulting in 27 deaths. Ahmad Tejan Kabbah won the presidency in a run-off on 15 March 1996. In May 1997, however, Major Johnny Paul Koromah led a coup that overthrew Kabbah. Civil war broke out

and armed gangs fought. In February 1998, Nigeria led a force of peacekeeping troops into Sierra Leone that ousted Koromah's ruling military council and restored President Kabbah to power. After the fighting was over, Freetown was heavily damaged and still had to deal with looters, vigilante gangs, disease, and food shortages. Approximately 250,000 people fled the country.

The Armed Forces Revolutionary Council and the Revolutionary United Front (RUF) resumed the war, seizing 500 UN personnel; however, it started a campaign of terror against civilians called "Operation No Living Thing." The rebels have killed civilians, and looted and destroyed villages. Victims have their hands or feet amputated as "messages" to the Kabbah government.

In October 1998, the restored government executed some two dozen people who had been convicted for taking part in the 1997 coup. Until March 2000, it appeared that the peace accords might be implemented. In early May 2000, the RUF resumed the war and advanced to within 25 miles of the capital. Diamond smuggling into Liberia is believed to be the chief factor in the rebel's refusal to demobilize.

13 GOVERNMENT

A new constitution came into force on 1 October 1991, but since that time it has been superseded by a number of coups led by the military. In May 1997, a military coup, led by Major Johnny Paul Koromah, overthrew the most recently elected government. However, in February 1998 Nigerian troops entered the country to

Photo credit: EPD/Office of the President of Sierra Leone.

Name:	Ahmed Tejan Kabbah
Position:	President of a constitutional democracy
Took office:	29 March 1996
Birthplace:	Pendemba, Sierra Leone
Birth date:	16 February 1932
Religion:	Islam
Education:	University College, Wales, studied economics; later received a law degree
Spouse:	Patricia Tucker Kabbah
Of interest:	Though a Muslim, Kabbah attended Catholic schools.

restore the elected government. Elections are due in December 2001, though they are uncertain given the state of war in Sierra Leone.

14 POLITICAL PARTIES

A multiparty presidential election was held in February 1996 and Ahmed Tejan Kabbah of the National Peoples Party won in a run-off. There were 15 parties registered for the 1996 elections. In 1997 the elected government was overthrown by Major Johnny Paul Koromah, a member of the newly formed Armed Forces Revolutionary Council, but in February 1998 he fled the country after Nigerian troops entered the country to restore the elected government.

15 JUDICIAL SYSTEM

Magistrates hold court in the various districts and in Freetown, administering the English-based code of law. Appeals from magistrates' courts are heard by the High Court, which also has unlimited original civil and criminal jurisdiction. Appeals from High Court decisions may be made to the Court of Appeal and finally to the Supreme Court, consisting of a chief justice and not fewer than three other justices. The National Provisional Ruling Council (NPRC) formed after the 1992 military coup has not altered the previously existing judicial system, but it has set up special commissions of inquiry to handle some cases.

16 ARMED FORCES

In 2000, the Sierra Leone armed services had 3,000 members following the 1997 civil war and the restoration of President Kabbah. There were 200 naval (coast guard) personnel with three patrol craft. Military service is voluntary. Sierra Leone

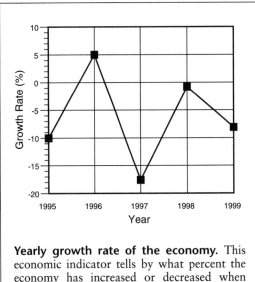

Yearly growth rate of the economy. This economic indicator tells by what percent the economy has increased or decreased when compared with the previous year.

hosts peacekeeping forces from Guinea, Ghana, and Nigeria.

17 ECONOMY

Although Sierra Leone is a potentially rich country with diverse resources, which include diamonds, gold, rutile, bauxite, and a variety of agricultural products, the economy has been severely depressed over the past two decades due to civil unrest. At one point, agriculture employed 70% of the labor force.

18 INCOME

In 1998, Sierra Leone's gross domestic product (GDP) was $2.7 billion, or about $530 per person. In 1999, the average annual inflation rate was 37%, resulting in a decline in GDP of about 8%.

19 INDUSTRY

The Wellington Industrial Estate, covering 46 hectares (113 acres) just east of Freetown, was developed in the 1960s by the government to encourage investments. Its factories produce a variety of products, including cement, nails, shoes, oxygen, cigarettes, beer and soft drinks, paint, and knitted goods. Timber for prefabricated buildings is milled, and another factory produces modern furniture.

20 LABOR

Agriculture is the occupation of at least two-thirds of the labor force; manufacturing engages only 2% of the labor force. Only 70,200 Sierra Leoneans were wage earners as of 1988 (in establishments with six or more workers). The 1991 constitution provides for the right of association, and all workers have the right to join trade unions of their choice.

Minimum age laws exist to regulate child labor, but they are not enforced; children routinely work in agriculture and in small businesses. There is no minimum wage.

21 AGRICULTURE

Agriculture is the primary occupation in Sierra Leone, employing at least two-thirds of the labor force and accounting for 52% of GDP. Rice is the most important subsistence crop and, along with millet in the northeast, is a food staple; an estimated 411,000 tons were produced in 1998. Other domestic food crops include cassava, yams, peanuts, corn, pineapples, coconuts, tomatoes, and pepper. Agricultural exports include coffee, cocoa, palm

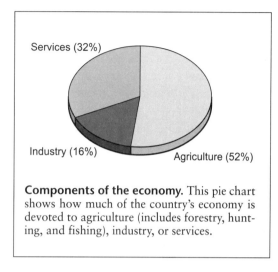

Components of the economy. This pie chart shows how much of the country's economy is devoted to agriculture (includes forestry, hunting, and fishing), industry, or services.

Services (32%)
Industry (16%)
Agriculture (52%)

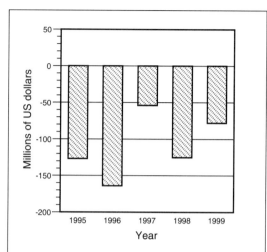

Yearly balance of trade measured in millions of US dollars. The balance of trade is the difference between what a country sells to other countries (its exports) and what it buys (its imports). If a country imports more than it exports, it has a negative balance of trade (a trade deficit). If exports exceed imports there is a positive balance of trade (a trade surplus).

kernels, piassava, kola nuts, and ginger. Coffee production was about 31,000 tons in 1998. Piassava, a raffia palm fiber used for broom and brush bristles, is grown in the swampy areas of the extreme south.

22 DOMESTICATED ANIMALS

Estimates of livestock in 1998 were 400,000 head of cattle, 350,000 sheep, 190,000 goats, and 50,000 hogs. Large numbers of cattle are kept, mainly by nomads in the grasslands area of the northeast. Poultry farmers had an estimated six million chickens in 1998.

23 FISHING

The fishing industry includes industrial, freshwater, and shellfish fisheries. Total fish and shellfish production in 1997 was 68,739 tons. Shrimp is the main export.

24 FORESTRY

Although much of Sierra Leone was once forested, intensive farming gradually elim-

inated most of the forest area. There are still about two million hectares (4.9 million acres) of forests and woodland. In 1997, an estimated total of 3.3 million cubic meters (4.3 million cubic yards) of roundwood was harvested, 96% of it for fuel.

25 MINING

Diamonds, first discovered in 1930, are widely scattered over a large area but particularly along the upper Sewa River. Production was reported at 255,000 carats in 1996. It is believed that many of the diamonds close to the earth's surface are smuggled out of the country. Other known minerals are antimony, cassiterite, columbite, corundum, fluorspar, ilmenite, lead,

Selected Social Indicators

The statistics below are estimates for the period 1996 to 2000. For comparison purposes, data for the United States and averages for low-income countries and high-income countries are also given.

Indicator	Sierra Leone	Low-income countries	High-income countries	United States
Per capita gross national product (GNP)†	$440	$1,870	$25,690	$31,910
Population growth rate	3%	2.1%	0.7%	1.1%
People per square kilometer of land	69	73	29	30
Life expectancy in years	37	59	78	77
Number of physicians per 1,000 people	<0.1	1.0	2.5	2.5
Number of pupils per teacher (primary school)	n.a.	41	17	14
Illiteracy rate (15 years and older)	63%	34%	<5%	3%
Television sets per 1,000 people	13	85	693	844
Energy consumed per capita (kg of oil equivalent)	72	550	5,366	7,937

† The GNP is the total dollar value of all goods and services produced by a country in a year. The per capita GNP is calculated by dividing a country's GNP by its population and adjusting for relative purchasing power. About 15% of the world's 6.1 billion people live in high-income countries, while 40% live in low-income countries.

n.a. = data not available   > = greater than   < = less than

Sources: World Bank. *World Development Indicators.* Washington, D.C.: The World Bank, 2001; Central Intelligence Agency. *The World Factbook.* Washington, D.C.: Government Printing Office, 2000.

lignite, magnetite, molybdenum, monazite, platinum, silver, tantalite, tin, titanium, tungsten, and zinc.

26 FOREIGN TRADE

Sierra Leone exports primary minerals and agricultural commodities, and it imports food and machinery. The principal exports are rutile (27%), diamonds (45%), coffee (3.5%), and cocoa (1.7%). Principal imports are foodstuffs, machinery and transport equipment, and chemicals.

Sierra Leone's leading export partner (in millions of US dollars) in 1998 was Belgium (60), followed by the United States (11), and Spain (9). Imports to Sierra Leone came from the United Kingdom (40), the United States (26), and Belgium (15).

27 ENERGY AND POWER

Total national production of electricity increased to 235 million kilowatt hours in 1998, of which about 60% was generated by public utilities. Installed capacity in 1998 was 126,000 kilowatts. Apart from wood, lignite is the only natural fuel found, but known deposits are not being economically mined.

28 SOCIAL DEVELOPMENT

Since 1946, the Welfare Department has sponsored child welfare and domestic affairs programs, promoted youth groups, and set up programs for the care of the aged, the blind, and the mentally handicapped. In 1955, these services were reorganized into the Ministry of Social Welfare. A National Coordinating Committee concerned with community development and social services also has been set up. The constitution guarantees equal rights for females, and women have held prominent positions in government. However, discrimination and violence against women are frequent.

29 HEALTH

In 1992, only 38% of the population had access to health care services. That year, there were seven doctors per 100,000 people. In 1990, there was one hospital bed per 1,000 inhabitants. Sierra Leone has 52 hospitals.

With technical assistance from World Health Organization (WHO) and United Nations Children's Fund (UNICEF), a disease-control unit reduced the incidence of sleeping sickness and yaws and began a leprosy-control campaign. Malaria, tuberculosis, and schistosomiasis remain serious health hazards, however, as is malnutrition, with the calorie supply meeting only 83% of minimum requirements in 1992. Life expectancy in 2000 was only 37 years, one of the lowest in the world. UNICEF estimated that Sierra Leone had the world's highest mortality rate in 1994.

30 HOUSING

Many of the older two-story wooden houses in Freetown are being replaced by structures built largely of concrete blocks, with corrugated iron or cement-asbestos roofs. Building is controlled in the major

towns, and designs are subject to approval. Village houses in the provinces are traditionally made of sticks, with mud walls and thatch or grass roofs, and they may be circular or rectangular in shape.

31 EDUCATION

In 1990, Sierra Leone's 1,795 primary schools had 10,850 teachers and a total enrollment of 367,426 pupils, and secondary schools had 102,474 pupils and 5,969 teachers. Primary education is neither free nor compulsory. In 1999, the adult illiteracy rate was estimated to be 63%.

Fourah Bay College, the oldest institution of higher learning in West Africa, was founded in 1827 by the Church Missionary Society, primarily to provide theological training. In 1967, the University of Sierra Leone was chartered with two constituent colleges, Fourah Bay (in Freetown) and Njala University College (in Moyamba District). In 1990, all higher level institutions were reported to have 4,742 pupils and 600 teaching personnel.

32 MEDIA

Radio Sierra Leone, the oldest broadcasting service in English-speaking West Africa, broadcasts mainly in English, with regular news and discussion programs in several native languages, and a weekly program in French. In 1999 there were two radio stations, as well as one television station. In 2000 there were 251 radios and 13 television sets per 1,000 population. International cablegram, telex, and telephone services are provided by Sierra Leone External Telecommunications.

The only daily newspaper is the government-owned *Daily Mail* (with a 1999 circulation of about 20,000), but there are several privately owned weekly newspapers.

33 TOURISM AND RECREATION

Sierra Leone has magnificent beaches, including Lumley Beach on the outskirts of Freetown, perhaps the finest in West Africa. Natural scenic wonders include the Loma Mountains. There are several modern hotels in Freetown, as well as a luxury hotel and casino at Lumley Beach. The main provincial towns have smaller hotels, and a number of government rest houses are located throughout the country. International tourist arrivals numbered about 22,000 in 1996, and tourism receipts totaled $10 million.

34 FAMOUS SIERRA LEONEANS

Sir Samuel Lewis (1843–1903) was a member of the Legislative Council for more than 20 years and the first mayor of Freetown. Sir Milton Augustus Strieby Margai (1895–1964) was the first prime minister of Sierra Leone, a post he held until his death. Siaka Probyn Stevens (1905–88), founder of the APC political party, was prime minister from 1968 to 1971 and became the republic's first president from 1971 to 1985.

35 BIBLIOGRAPHY

Alie, Joe A. D. *A New History of Sierra Leone.* New York: St. Martin's, 1990.

Binns, Margaret. *Sierra Leone.* Oxford, England; Santa Barbara, Calif.: Clio Press, 1992.

Foray, Cyril P. *Historical Dictionary of Sierra Leone.* Metuchen, N.J.: Scarecrow, 1977.

Fyfe, Christopher. *A Short History of Sierra Leone.* New York: Longman, 1979.

Greene, Graham. *The Heart of the Matter.* New York: Viking, 1948.

White, E. Frances. *Sierra Leone's Settler Women Traders: Women on the Afro-European Frontier.* Ann Arbor: University of Michigan Press, 1987.

SINGAPORE

Republic of Singapore

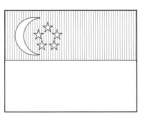

CAPITAL: Singapore.

FLAG: The flag consists of a red stripe at the top and a white stripe on the bottom. On the red stripe, at the hoist, are a white crescent opening to the fly and five white stars.

ANTHEM: *Long Live Singapore.*

MONETARY UNIT: The Singapore dollar (s$) of 100 cents is a freely convertible currency. There are coins of 1, 5, 10, 20, and 50 cents and 1 dollar and notes of 2, 5, 10, 20, 50, 100, 500, 1,000, and 10,000 dollars. s$1 = us$0.59762 (or us$1 = s$1.6733).

WEIGHTS AND MEASURES: The metric system is in force, but some local measures are used.

HOLIDAYS: Major Western, Chinese, Malay, and Muslim holidays are celebrated, some of which fall on annually variable dates because of the calendars used. Major holidays include New Year's Day, 1 January; Chinese New Year; Good Friday; Vesak Day (Buddhist festival); Labor Day, 1 May; Hari Raya Puasa (Muslim festival); National Day, 9 August; Hari Raya Haji (Malay Muslim festival); Dewali; Christmas, 25 December.

TIME: 8 PM = noon GMT.

1 LOCATION AND SIZE

The Republic of Singapore, the second smallest country in Asia, consists of Singapore Island and several smaller adjacent islets. Situated in the Indian Ocean off the southern tip of the Malay Peninsula, Singapore has an area of 632.6 square kilometers (244.2 square miles), slightly less than 3.5 times the size of Washington, D.C. Singapore is connected to the nearby western portion of Malaysia by a causeway across the narrow Johore Strait. Singapore's capital city, Singapore, is located on the country's southern coast.

2 TOPOGRAPHY

Singapore Island is mostly low-lying, green, rolling country with a small range of hills at the center. The highest point of the island is Timah Hill (176 meters/577 feet). There are sections of rainforest in the center and large mangrove swamps along the coast. Singapore's harbor is wide, deep, and well protected.

3 CLIMATE

The climate is tropical, with heavy rainfall and high humidity. The range of temperature is slight; the average annual maximum is 31°C (88°F), and the average minimum 24°C (75°F). The annual rainfall of 228 centimeters (90 inches) is distributed fairly evenly throughout the year, ranging from 39 centimeters (15 inches) in December to 28 centimeters (11 inches) in May. It rains about every other day.

Geographic Profile

Geographic Features

Size ranking: 175 of 192
Highest elevation: 176 meters (577 feet) at Timah Hill (Bukit Timah)
Lowest elevation: Sea level at the Singapore Strait

Land Use†

Arable land: 2%
Permanent crops: 6%
Permanent pastures: <1%
Forests: 5%
Other: 86%

Weather††

Average annual precipitation: 228 centimeters (90 inches)
Average temperature in January: 26.1°C (79.0°F)
Average temperature in July: 27.4°C (81.3°F)

†*Arable land:* Land used for temporary crops, like meadows for mowing or pasture, gardens, and greenhouses. *Permanent crops:* Land cultivated with crops that occupy its use for long periods, such as cocoa, coffee, rubber, fruit and nut orchards, and vineyards. *Permanent pastures:* Land used permanently for forage crops. *Forests:* Land containing stands of trees. *Other:* Any land not specified, including built-on areas, roads, and barren land.

††The measurements for precipitation and average temperature were taken at weather stations closest to the country's largest city. Precipitation and average temperature can vary significantly within a country, due to factors such as latitude, altitude, coastal proximity, and wind patterns.

4 PLANTS AND ANIMALS

The dense tropical forest that originally covered Singapore has mostly been cleared. There is some rainforest in the central area of the island, however, as well as extensive mangrove (trees with dense roots) swamps along the coast.

5 ENVIRONMENT

Air pollution from transportation vehicles is a problem in the nation's growing urban areas. Singapore does not have enough water to support the needs of its people. The nation uses 4% of its water for farming and 51% for industrial purposes. Pollution from the nation's oil industry also is a significant problem. Waste water is treated and recycled to conserve water supplies.

In 1994, 19 plant species were considered to be in danger of extinction.

6 POPULATION

Singapore's 2000 estimated population was 3.57 million; it was 2.7 million at the time of the 1990 census. The population projection for 2005 is nearly 3.8 million. The population density in 2000, estimated at 6,384 persons per square kilometer (16,534 per square mile), is the highest of any nation in the world (excluding Monaco).

7 MIGRATION

Immigration, rather than natural increase, was the major factor in Singapore's fast population growth through the mid-twentieth century. In November 1965, following separation from Malaysia, Singapore's newly independent government introduced measures to restrict the flow of Malaysians entering the country in search of work, who had averaged 10,000 a year up to 1964. Immigration is now generally restricted to those with capital or with special skills. In 1999, the immigration rate was 2.83 migrants per 1,000 population.

8 ETHNIC GROUPS

The people of Singapore are mainly of Chinese origin. Of an estimated 2000 population of more than 3.5 million, about 77.6% were ethnic Chinese (most of them, however, born in Singapore or in neighboring Malaysia). Some 14.9% were Malays; 6.4% were South Asian, (including Indians, Pakistanis, Bangladeshis, and Sri Lankans).

9 LANGUAGES

There are four official languages: Chinese (Mandarin dialect), Malay, English, and Tamil. English is the principal language of government and the school system, and is widely used in commerce. Malay is the national language. In 1990, Chinese dialects were the first language of 36.7% of the population and Mandarin of 26%. English was used by nearly 20%.

10 RELIGIONS

The Chinese for the most part (54% in 1991) adhere in varying degrees to Buddhism, Taoism, and Confucianism. Malays and persons with origins in the Pakistani and Bangladeshi portions of the Indian subcontinent—about 15% of the population—are almost exclusively Muslims. Most of the Indian minority are Hindus. The Christian population was estimated in 1999 at 13%.

11 TRANSPORTATION

With a natural deepwater harbor that is open year-round, Singapore now ranks as the largest container port in the world, with facilities that can accommodate supertankers. Ships of some 600 shipping lines, flying the flags of nearly all the mar-

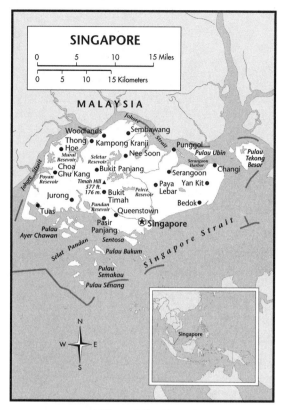

LOCATION: 1°9′ to 1°29′N; 103°38′ to 104°6′E.
TERRITORIAL SEA LIMIT: 3 miles.

itime nations of the world, regularly call at Singapore. In 1998, Singapore itself had 875 ships totaling 19.7 million gross registered tons.

There are two major airports: Singapore Changi International Airport and Seletar Airport. Singapore Airlines carried 13 million passengers in 1997.

In 1995, there were 460,862 motor vehicles, of which 324,000 were automobiles. They traveled on 3,017 kilometers (1,875 miles) of roads in 1997. Singapore's sole rail facility is a 38.6-kilometer (24-mile) section of the Malayan

Photo credit: Corel Corporation.

Worshippers at Sri Veeramakaliamman Temple, Singapore.

Railways, which links Singapore to Kuala Lumpur, Malaysia.

12 HISTORY

Singapore is thought to have been a thriving trading center in the thirteenth and fourteenth centuries, until it was devastated by a Javanese (island of present-day Indonesia) attack in 1377. However, it was an almost uninhabited island when Sir Stamford Raffles, in 1819, established a trading station there of the British East India Company. In 1826 it was incorporated with Malacca (Melaka, Malaysia) and Penang (Pinang, Malaysia) to form the Straits Settlements, which was the form of its legal status and administration up to World War II (1939–45). The trading center grew into the city of Singapore and attracted large numbers of Chinese, many of whom became merchants, until it became a largely Chinese-populated community.

A Nation Built on Trade

With its excellent harbor, Singapore also became a flourishing commercial center and the leading seaport of Southeast Asia, handling the vast export trade in tin and rubber from British-ruled Malaya (present-day Malaysia). In 1938, the British completed construction of a large naval base on the island, which the Japanese captured in February 1942 during World War II, following a land-based attack from the Malay Peninsula to the north.

Recaptured by the United Kingdom in 1945, Singapore was detached from the Straits Settlements to become a separate crown colony in 1946. In 1959, Singapore became a self-governing state, and on 16 September 1963, it joined the new Federation of Malaysia (formed by bringing together the previously independent Malaya and Singapore and the formerly British-ruled northern Borneo territories of Sarawak and Sabah).

Independence

However, Singapore, with its mostly urban Chinese population and highly commercial economy, found itself at odds with the Malay-dominated central government of Malaysia. Frictions mounted, and on 9

August 1965, Singapore separated from Malaysia to become wholly independent in its own right as the Republic of Singapore. Singapore, Indonesia, Malaysia, the Philippines and Thailand formed the Association of South-East Asian Nations (ASEAN) in 1967. Brunei became a member of ASEAN in 1984. Harry Lee Kuan Yew, a major figure in the move toward independence, served as Singapore's first prime minister.

The People's Action Party (PAP) founded in 1954 has been the dominant political party, winning every general election since 1959. The PAP's popular support has rested on economic growth and improved standards of living along with unrelenting repression of opposition leaders. The PAP won all parliamentary seats in the general elections from 1968 to 1980.

In May and June 1987, the government detained 22 persons for alleged involvement in a "Marxist conspiracy." These detentions triggered an international response on human rights critical of the detentions without trial and allegations of torture of the detainees. Most of the alleged conspirators were released by December, but eight were rearrested in April 1988 after issuing a joint press statement regarding the circumstances of their detention.

On 28 November 1990, Lee Kuan Yew, prime minister of Singapore for more than thirty-one years, transferred the prime ministership to Goh Chok Tong, the former first deputy prime minister. Singapore's first direct presidential elections were held on 28 August 1993, and Ong Teng Cheong became the first elected president.

A Nation of Strict Laws

Laws are strictly enforced in Singapore. An incident that garnered worldwide attention was the Singapore government's arrest in October 1993 of nine foreign youths charged with vandalism of some 70 cars which were spray painted. Michael Fay, an American student suspected of being the leader, admitted his guilt under police interrogation and was sentenced to four months in prison, a fine of US$2,230, and six strokes of the cane.

On 7 March 1994, US president Bill Clinton urged Singapore to reconsider the flogging of Fay, but Fay's appeal was dismissed. A plea to the Singaporean president for clemency (mercy) was rejected, but as a "goodwill gesture towards President Clinton," the sentence of caning was reduced from six strokes to four. The sentence was carried out on 5 May 1994.

In 1994, the Singapore High Court ruled in favor of the government in a libel suit against the *International Herald Tribune*. The newspaper had published an editorial stating that Prime Minister Goh was simply a figurehead.

Parliamentary elections were held in 1997 and the PAP retained its vast majority.

13 GOVERNMENT

The constitution of the Republic of Singapore provides for a single-chamber parliamentary form of government. Singapore

Photo credit: EPD/Government of Singapore.

Name:	Goh Chok Tong
Position:	Prime minister of a parliamentary republic
Took office:	28 November 1990
Birthplace:	Singapore
Birth date:	20 May 1941
Education:	University of Singapore, Bachelor of Arts degree in economics, 1964; Williams College, Master of Arts degree in development economics
Spouse:	Tan Choo Leng (a lawyer)
Children:	Two children
Of interest:	Goh criticizes the West for its supposed abandonment of family values.

practices universal suffrage, and voting has been compulsory for all citizens over 21 since 1959. In 1993, the unicameral legislature consisted of an 81 elected-member parliament and six nominated members (NMPs) appointed by the president.

The prime minister, who commands the confidence of a majority of parliament, acts as effective head of government, and appoints the cabinet. The president is elected for a term of six years. In 1996, the parliament enacted laws that limited the president's power to veto legislation (a right only granted in 1991).

Singapore has no local government divisions.

14 POLITICAL PARTIES

There were 22 registered political parties at the beginning of 1993. The ruling People's Action Party (PAP) of former Prime Minister Lee Kuan Yew has dominated the country since 1959. The main opposition parties are the Singapore Democratic Party (SDP) and the Workers' Party (WP). Smaller minority parties are the United People's Front, the Singapore Malays' National Organization, and the Singapore Solidarity Party. The Malay Communist Party and the underground Malayan National Liberation Front are illegal.

In the 1997 parliamentary elections, the PAP maintained its control by winning 81 of 83 seats up for election.

15 JUDICIAL SYSTEM

The judiciary includes the Supreme Court as well as district, magistrate, and special courts. Minor cases are heard in the country's ten magistrate courts and in district courts (two civil and four criminal), each presided over by a district judge. The

Supreme Court is headed by a chief justice and is divided into the High Court and the Court of Appeal. In its appeals jurisdiction, the High Court hears criminal and civil appeals from the magistrate and district courts.

16 ARMED FORCES

Required national military service has been in effect since 1967. Male citizens are called up for 24 months' full-time military service at age 18. Singapore's armed forces numbered 73,000 (with 39,800 draftees) in 2000.

In 2000, the army had an estimated 50,000 personnel, including three combined arms divisions; the navy had 9,500 personnel and a fleet of 24 ships, including six corvettes and 18 missile gunboats. The 1999 defense budget was US$4.2 billion, or 5.1% of the gross domestic product (GDP).

17 ECONOMY

Historically, Singapore's economy was based primarily on its role as a trading center for neighboring countries, which developed from its strategic geographic location. Its most significant natural resource is a deep-water harbor. By the early 1980s, Singapore had built a strong, diversified economy, giving it an economic importance in Southeast Asia out of proportion to its small size.

In the late 1980s, Singapore began to further diversify its economy, making it capable of providing manufacturing, financial, and communications facilities for multinational firms. One of the fastest-

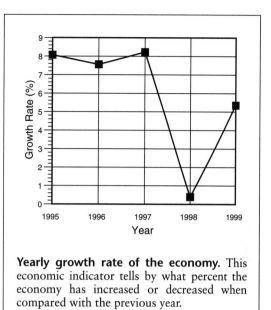

Yearly growth rate of the economy. This economic indicator tells by what percent the economy has increased or decreased when compared with the previous year.

growing sectors of Singapore's economy was international banking and finance, ranking Singapore behind Tokyo and Hong Kong among financial service centers in Southeast Asia region.

The inflation rate based on consumer prices in 1996 was 1.3%. Manufacturing was dominated by the production of computer peripherals and oil processing. Since 1992, property prices have doubled and residential property prices were still climbing in mid-1995. The main constraints on Singapore's economic performance are labor shortages, rising labor costs, and erosion of productivity. The gross domestic product (GDP) grew by more than 10% in 1993 and 1994, but growth cooled to 8% in 1995 and, after a slight improvement in 1997, dropped below 1% in 1998.

18 INCOME

In 1998, Singapore's gross domestic product (GDP) was $91.7 billion, or approximately $21,828 per person. In 1999, the average annual inflation rate was -0.3%, resulting in a growth rate in GDP of more than 5%.

19 INDUSTRY

Manufacturing grew by an average annual rate of about 20% during the 1962–74 period, and it registered an average annual increase of more than 10% from 1975–81. Industry in 1998 accounted for 35% of the gross domestic product (GDP).

The electronics industry is the most important sector of manufacturing. Singapore is the world's leading supplier of disk drives. Telecommunications and other computer equipment also is manufactured.

Petroleum refining is a well-established industry in Singapore. After Rotterdam, the Netherlands, and Houston, Texas, Singapore is the world's third-largest refining center. Production capacity is one million barrels a day. Other major industries are oil drilling equipment, rubber processing and rubber products, processed food and beverages, ship repair, entrepôt (intermediary) trade, financial services, and biotechnology.

20 LABOR

In 1999, Singapore's employed work force totaled 1.9 million. Of this number, 30% were employed in manufacturing and

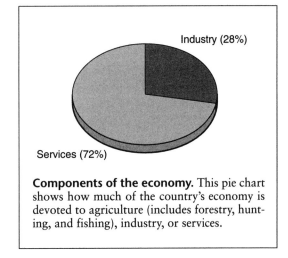

Components of the economy. This pie chart shows how much of the country's economy is devoted to agriculture (includes forestry, hunting, and fishing), industry, or services.

70% in the service sector. About 24% of the work force consists of foreigners. The unemployment rate was 3.2% in 1998.

There is no minimum wage legislation. The standard legal workweek is 44 hours over six days. In 1999, there were 82 registered trade unions in Singapore.

21 AGRICULTURE

Urbanization and industrialization have taken almost all the land away from agricultural activity in post-World War II (post-1945) Singapore. Many of the rubber and coconut plantations that dominated Singapore's landscape before the war have disappeared altogether. Housing for a growing population—and factories for its employment—stand where rubber and coconut trees used to grow.

Only about 1.6% of the land area is used for farming. In 1999, production of fresh vegetables totaled 5,000 tons, resulting in a decreased need to rely on foreign produce imports. Despite this improve-

Photo credit: Cory Langley.

A freighter docked at a pier. Singapore's most significant natural resource is a deep-water harbor.

ment, the value of Singapore's agricultural imports still far exceeded the value of its agricultural products. Orchids are grown for export.

22 DOMESTICATED ANIMALS

Singapore has been self-sufficient (or nearly so) in the production of pork, poultry, and eggs since 1964. However, hog farming is being phased out because of environmental pollution; domestic pork requirements are increasingly being met by imports. In 1998, the livestock population included two million chickens and 190,000 pigs. Also that year, about 16,000 tons of eggs also were produced.

The Pig and Poultry Research and Training Institute and Lim Chu Kang Veterinary Experimental Station conduct research on feeding, housing, breeding, management, and disease control.

23 FISHING

Local fishermen operate chiefly in inshore waters, but some venture into the South China Sea and the Indian Ocean. Traditional fishing methods are used along coastal waters, but there is a trend toward mechanization in both offshore and deep-sea fishing. In 1997, Singapore's fishermen caught 13,338 tons of fish.

Aquaculture (fish-raising) concentrates on the breeding of grouper, sea bass, mussels, and shrimp. By the end of 1985, 60 marine fish farms were in operation. By 1997, Singapore was contributing 4.8% to the world's total exports of fresh, chilled, and frozen fish.

24 FORESTRY

There is little productive forestry left on the island, but Singapore continues to have a fairly sizable sawmilling industry, processing timber imported largely from Malaysia (with some additional imports from Indonesia). Both Malaysia and Indonesia are expanding their processing capacities, however, and the industry is declining in Singapore in the face of the government's policy shift to high-technology industries.

25 MINING

There is no mining in Singapore.

26 FOREIGN TRADE

Since World War II (post-1945), Singapore has changed from a trading center for its neighbors in Southeast Asia to an exporting country in its own right. Machinery and transport equipment constituted the leading import and also headed the export list, followed by mineral fuels. In 1999, exports amounted to $114 billion and imports totaled $111 billion.

Singapore's main trading partners are the ASEAN group (principally Malaysia), the United States, China, and Japan.

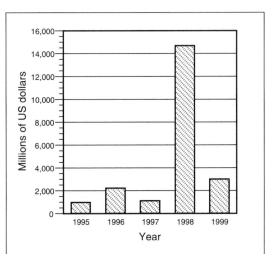

Yearly balance of trade measured in millions of US dollars. The balance of trade is the difference between what a country sells to other countries (its exports) and what it buys (its imports). If a country imports more than it exports, it has a negative balance of trade (a trade deficit). If exports exceed imports there is a positive balance of trade (a trade surplus).

27 ENERGY AND POWER

Electricity generated in 1998 totaled 26.5 billion kilowatt hours. All power was generated thermally, largely from imported mineral fuels. Singapore, a major petroleum-refining center, produced gasoline in 1994 at a rate of 100,490 barrels per day; distillate fuel oil, 372,200; residual fuel oil, 288,120; jet fuel, 147,740; and kerosene, 19,060. The total output of 1.2 million barrels per day ranked Singapore among the top producers in East Asia in 1998, with Japan, China, and South Korea (Republic of Korea).

28 SOCIAL DEVELOPMENT

Besides institutionalized care, the Ministry of Community Development administers foster and homemaker service programs for needy young persons. The government operates child care centers and welfare homes for aged and destitute persons. Social welfare assistance also is provided by mutual-benefit organizations and voluntary services.

The Central Provident Fund, a public pension and retirement program, provides lump-sum benefits for old age, disability, death, sickness, and maternity. Employers fund workers' compensation benefits for job-related injuries.

Women's legal rights are equal to those of men in most areas, including civil liberties, employment, business, and education. Women comprise 42% of the labor force and are well represented in the professions. However, they still fill most low-paying clerical positions, and their average salary is only 75% that of men.

Prison conditions are considered good, but there are reports of mistreatment of prisoners. Caning is a common form of punishment.

29 HEALTH

Singapore's population enjoys one of the highest health levels in all of Southeast Asia due largely to good housing, sanitation, and water supply, as well as the best hospitals and other medical facilities in the region. Nearly all of the population has access to safe drinking water, and 99% has adequate sanitation. Nutritional standards are among the highest in Asia. Life expectancy is 78 years.

In 1990, there were 19 hospitals. In 1997, there were 3.6 hospital beds per

Photo credit: Corel Corporation.

Teenage girl dressed for a parade, Singapore.

1,000 people. In 1991, there were 3,779 doctors and 10,240 nurses. There were 1.4 doctors per 1,000 people in 2000. In the same year, 100% of the population had access to health care services.

The principal causes of death are heart disease and cancer. Other leading causes of death are communicable diseases and maternal/perinatal causes, noncommunicable diseases, and injuries.

30 HOUSING

In 1985, as a result of government-sponsored efforts, 2.1 million persons—or 84% of the total population of Sin-

Selected Social Indicators

The statistics below are estimates for the period 1996 to 2000. For comparison purposes, data for the United States and averages for low-income countries and high-income countries are also given.

Indicator	Singapore	Low-income countries	High-income countries	United States
Per capita gross national product (GNP)†	$22,310	$1,870	$25,690	$31,910
Population growth rate	1.5%	2.1%	0.7%	1.1%
People per square kilometer of land	6,384	73	29	30
Life expectancy in years	78	59	78	77
Number of physicians per 1,000 people	1.4	1.0	2.5	2.5
Number of pupils per teacher (primary school)	n.a.	41	17	14
Illiteracy rate (15 years and older)	7.6%	34%	<5%	3%
Television sets per 1,000 people	308	85	693	844
Energy consumed per capita (kg of oil equivalent)	7,681	550	5,366	7,937

† The GNP is the total dollar value of all goods and services produced by a country in a year. The per capita GNP is calculated by dividing a country's GNP by its population and adjusting for relative purchasing power. About 15% of the world's 6.1 billion people live in high-income countries, while 40% live in low-income countries.

n.a. = data not available   > = greater than   < = less than

Sources: World Bank. *World Development Indicators.* Washington, D.C.: The World Bank, 2001; Central Intelligence Agency. *The World Factbook.* Washington, D.C.: Government Printing Office, 2000.

gapore—lived in 551,767 apartments under the management of the Housing and Development Board. Some 397,180 units had been sold to the public. In 1990, 84% of all housing units were apartments, 7% were bungalows and terrace houses, 5% were condominiums, and 1% were dwellings with attap or zinc roofs. The total number of housing units in 1992 was 758,000.

31 EDUCATION

Literacy in 2000 was about 92.4%. All children who are citizens are entitled to free primary education. Primary schooling is available in all four official languages. Upon completion of primary school, students can receive vocational training, or if they qualify, they can take four or five years of secondary schooling leading to two-year courses in junior colleges or three-year courses in school centers at the pre-university level.

In 1996, there were 198 primary schools in Singapore and an estimated 145 secondary schools and junior colleges. The total school population in 1998 was 269,668 primary and 207,719 secondary and pre-university students. Fifteen vocational institutes offered training courses in the metal, woodworking, electrical, electronic, and building trades.

The National University of Singapore was established on 8 August 1980 through the merger of the University of Singapore and Nanyang University. In addition, there are the Singapore Technical Institute, Ngee Ann Polytechnic, Singapore Polytechnic, and Nanyang Technological Institute.

32 MEDIA

Postal, telephone, and telegraph services in Singapore are among the most efficient in Southeast Asia. Service is available on a 24-hour basis for worldwide telegraph, telephone, and telex communication. There were 1.4 million telephones in 1997.

The Singapore Broadcasting Corp., created in 1980, operates radio and television services. Radio Singapore broadcasts in Chinese, Malay, English, and Tamil. Television Singapore, inaugurated in 1963, operates daily on four channels. There were 739 radios and 308 television sets per 1,000 population in 1997. Singapore had 188 Internet hosts per 1,000 population in 1998.

Singapore has 10 daily newspapers, with at least one printed in each of the four official languages. The total circulation of daily papers in 1995 was 930,000. The oldest and most widely circulated daily is the English-language *Straits Times,* founded in 1845.

Although freedom of the press is guaranteed by law, the International Press Institute has on various occasions cited Singapore for interference with press freedom. In August 1986, parliament passed a bill enabling the government to restrict sales and distribution of foreign publications "engaging in domestic politics." Two months later, the government announced that the distribution of *Time* magazine would be reduced because the magazine had refused to print the entire text of a letter from a government official. In 1987, similar distribution restrictions were placed on the *Asian Wall Street Journal.*

In 1999, Singapore's largest newspapers, with their estimated daily circulations, were the *Straits Times* (English, 313,000); *Lian He Zao Bao* (Chinese, 205,000); *Lian He Wan Bao* (Chinese, 85,000); *Shin Min Daily News* (Chinese, 102,000); *Berita Harian* (Malay, 44,700); and the *Business Times* (English, 23,000).

33 TOURISM AND RECREATION

Singapore's tourist volume has increased steadily. In 1997, 7.2 million tourists visited Singapore, mostly from East Asia. That year, Singapore earned $6.8 billion from tourism.

Shopping, with bargaining the usual practice, is a major tourist attraction. Points of interest include the Van Kleef Aquarium at Fort Canning Park, the Singapore Zoological and Botanical Gardens, and the resort island of Sentosa. Singapore has a number of tourist attractions, including an amusement park at Haw Pav Village, site of historic Chinese statues, and the restored Alkaff Mansion.

Singapore has many sports clubs and associations, notably in the areas of badminton (in which Singaporeans have distinguished themselves internationally), basketball, boxing, cricket, cycling, golf, hockey, horse racing, motoring, polo, swimming, tennis, and yachting.

34 FAMOUS SINGAPOREANS

Sir Thomas Stamford Bingley Raffles (1781–1826) played a major role in the establishment of a British presence on Singapore Island in 1819, introducing policies that greatly enhanced Singapore's wealth and suppressing the slave trade.

The English writer and educator Cyril Northcote Parkinson (1909–93), formerly a professor at the University of Singapore, became internationally known as the originator of Parkinson's Law.

One of Singapore's dominant contemporary figures was Lee Kuan Yew (b.1923), prime minister of the Republic of Singapore from 1965 to 1990.

35 BIBLIOGRAPHY

Brown, M. *Singapore*. Chicago: Children's Press, 1989.

Chew, Ernest, and Edwin Chew, eds. *A History of Singapore*. New York: Oxford University Press, 1991.

Jayapal, Maya. *Old Singapore*. New York: Oxford University Press, 1992.

LePoer, Barbara Leitch, ed. *Singapore: A Country Study*. 2d ed. Washington, D.C.: Library of Congress, 1991.

Minchin, James. *No Man Is an Island: A Portrait of Singapore's Lee Kuan Yew*. 2d ed. Sydney: Allen & Unwin, 1990.

Wee, Jessie. *Singapore*. Philadelphia: Chelsea House, 2000.

SLOVAKIA

Slovak Republic
Slovenska Republika

CAPITAL: Bratislava

FLAG: Horizontal bands of white (top), blue, and red superimposed with a crest of a white double cross on three blue mountains.

ANTHEM: *Nad Tatru sa blyska (Over Tatra it lightens).*

MONETARY UNIT: The currency of the Slovak Republic is the Slovak koruna (Sk) consisting of 100 hellers, which replaced the Czechoslovak Koruna (Kcs) on 8 February 1993. There are coins of 10, 20, and 50 hellers and 1, 2, 5, and 10 korun, and notes of 20, 50, 100, 500, 1,000, and 5,000 korun. Sk1 = $0.02377 (or $1 = Sk42.059).

WEIGHTS AND MEASURES: The metric system is the legal standard.

HOLIDAYS: New Year's Day, 1 January; May Day, 1 May; Anniversary of Liberation, 8 May; Day of the Slav Apostles, 5 July; Anniversary of the Slovak National Uprising, 29 August; Reconciliation Day, 1 November; Christmas, 24–26 December. Movable holiday is Easter Monday.

TIME: 1 PM = noon GMT.

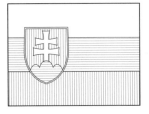

1 LOCATION AND SIZE

Slovakia, a landlocked country located in Eastern Europe, is about twice the size of the state of New Hampshire with a total area of 48,845 square kilometers (18,859 square miles). It has a total boundary length of 1,355 kilometers (842 miles). Slovakia's capital city, Bratislava, is located on the southwestern border of the country.

2 TOPOGRAPHY

The topography of Slovakia features rugged mountains in the central and northern part of the country, and lowlands in the south. More than one-third of the land is forest. The Tatry Mountains along the Polish border are surrounded by many lakes and deep valleys.

3 CLIMATE

In July the average temperature is 21°C (70°F). The average temperature in January is –1°C (30°F). Rainfall averages roughly 49 centimeters (19.3 inches) a year, and can exceed 200 centimeters (80 inches) annually in the Tatry (Tatras) Mountains.

4 PLANTS AND ANIMALS

There are areas of steppe grassland. Mammals include fox, rabbits, and wild pig. A wide variety of birds inhabit the valleys of Slovakia. Carp, pike, and trout are found in the country's rivers, lakes, and streams.

5 ENVIRONMENT

Both Slovakia and its neighbor, the Czech Republic, suffer from air, water, and land pollution caused by industry, mining, and

---

Geographic Profile

Geographic Features

Size ranking: 126 of 192
Highest elevation: 2,655 meters (8,711 feet) at
    Gerlachovsky
Lowest elevation: 94 meters (308 feet) at the Bodrok
    River

Land Use

Arable land:	31%
Permanent crops:	3%
Permanent pastures:	17%
Forests:	41%
Other:	8%

Weather

Average annual precipitation: 49 centimeters (19.3
    inches). Annual precipitation can exceed 200
    centimeters (80 inches) high in the Tatras
    Mountains.
Average temperature in January: –1°C (30°F)
Average temperature in July: 21°C (70°F)

---

agriculture. The air in both nations is contaminated by sulfur dioxide emissions. The two republics use 9% of available water for farming and 68% for industry. The land has suffered from the loss of forest cover, erosion, and acid rain.

In 1994, two mammal species and 18 types of birds were endangered, and 29 types of plants were threatened with extinction.

6 POPULATION

The population of Slovakia was estimated at 5.4 million in 2000. The US Bureau of the Census has projected a population of 5.5 million for the year 2005. The population density in 1998 was about 112 persons per square kilometer (290 per square mile). Bratislava, the capital, had a population of 471,000 in 2000.

7 MIGRATION

As of 1999, Slovakia hosted 490 refugees, most of whom are Bosnians or Kosovars who have been permitted to live temporarily in Slovakia. The net immigration rate in 1999 was 0.29 immigrants per 1,000 population.

8 ETHNIC GROUPS

The population was 85.7% Slovak according to the latest estimates. Hungarians, heavily concentrated in southern border areas, totaled 10.7%; Romany Gypsies, 1.5%; Ruthenians, 0.3%; and Czechs, 1%. There were smaller numbers of Germans, Poles, and Ukrainians.

9 LANGUAGES

Slovak is the official language. It belongs to the western Slavic group and is written in the Roman alphabet. There are only slight differences between Slovak and Czech. Minority languages include Hungarian.

10 RELIGIONS

In 1998 an estimated 60.3% of the population was Roman Catholic, although estimates vary widely, with some being lower. Other churches with substantial memberships are the Slovak Evangelical Church of the Augsburg Confession (329,000 members in 1991) and the Orthodox Church (54,000 members in 1991). In the same year there also were 3,300 Jews, a remnant of what had been a much larger population prior to World War II (1939–45).

SLOVAKIA

0	25	50 Miles
0	25	50 Kilometers

LOCATION: 47°44′ to 49°37′; 16°51′ to 22°34′E. **BOUNDARY LENGTHS:** Total boundary lengths, 1,355 kilometers (842 miles); Austria, 91 kilometers (57 miles); Czech Republic, 215 kilometers (134 miles); Hungary, 515 kilometers (320 miles); Poland, 444 kilometers (275 miles); Ukraine, 90 kilometers (56 miles).

11 TRANSPORTATION

There were some 3,660 kilometers (2,274 miles) of railroads in 1996. The road system totaled 38,000 kilometers (26,613 miles) in 1998. As an inland country, Slovakia relies on the Danube (Dunaj) River for transportation of goods. Bratislava and Komárno are the major ports on the Danube (Dunaj). Air service in Slovakia is primarily through Ivanka Airport at Bratislava. In 1997, 81,000 passengers were carried on scheduled domestic and international airline flights.

12 HISTORY

The first recorded inhabitants of the present-day Slovak Republic settled there about 50 BC. Early ethnic groups included Celts, Slavs, and Franks. The Moravian Empire thrived in parts of Slovakia but was destroyed at the end of the ninth century by invading Magyars (Hungarians).

Although the first Christian missionaries active in the area were Orthodox, it was the Roman church that eventually established dominance. Some contact with the Czechs, who speak a closely related

Photo credit: Dusan Keim.

Old town in Bratislava, capital of Slovakia.

language, began in the early fifteenth century, as refugees from the Hussite (nationalist and religious movement founded by John Huss) religious wars in Bohemia moved east.

In 1526, the Kingdom of Hungary was divided into three parts. "Royal Hungary," which included Slovakia, came under the rule of the Habsburg dynasty. Bratislava was the Habsburg capital until the end of the seventeenth century. Slovak nationalism gained force in the late eighteenth century, with the attempt by the Habsburg rulers to spread the German language and customs throughout the

empire, and again during the 1848 Revolution.

When World War I (1914–18) began, the Slovaks joined with the Czechs and other oppressed nationalities of the Austro-Hungarian Empire in demanding their own states. The Czechs declared independence on 28 October 1918, and the Slovaks seceded from Hungary two days later, to create the Czecho-Slovak Republic.

The relationship between the two parts of the new state was an uneasy one. The Czech lands were more developed economically, and Czechs dominated the political system. Many Slovak nationalists wanted complete independence.

World War II

After first occupying what is now the north Czech Republic in 1938, German leader Adolf Hitler took over the remainder of the Czechoslovakian lands on 15 March 1939, ending the first republic. Slovak nationalists argued that once the breakup of Czechoslovakia had begun, they too should secede. The Slovak government declared its independence, establishing the Slovak Republic, with Dr. Jozef Tiso as its head of state. Tiso allowed the Germans to occupy Slovakia and followed the Nazis' policies. Tiso had some support, but on 29 August 1944 an underground resistance movement organized the Slovak National Uprising against German control. The uprising began in Banská Bystrica but it soon weakened due to lack of support from the Allies (countries fighting against Germany).

During World War II (1939–45), Slovak leaders like Stefan Osusky and Juraj Slavik cooperated with Edward Benes's Czechoslovak government-in-exile, headquartered in London. In December 1943, a Slovak National Council was formed in opposition to the government, with both democratic and communist members. When the war ended, the Slovak National Council took control of the country. In 1945, negotiations between the Czech leaders Edward Benes and Klement Gottwald and the Soviet Union's Josef Stalin led to the formation of a postwar Czechoslovakian government.

Communism and Soviet Influence

The new National Front government ran Czechoslovakia as a democracy until 1948, when a military coup with backing from the Soviet Union forced President Benes to accept a government headed by Klement Gottwald, a communist. A wave of purges and arrests rolled over the country from 1949 to 1954. Gottwald died a few days after Stalin, in March 1953. His successors clung to harsh Stalinist (dictatorial) methods of control, holding Czechoslovakia in a tight grip until well into the 1960s.

Soviet leader Nikita Khrushchev led a movement of liberalization in the Soviet Union. This atmosphere encouraged liberals within the Czechoslovak party to try to emulate his leadership style. In January 1968, Alexander Dubček was named head of the Czechoslovak Communist Party, the first Slovak ever to hold the post. Under Dubček, Czechoslovakia embarked on a radical liberalization, termed "socialism with a human face." The leaders of the Soviet Union and other eastern bloc (communist) nations viewed these developments—termed the "Prague Spring"—with alarm. Communist leaders issued warnings to Dubček.

Finally, on the night of 20–21 August 1968, military units from almost all the Warsaw Pact (communist) nations invaded Czechoslovakia, to "save it from counter-revolution." Dubček and other officials were arrested, and the country was placed under Soviet control. A purge of liberals followed, and Dubček was expelled from the Communist Party. Between 1970 and 1975 nearly one-third of the party was dismissed, as the new Communist Party leader, Gustav Husak, consolidated his power, reuniting the titles of party head and republic president.

In the 1980s, liberalization in the Soviet Union, under the concepts of *perestroika* (restructuring) and *glasnost* (openness), once again set off political change in Czechoslovakia. After ignoring Soviet leader Mikhail Gorbachev's calls for Communist Party reform, in 1987 Husak announced his retirement. His replacement was Milos Jakes.

The Velvet Revolution

In November 1989, thousands gathered in Prague's Wenceslas Square, demanding free elections. This "velvet revolution," so-called because it was not violent, ended on 24 November, when Jakes and all his government resigned. Vaclav Havel, a Czech playwright and dissident, was named president on 29 December 1989, while Dubček was named leader of the National Assembly.

There was less enthusiasm for returning to an economic system of private ownership in Slovakia than among the Czechs. Vladimir Meciar, the Slovak premier, was a persuasive voice for growing Slovak separatism from the Czechs. In July 1992, the new Slovak legislature issued a declaration of sovereignty and adopted a new constitution as an independent state, to take effect 1 January 1993. By the end of 1992, it was obvious that separation was inevitable. The two prime ministers, Klaus and Meciar, agreed to the peaceful separation—the so-called "velvet divorce," which took effect 1 January 1993.

The new Slovak constitution created a 150-seat National Assembly, which elects the head of state, the president. The Meciar government rejected the political and economic liberalization that the Czechs were pursuing, attempting instead to retain a socialist-style government. Swift economic decline, especially compared to the Czechs' growing prosperity, caused him to lose a vote of no-confidence in March 1994. Michal Kovac was elected to a five-year term in February 1993 and appointed Meciar prime minister in December 1994. However, Meciar again was slow to implement economic reforms, and Kovac stopped much of Meciar's more authoritarian legislation. Kovac's term, however, ended in March 1998 and Meciar abstained from voting in parliament for a new president, thus keeping the position vacant. Meciar assumed presidential duties and began building up his base of power. Tens of thousands of protesters

Photo credit: EPD/Government of the Slovak Republic.

Name:	Mikulas Dzurinda
Position:	Prime minister of a parliamentary democracy
Took office:	30 October 1998
Birthplace:	Spissky Sturtok, Slovakia
Birth date:	4 February 1955
Education:	University of Transportation and Telecommunications, studied economics; economic research at an institute in Zilina
Children:	Two daughters

marched in Bratislava against Meciar's administration.

Michal Kovac was elected for a five–year term as president by the National Parliament in 1994. In the 1999 elections, Rudolf Schuster replaced Kovac as president.

Under new election laws, the Slovak Democratric Coalition was formed in 1997. Their candidate, Mikulas Dzurinda, was elected prime minister in the 1998 elections.

13 GOVERNMENT

The constitution that the Slovak National Assembly adopted in July 1992 created a single-chamber legislature of 150 members. The government is formed by the leading party, or coalition of parties, and headed by a prime minister. The president is head of state. Slovakia is currently divided into 38 districts.

14 POLITICAL PARTIES

At one time, the most popular party was Meciar's Movement for a Democratic Slovakia. The Party of the Democratic Left, the Christian Democratic Movement, the Slovak Democratic Coalition, and the Association of Slovak Workers are other leading parties.

15 JUDICIAL SYSTEM

The judicial system consists of a republic-level Supreme Court; regional courts in Bratislava, Banská Bystrica, and Košice; and 38 local courts responsible for individual districts. The highest judicial body, the ten-judge Constitutional Court in Košice, rules on the constitutionality of laws as well as the decisions of lower level courts.

16 ARMED FORCES

The total active armed forces of Slovakia number 44,800, including 23,800 army

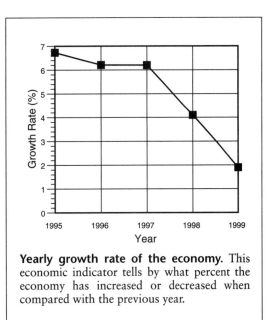

Yearly growth rate of the economy. This economic indicator tells by what percent the economy has increased or decreased when compared with the previous year.

personnel and 12,000 air force personnel. Additionally, there is an estimated reserve national guard force of 20,000. The defense budget for 1998 was $436 million.

17 ECONOMY

The economy of Slovakia is highly industrialized, although the industrial structure is less developed than that of the Czech Republic. Agriculture, which had been the most important area of the economy before the communist era, now plays a smaller role than industry. The growth rate of the gross domestic product in 1999 was about 2%.

18 INCOME

In 1998, Slovakia's gross domestic product (GDP) was $445 billion, or about $8,300 per person. In 1999, the average annual inflation rate was 7.4%, resulting in a GDP of about 2%.

19 INDUSTRY

Major industries include heavy engineering, armaments, iron and steel production, nonferrous metals, and chemicals.

20 LABOR

As of 1998, there were three million members of the Slovak workforce. Agriculture accounted for 10% of employment; manufacturing, 26.5%; construction, 9%; commerce, 12.3%; services (including government), 25%; and other sectors, 20%. Registered unemployment was 11.9% (297,500 persons) in 1998. About 45% of all workers were labor union members in 1999. Minimum wage was $86 per month, with an average 42.5-hour workweek in 1999.

21 AGRICULTURE

Some 34% of the total land area is under cultivation. Important crops in Slovakia in 1998 (in thousands of tons) included: wheat, 1,789; barley, 875; corn, 637; potatoes, 412; rye, 96; and sugar beets, 1,331. Barley and hops are important agricultural exports.

22 DOMESTICATED ANIMALS

Some 17% of the total area is classified as meadow and pasture. In 1998, there were about two million pigs, 803,000 head of cattle, 417,000 sheep, 12,000 horses, and 14 million chickens. Meat production in 1998 was 368,000 tons, with pork accounting for 62%; beef, 11%; and poultry, 20%.

23 FISHING

Fishing is only a minor source of the domestic food supply. The total catch in 1997 was 2,640 tons, with common carp and rainbow trout the dominant species.

24 FORESTRY

Slovakian forest product exports include paper, wood, and furniture. In 1997, roundwood production amounted to 5.9 million cubic meters. Forests covered an estimated 41% of Slovakia in 1995.

25 MINING

Nonfuel mineral resources include antimony ore, mercury, iron ore, copper, lead, zinc, precious metals, magnesite, limestone, dolomite, gravel, brick soils, ceramic materials, and stonesalt.

26 FOREIGN TRADE

Slovakia's most valuable exports in 1999 were manufactured goods (43%), machinery and transport equipment (37%), chemicals (9%), and raw materials (4%). The Czech Republic accounts for roughly one-third of Slovakia's foreign trade. Other leading trade partners in 1998 were Germany, Russia, the United States, and Poland.

27 ENERGY AND POWER

As of 1998, of the total 7.4 million kilowatts of electrical generating capacity, nuclear plants accounted for about 44% of total electricity production; thermal power plants, 36%; and hydroelectric plants, 20%. Coal mining produced some three million tons of lignite in 1995. There

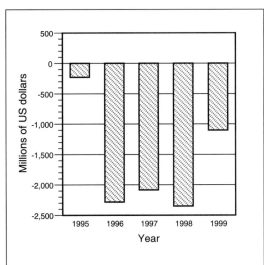

Yearly balance of trade measured in millions of US dollars. The balance of trade is the difference between what a country sells to other countries (its exports) and what it buys (its imports). If a country imports more than it exports, it has a negative balance of trade (a trade deficit). If exports exceed imports, there is a positive balance of trade (a trade surplus).

are petroleum refineries at Bratislava, Strážske, and Zvolen.

28 SOCIAL DEVELOPMENT

Slovak law guarantees the equality of all citizens and prohibits discrimination. Health care, retirement benefits, and other social services are provided regardless of race, sex, religion, or disability. Women and men are equal under the law, enjoying the same property, inheritance, and other rights, and receiving equal pay for equal work. Slovakia's Roma (Gypsy) population experiences higher levels of unemployment and housing discrimination than ethnic Slovaks. There were incidents of ethnically motivated attacks against Roma reported in 1999.

29 HEALTH

Life expectancy was 73 years, and infant mortality was 10 per 1,000 live births in 1999. The country had three physicians and 7.5 hospital beds per 1,000 population in 2000. Tuberculosis has been on the rise in Slovakia; there were 28 diagnosed cases per 100,000 population in 1996.

30 HOUSING

With a shortage of 500,000 apartments, the Slovak Republic planned to build 200,000 new ones by the year 2000. As of 1992, 80,000 people were on waiting lists.

31 EDUCATION

Slovakia has an estimated adult literacy rate of more than 99%. Education is compulsory for 10 years, approximately up to the age of 15.

In 1997, 329,880 children attended the elementary schools, and 677,377 students attended general secondary schools. Another 237,130 pupils attended the 493 specialized and technical secondary schools in 1994.

Slovakia has 13 universities, with the oldest being Cornenius (Komensky) University in Bratislava. In 1997, 101,764 students were enrolled at the universities.

32 MEDIA

There are 24 radio stations and 41 television stations. There were 68,500 Internet hosts in 1996. Major newspapers, with their estimated 1999 circulations, are *Pravda* (165,000), *Práca* (80,000) and *Novy Cas* (250,000).

Selected Social Indicators

The statistics below are estimates for the period 1996 to 2000. For comparison purposes, data for the United States and averages for low-income countries and high-income countries are also given.

Indicator	Slovakia	Low-income countries	High-income countries	United States
Per capita gross national product (GNP)†	$10,430	$1,870	$25,690	$31,910
Population growth rate	0.1%	2.1%	0.7%	1.1%
People per square kilometer of land	112	73	29	30
Life expectancy in years	73	59	78	77
Number of physicians per 1,000 people	3	1.0	2.5	2.5
Number of pupils per teacher (primary school)	22	41	17	14
Illiteracy rate (15 years and older)	<1%	34%	<5%	3%
Television sets per 1,000 people	417	85	693	844
Energy consumed per capita (kg of oil equivalent)	3,136	550	5,366	7,937

† The GNP is the total dollar value of all goods and services produced by a country in a year. The per capita GNP is calculated by dividing a country's GNP by its population and adjusting for relative purchasing power. About 15% of the world's 6.1 billion people live in high-income countries, while 40% live in low-income countries.

n.a. = data not available   > = greater than   < = less than

Sources: World Bank. *World Development Indicators.* Washington, D.C.: The World Bank, 2001; Central Intelligence Agency. *The World Factbook.* Washington, D.C.: Government Printing Office, 2000.

33 TOURISM AND RECREATION

Slovakia's outdoor tourist attractions include mountains (the most famous being the Tatry Mountains), forests, cave formations, and more than 1,000 mineral and hot springs. In addition, tourists can visit ancient castles, monuments, chateaux, museums, and galleries. There are more than 1,000 hotels in Slovakia. In 1997, 814,138 tourists arrived in Slovakia and spent an estimated $546 million.

34 FAMOUS SLOVAKS

The greatest Slovak poet, Pavel Hviezdoslav (1849–1921), contributed to the awakening of Slovak nationalism. The Robin Hood of the Slovaks, Juraj Jánošík (1688–1713), fought the Hungarians.

Milan Rastislav Štefánik (1880–1919) was a famous military leader. Alexander Dubček (1921–92) was first secretary of the Czechoslovak Communist Party (1968–69) until the invasion of Czechoslovakia by the Warsaw Pact (communist) nations in 1968. In 1989 he was elected the Federal Assembly's first speaker.

35 BIBLIOGRAPHY

Kinkade, Sheila. *Children of Slovakia.* Minneapolis: Carolrhoda Books, 2001.

Mikus, Joseph A. *Slovakia and the Slovaks.* Washington, D.C.: Three Continents Press, 1977.

Momatiuk, Yva, and John Eastcott. "Slovakia's Spirit of Survival." *National Geographic,* January 1987, 120–146.

Skalnik, Carol. *The Czech and Slovak Republics: Nation vs. State.* Boulder, Colo.: Westview Press, 1997.

Slovakia in Pictures. Minneapolis: Lerner, 1995.

SLOVENIA

Republic of Slovenia
Republika Slovenije

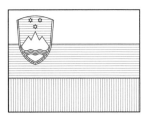

CAPITAL: Ljubljana

FLAG: Equal horizontal bands of white (top), blue, and red with seal superimposed on upper hoist side.

ANTHEM: *Zive naj vsi narodi.* (The national anthem begins, "Let all nations live . . .")

MONETARY UNIT: The currency of Slovenia is the tolar (Slt), which consists of 100 stotinov. There are coins of 50 stotinov and 1, 2, and 5 tolars, and notes of 10, 20, 50, and 200 tolars. Slt1 = $0.00512 (or $1 = Slt195.06).

WEIGHTS AND MEASURES: The metric system is in force.

HOLIDAYS: New Year, 1–2 January; Prešeren Day, Day of Culture, 8 February; Resistance Day, 27 April; Labor Days, 1–2 May; National Statehood Day, 25 June; Assumption, 15 August; Reformation Day, 31 October; All Saints' Day, 1 November; Christmas Day, 25 December; Independence Day, 26 December. Movable holidays are Easter Sunday and Monday.

TIME: 1 PM = noon GMT.

1 LOCATION AND SIZE

Located in central Europe, Slovenia is slightly larger than the state of New Jersey with a total area of 20,296 square kilometers (7,836 square miles). Slovenia has a total boundary length of 999 kilometers (621 miles). The capital city, Ljubljana, is located near the center of the country.

2 TOPOGRAPHY

The topography of Slovenia features a small coastal strip on the Adriatic Sea, an alpine region adjacent to Italy, and mixed mountains and valleys with numerous rivers in the east.

3 CLIMATE

Slovenia's climate is Mediterranean on the coast, and continental in the plateaus and valleys to the east. July's mean temperature is 22°C (72°F). The mean temperature in January is 1°C (33°F). Rainfall averages 62 centimeters (24 inches) a year.

4 PLANTS AND ANIMALS

Ferns, flowers, mosses, and common trees populate the landscape. Wild animals include deer, brown bear, rabbit, fox, and wild boar. Farmers plant vineyards on the hillsides and raise livestock in the fertile lowlands of the country.

5 ENVIRONMENT

The Sava River is polluted with domestic and industrial waste; heavy metals and toxic chemicals can be found along coastal water near Koper. Metallurgical and chemical emissions have damaged the forests.

6 POPULATION

The population of Slovenia was estimated at nearly 2 million in 2000. A population of nearly 2 million also is projected by the US Census Bureau for 2005. The population density in 1998 was about 99 persons per square kilometer (256 per square mile). Ljubljana, the capital, had a population of 278,000 in 2000.

7 MIGRATION

In 1995, Slovenia was harboring 29,000 refugees from the former Yugoslav Socialist Federal Republic, which broke apart in 1991; by 1999, almost 10,000 still remained. In 1999 the net emigration rate was .23 emigres per 1,000 population.

8 ETHNIC GROUPS

In 1998, the population was 91% Slovene. Croats comprised 3%; Serbs, 2%; and Muslims, 1%.

9 LANGUAGES

Like Serbo-Croatian, Macedonian, and Bulgarian, Slovene is a language of the southern Slavic group. It is closest to Serbo-Croatian. Slovene is written in the Roman alphabet.

10 RELIGIONS

Membership in the Roman Catholic Church was estimated in 1998 at 70.8% of the population. There also is a Slovenian Old Catholic Church and some Eastern Orthodox Churches. The only well-established Protestant group is the Evangelical Lutheran Church of Slovenia, which accounted for 1% in 1998.

Geographic Profile

Geographic Features

Size ranking: 150 of 192
Highest elevation: 2,863 meters (9,396 feet) at Mount Triglav
Lowest elevation: Sea level at the Adriatic Sea

Land Use†

Arable land:	12%
Permanent crops:	3%
Permanent pastures:	28%
Forests:	51%
Other:	6%

Weather††

Average annual precipitation: 62 centimeters (24 inches)
Average temperature in January: 1°C (33°F)
Average temperature in July: 22°C (72°F)

†*Arable land:* Land used for temporary crops, like meadows for mowing or pasture, gardens, and greenhouses. *Permanent crops:* Land cultivated with crops that occupy its use for long periods, such as cocoa, coffee, rubber, fruit and nut orchards, and vineyards. *Permanent pastures:* Land used permanently for forage crops. *Forests:* Land containing stands of trees. *Other:* Any land not specified, including built-on areas, roads, and barren land.

††The measurements for precipitation and average temperature were taken at weather stations closest to the country's largest city. Precipitation and average temperature can vary significantly within a country, due to factors such as latitude, altitude, coastal proximity, and wind patterns.

---

11 TRANSPORTATION

As of 1998, there were some 1,200 kilometers (746 miles) of railway tracks. With more than 150 passenger stations and 140 freight stations, almost every town in Slovenia can be reached by train. In 1997, Slovenia had 14,830 kilometers (9,215 miles) of roads. Slovenia has two expressways: one connects Ljubljana and Postojna with the coastal region; the other links Ljubl-

LOCATION: 46°15′N; 15°10′E. **BOUNDARY LENGTHS:** Total boundary lengths, 999 kilometers (621 miles); Austria 262 kilometers (163 miles); Croatia, 455 kilometers (283 miles); Italy, 199 kilometers (124 miles); Hungary, 83 kilometers (52 miles).

jana with Kranj and the Karawanken tunnel to Austria.

The principal marine port is Koper. Slovenian owners control 14 vessels (1,000 gross registered tons or more) totaling 229,727 gross registered tons.

12 HISTORY

The Slovenes are one of a large group of Slavic nations. An agricultural people, the Slovenes settled from around AD 550 in the Roman Noricum (present-day Austria and Germany) area of the eastern Alps and in the western Pannonian plains (present-day Hungary). Part of the Slavic Kingdom of Samo in the mid-seventh century, the settlement continued its existence as a Duchy of the Slovenes after Samo's death in AD 659, eventually coming under the control of the numerically stronger Bavarians (southern Germans).

The eastward expansion of the Franks (west Germans) in the ninth century brought all Slovene lands under Frankish control. Under the feudal system, various families of mostly Germanic nobility were granted fiefdoms (areas of control) over Slovene lands and competed among themselves to increase their holdings.

The Austrian Habsburgs grew steadily in power and by the fifteenth century became the leading feudal family in control of most Slovene lands. Rebellions by Slovene and Croat peasants in the fifteenth to eighteenth centuries were cruelly repressed.

The Protestant Reformation (mid-1500s) gave a boost to the Slovenians' sense of national identity through the efforts of Protestant Slovenes to provide printed Slovenian language materials to support their cause. When the ideas of the French Revolution (late 1700s) spread through Europe and Napoleon Bonaparte seized power at the end of the eighteenth century, the Slovenes were ready to join in the effort to eliminate the aristocracy.

When Napoleon defeated Austria, Slovenia became part of his Illyrian Provinces (1809–13). The Slovene language was encouraged in the schools and also used, along with French, as an official language. Austria, however, regained the Illyrian Provinces in 1813 and reestablished its direct control over the Slovene lands.

The 1848 "spring of nations" brought about various demands for national freedom of Slovenes and other Slavic nations of Austria. The revolts of 1848 were repressed after a few years and dictatorial regimes kept under control any movements in support of national rights.

In 1867, the region's German and Hungarian majorities agreed to the reorganiza-tion of the state into a "Dualistic" Austro-Hungarian Monarchy in order to better control the minority elements in each half of the empire. However, the addition of Bosnia and Herzegovina to Austria through occupation and annexation increased the power of the region's Slovenes, Croats, and Serbs in an arrangement that eventually would allow these South Slavic groups ("Yugoslavs") to form their own joint nation state. However, the German leadership's policies prevented any compromise, and nationalist strife in the region helped to ignite World War I (1914–18).

World War I brought about the breakup of centuries-old ties between the Slovenes and the Austrian monarchy, and the Croats/Serbs and the Hungarian crown. On 29 October 1918, the National Council for all Slavs of former Austro-Hungary proclaimed the separation of the South Slavs from Austro-Hungary and the formation of a new state of Slovenes, Croats, and Serbs.

Creation of Yugoslavia

A united "Kingdom of Serbs, Croats, and Slovenes" was declared on 1 December 1918, and it included a strongly centralized government ruled, after 1921, by King Alexander of Serbia. However, the Slovenes and Croats, while freed from Austro-Hungarian domination, did not win the political and cultural self-rule for which they had hoped.

The period between 1921 and 1929 was a confused one, with a series of 23 governments. On 6 January 1929, the king dissolved the parliament, abolished the 1921 constitution, and established his own personal dictatorship as a temporary arrangement. On 3 October 1929, the country was renamed the Kingdom of Yugoslavia. King Alexander was assassinated in Marseille, France, on 9 October 1934 by agents of the extreme Croatian nationalist group, the Ustaša.

Hitler unleashed German forces on Yugoslavia on 6 April 1941, bombing Belgrade and other cities without any warning or formal declaration of war. The Yugoslav government fled the country, and the Nazis set up a government run by the Ustaša, which initiated a bloody orgy of mass murders of Serbs.

Slovenia was divided in 1941 among Germany, Italy, and Hungary. Resistance movements were initiated by nationalist groups and by communist-dominated Partisans. Spontaneous resistance to the Partisans by the noncommunist peasantry led to a bloody civil war in Slovenia. The other Yugoslav states also suffered civil war. All were now largely under foreign occupiers, who encouraged the bloodshed.

With the entry of the Soviet Union's armies into Yugoslav territory in October 1944, the Partisans swept over Yugoslavia in pursuit of the retreating German forces. The Partisans took over Croatia, launching a campaign of executions and large-scale massacres.

All of the republics of the former Federal Socialist Republic of Yugoslavia share a common history between 1945 and 1991, the year of Yugoslavia's breakup. The World War II (1939–45) Partisan resistance movement, controlled by the Communist Party of Yugoslavia and led by Marshal Josip Broz Tito, won a civil war waged against nationalist groups.

A conflict erupted between Tito and the Russian leader Josef Stalin in 1948, and Tito was expelled from the Soviet Bloc (communist countries allied with the Soviet Union). Yugoslavia then developed its own brand of communism based on workers' councils and self-management of enterprises and institutions. Yugoslavia became the leader of the nonaligned group of nations (those countries who were neither allies of the United States nor the Soviet Union).

The Yugoslav communist regime relaxed its central controls somewhat. This allowed for the development of more liberal wings of communist parties, especially in Croatia and Slovenia. Also, nationalism reappeared, with tensions especially strong between Serbs and Croats in the Croatian republic. This led Tito to repress the Croatian and Slovenian "springs" (freedom movements like the one in Czechoslovakia in 1968) in 1970–71.

Independence for Yugoslavia

The 1974 constitution shifted much of the decision-making power from the federal level to the republics, further decentralizing the political process. Following Tito's death in 1980, there was an economic crisis. Severe inflation and inability to pay the nation's foreign debts led to tensions between the different republics and demands for a reorganization of the Yugo-

Children play on an abandoned field gun in the refugee center of Bloke, about 40 miles southwest of Ljubljana, Slovenia. The center currently has 474 refugees from Bosnia; 250 of them are children under 16.

slav federation into a confederation of sovereign states.

Pressure towards individual autonomy for the regions, as well as a market economy, grew stronger, leading to the formation of noncommunist political parties. By 1990 these parties were able to win majorities in multiparty elections in Slovenia and then in Croatia, ending the era of Communist Party monopoly of power.

Slovenia and Croatia declared their independence on 25 June 1991. On 27 June 1991, the Yugoslav army tried to seize control of Slovenia but was met by heavy resistance from Slovenian "territorial guards." The "guards" surrounded

Yugoslav army tank units, isolated them, and engaged in close combat. In most cases, the Yugoslav units surrendered to the Slovenian forces. More than 3,200 Yugoslav army soldiers surrendered and were well-treated by the Slovenes, who gained favorable publicity by having the prisoners call their parents all over Yugoslavia to come to Slovenia and take their sons back home.

The war in Slovenia ended in ten days due to the intervention of the European Community (nations of Europe), which negotiated a ceasefire. Thus Slovenia was able to remove itself from Yugoslavia with a minimum of casualties, although the military operations caused considerable damage to property estimated at almost $3 billion.

On 23 December 1991, a new constitution was adopted by Slovenia establishing a parliamentary democracy with a two-chamber legislature. International recognition came first from Germany on 18 December 1991, from the European Community (EC) on 15 January 1992, and finally from the United States on 7 April 1992. Slovenia was accepted as a member of the United Nations on 23 April 1992 and has since become a member of many other international organizations.

In December 1992, a coalition government was formed by the Liberal Democrats, Christian Democrats, and the United List Group of Leftist Parties.

In the 1970s, in the region of Slovenia, the standard of living was close to the one in neighboring Austria and Italy. However, the burdens imposed by the cost of maintaining a large Yugoslav army and the repayments on a $20 billion international debt caused a lowering of its living standard over the 1980s. The situation worsened with the trauma of secession from Yugoslavia, the war damages suffered, and the loss of the former Yugoslav markets.

In spite of all these problems Slovenia has made good progress since independence in improving its productivity, controlling inflation, and reorienting its exports to western Europe.

13 GOVERNMENT

Slovenia is a republic based on a constitution adopted on 23 December 1991. The president is Dr. Milan Kučan, elected in

Photo credit: EPD/Government of Slovenia.

Name:	Milan Kucan
Position:	President of a parliamentary democratic republic
Took office:	22 April 1990
Birthplace:	Krizevci, northeastern Slovenia
Birth date:	14 January 1941
Education:	University of Ljubljana, law degree, 1963
Of interest:	Kucan has received several awards, including a medal of the Order of Pope Pius from Pope John Paul II in 1993.

1990 and reelected in 1997. The prime minister was Dr. Janez Drnovšek, whose coalition collapsed in April 2000, and has yet to be replaced.

The constitution provides for a National Assembly as the highest legislative authority with 90 seats. Deputies are elected to four-year terms of office. The National Council, with 40 seats, has an advisory role. Council members are elected to five-year terms of office and may propose laws to the National Assembly, request it to review its decisions, and may demand the calling of a constitutional referendum.

The executive branch consists of a President of the Republic who also is Supreme Commander of the Armed Forces, and is elected to a five-year term of office, limited to two consecutive terms. The president calls for elections to the National Assembly, proclaims the adopted laws, and proposes candidates for prime minister to the National Assembly. Since 1993, the government has consisted of 15 ministries instead of the previous 27.

The National Assembly is attempting to reform the inefficient local government system inherited from the former Yugoslavia.

14 POLITICAL PARTIES

The last parliamentary elections were held on 10 November 1996, with seven parties receiving enough votes to gain representation in the National Assembly. The Liberal Democratic Party held 25 seats; Slovene People's Party, 19; Social Democrats of Slovenia, 16; Christian Democrats, 10; and United List (former communists and allies), 10. Other parties include DESUS, Slovene National Party, Italian Minority, and Hungarian Minority.

15 JUDICIAL SYSTEM

The judicial system consists of local and district courts and a Supreme Court that hears appeals. A nine-member Constitutional Court resolves jurisdictional disputes and rules on the constitutionality of legislation and regulations. The Constitutional Court also acts as a final court of appeal in cases requiring constitutional interpretation.

The constitution guarantees the independence of judges. Judges are appointed to permanent positions subject to an age limit. The constitution affords criminal defendants a presumption of innocence, open court proceedings, the right to an appeal, a prohibition against double jeopardy, and a number of other due process protections.

16 ARMED FORCES

The Slovenian armed forces number 9,550 active duty soldiers and 61,000 reservists who are required to give seven months of service. Their equipment is dated, Warsaw-pact material. Defense spending amounted to 1.8% of the gross domestic product (GDP) in 1998.

17 ECONOMY

Before its independence, Slovenia was the most highly developed and wealthiest republic of the former Yugoslav Socialist Federal Republic (which broke apart in 1991), with a per person income more than double that of the Yugoslav average, and nearly comparable to levels in neighboring Austria and Italy. The painful transition to a market-based economy has

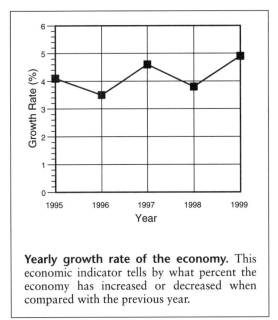

Yearly growth rate of the economy. This economic indicator tells by what percent the economy has increased or decreased when compared with the previous year.

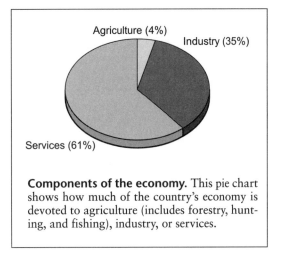

Components of the economy. This pie chart shows how much of the country's economy is devoted to agriculture (includes forestry, hunting, and fishing), industry, or services.

been aggravated by the disruption of intra-Yugoslav trade.

Slovenia deregulated prices and in November 1992 adopted a law that has enabled private businesses to expand. Managers and workers at state-owned companies were given the opportunity to purchase up to 60% of their companies.

18 INCOME

In 1998, Slovenia's gross domestic product (GDP) was $20.4 billion, or about $10,300 per person.

19 INDUSTRY

Manufacturing is the most prominent economic activity and is widely diversified. Important manufacturing areas include electrical and nonelectrical machinery, metal processing, chemicals, textiles and clothing, wood processing and furniture, transport equipment, and food processing. Industrial production fell by 25% in the early 1990s due in part to the international sanctions against Serbia, a major trading partner.

20 LABOR

The labor force totaled 1 million in 1998. Of all employees, 40% were in manufacturing, 12.2% in commerce, 12% in agriculture (which comprised 4% of the GDP), and 28% in other sectors.

About 46% of those employed in 1998 were women. Unemployment stood at 7.7% in 1998. The 1991 constitution provides that the establishment, activities, and recruitment of members of labor unions shall be unrestricted. There are three main labor federations, with branches throughout the society.

21 AGRICULTURE

Some 285,000 hectares (704,000 acres), or 14% of the total land area, were in use as cropland in 1997. Slovenia was the least agriculturally active of all the republics of the former Yugoslav Socialist Federal Republic. Major crops produced in 1998 included wheat, 191,000 tons; corn, 355,000 tons; potatoes, 495,000 tons; sugar beets, 289,000 tons; and fruit, 267,000 tons (of which grapes accounted for 48%).

22 DOMESTICATED ANIMALS

As of 1998, about 502,000 hectares (1.2 million acres), or about 25% of the total land area, were permanent pastureland. Sheep and cattle breeding, as well as dairy farming, dominate the agricultural part of the economy. In 1998, the livestock population included pigs, 578,000; cattle, 446,000; sheep, 28,000; goats, 9,000; horses, 8,000; and chickens, 9 million. Meat production in 1998 included 42,000 tons of beef, 57,000 tons of pork, and 73,000 tons of poultry. Productivity rates for livestock and dairy farming are comparable to much of Western Europe. In 1998, 568,000 tons of milk and 24,000 tons of eggs were produced.

23 FISHING

The total catch in 1997 was 3,262 tons, 67% from marine fishing. Exports of fish products amounted to $5.1 million in 1997.

24 FORESTRY

Forests and woodlands cover about 51% of the total area; they are Slovenia's most important natural resource. Roundwood production was 400,000 cubic meters in

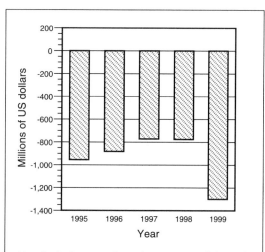

Yearly balance of trade measured in millions of US dollars. The balance of trade is the difference between what a country sells to other countries (its exports) and what it buys (its imports). If a country imports more than it exports, it has a negative balance of trade (a trade deficit). If exports exceed imports there is a positive balance of trade (a trade surplus).

1997. The furniture-making industry is a major consumer of Slovenia's forest products.

25 MINING

Slovenia's nonfuel mineral resources include lead-zinc and mercury (mined and smelted in Idrija). Imported ore is needed for the aluminum plant at Kidričevo, and for the iron- and steel-producing facilities at Jesenice.

26 FOREIGN TRADE

In 1999, Slovenian exports totaled $8.4 billion. Transport equipment and machinery accounted for 30%; other manufac-

Selected Social Indicators

The statistics below are estimates for the period 1996 to 2000. For comparison purposes, data for the United States and averages for low-income countries and high-income countries are also given.

Indicator	Slovenia	Low-income countries	High-income countries	United States
Per capita gross national product (GNP)†	$16,050	$1,870	$25,690	$31,910
Population growth rate	–0.1%	2.1%	0.7%	1.1%
People per square kilometer of land	99	73	29	30
Life expectancy in years	75	59	78	77
Number of physicians per 1,000 people	2.1	1.0	2.5	2.5
Number of pupils per teacher (primary school)	15	41	17	14
Illiteracy rate (15 years and older)	0.3%	34%	<5%	3%
Television sets per 1,000 people	556	85	693	844
Energy consumed per capita (kg of oil equivalent)	3,354	550	5,366	7,937

† The GNP is the total dollar value of all goods and services produced by a country in a year. The per capita GNP is calculated by dividing a country's GNP by its population and adjusting for relative purchasing power. About 15% of the world's 6.1 billion people live in high-income countries, while 40% live in low-income countries.

n.a. = data not available   > = greater than   < = less than

Sources: World Bank. *World Development Indicators.* Washington, D.C.: The World Bank, 2001; Central Intelligence Agency. *The World Factbook.* Washington, D.C.: Government Printing Office, 2000.

tured goods, 45%; chemicals, 10%; food and live animals, 3%; and raw materials, 3%. Imports that year totaled $9.7 billion. Machinery and transport equipment accounted for 31% of the total. Slovenia's main trading partners are Germany, Italy, Croatia, France, and Austria.

27 ENERGY AND POWER

In 1998, total electricity production amounted to more than 13 billion kilowatt hours. Slovenia is relatively well supplied with hydroelectricity. Several thermal plants and one nuclear power plant also supply electricity. Slovenia imports oil from the republics of the former Soviet Union and the developing world to supply a refinery at Lendava.

Coal is mined at Velenje; the mine produced 2.5 million tons of lignite in 1994. Natural gas is used extensively for industry and is supplied by the former Soviet Union and Algeria via 305 kilometers (190 miles) of natural gas pipelines.

28 SOCIAL DEVELOPMENT

The constitution provides for special protection against economic, social, physical, or mental exploitation or abuse of children. Women and men have equal status under the law. Discrimination against women or minorities in housing, jobs, or other areas, is illegal. Officially, both spouses are equal in marriage, and the constitution asserts the state's responsibility to protect the family. Women are well represented in business, academia, and government, although they still hold a disproportionate share of lower-paying jobs.

29 HEALTH

The life expectancy at birth was 75 years in 2000. The infant mortality rate dropped from 15 to 5 infant deaths per 1,000 live births during 1980–99.

30 HOUSING

No recent information is available.

31 EDUCATION

Slovenia has a high literacy rate. There were 824 primary schools with 98,866 students in 1997. At the secondary level, 13,919 teachers taught 214,042 students in 1994.

In Slovenia there are two universities, located at Ljubljana and Maribor. The University of Ljubljana, founded in 1919, has 25 faculties. In 1997, there were 51,009 enrolled university students.

32 MEDIA

In 1997, Slovenia had 691,240 telephones; as of 1999, there were 11 radio stations, and 23 television channels. In 2000, there were 416 radios and 556 televisions per 1,000 population. In 1995, there were six daily and 425 other newspapers and 250 periodicals. A total of 1,932 book titles were published in the same year.

33 TOURISM AND RECREATION

There are 75,000 beds available in hotels and other types of accommodations. Slovenia has convention centers in Ljubljana and three other cities, and international airports in Ljubljana and two other cities. Popular recreational activities include tennis, golf, mountain-climbing, canoeing, and fishing.

34 FAMOUS SLOVENIANS

Milan Kučan has been president of Slovenia since 1992. In 1551, Primož Trubar translated the New Testament into Slovene. The poet Valentin Vodnik (1754–1819) wrote poems in praise of Napoleon. Slovenian tennis star Mima Jausovec (b.1956) won the Italian Open in 1976 and the French Open in 1977.

35 BIBLIOGRAPHY

Benderly, Jill, and Evan Kraft. *Independent Slovenia*. New York: St. Martin's Press, 1994.

Fallon, Steve. *Slovenia*. Hawthorn, Vic.: Lonely Planet, 1998.

Glenny, Michael. *The Fall of Yugoslavia: The Third Balkan War*. New York: Penguin, 1992.

Gobetz, Edward, and Ruth Lakner, eds. *Slovenian Heritage*. Willoughby Hills, Ohio: Slovenian Research Center of America, 1980.

Harriman, Helga H. *Slovenia Under Nazi Occupation, 1941–1945*. New York: Studia Slovenica, 1977.

Plut-Pregelj, Leopoldina, and Carole Rogel. *Historical Dictionary of Slovenia*. Lanham, Md.: Scarecrow Press, Inc., 1996.

SOLOMON ISLANDS

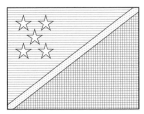

CAPITAL: Honiara.

FLAG: The flag consists of two triangles, the upper one blue, the lower one green, separated by a diagonal gold stripe; on the blue triangle are five white five-pointed stars.

ANTHEM: *God Save the Queen.*

MONETARY UNIT: The Solomon Islands dollar (SI$), a paper currency of 100 cents, was introduced in 1977, replacing the Australian dollar, and became the sole legal tender in 1978. There are coins of 1, 2, 5, 10, 20, and 50 cents and 1 dollar, and notes of 2, 5, 10, 20, and 50 dollars. SI$1 = US$0.19706 (or US$1 = SI$5.0745).

WEIGHTS AND MEASURES: The metric system is in force.

HOLIDAYS: New Year's Day, 1 January; Queen's Birthday, celebrated as a movable holiday in June; Independence Day, 7 July; Christmas, 25 December; Boxing Day, 26 December. Movable religious holidays include Good Friday, Easter Monday, and Whitmonday.

TIME: 11 PM = noon GMT.

1 LOCATION AND SIZE

The Solomon Islands consist of a chain of six large and numerous small islands situated in the South Pacific. The Solomon Islands have an area of 28,450 square kilometers (10,985 square miles), slightly larger than the state of Maryland.

The largest island is Guadalcanal, covering 5,302 square kilometers (2,047 square miles). The total coastline of the Solomon Islands is 5,313 kilometers (3,301 miles).

The capital city, Honiara, is located on the island of Guadalcanal.

2 TOPOGRAPHY

The topography varies from the volcanic peaks of Guadalcanal to low-lying coral atolls. The highest peak is Mt. Makarako-mburu, at 2,447 meters (8,029 feet), on Guadalcanal. Extensive coral reefs and lagoons surround the island coasts.

3 CLIMATE

The average daily temperature is about 26–27°C (79–81°F); annual rainfall averages 210 centimeters (83 inches); humidity is about 80%. Damaging cyclones occur periodically.

4 PLANTS AND ANIMALS

Dense rainforest covers about 90% of the islands, with extensive mangrove swamps and coconut palms along the coasts. The islands abound in small reptiles, birds, mammals, and insects. There are more than 230 kinds of orchids.

Geographic Profile

Geographic Features

Size ranking: 139 of 192
Highest elevation: 2,447 meters (8,029 feet) at Mount
   Makarakomburu (Mount Popomanasiu)
Lowest elevation: Sea level at the Pacific Ocean

Land Use†

Arable land:	1%
Permanent crops:	1%
Permanent pastures:	1%
Forests:	88%
Other:	9%

Weather††

Average annual precipitation: 210 centimeters (83
   inches)
Average temperature in January: 26.8°C (80.2°F)
Average temperature in July: 26.2°C (79.2°F)

†*Arable land:* Land used for temporary crops, like
meadows for mowing or pasture, gardens, and greenhouses. *Permanent crops:* Land cultivated with crops
that occupy its use for long periods, such as cocoa,
coffee, rubber, fruit and nut orchards, and vineyards.
Permanent pastures: Land used permanently for forage crops. *Forests:* Land containing stands of trees.
Other: Any land not specified, including built-on
areas, roads, and barren land.

††The measurements for precipitation and average
temperature were taken at weather stations closest to
the country's largest city. Precipitation and average
temperature can vary significantly within a country,
due to factors such as latitude, altitude, coastal proximity, and wind patterns.

5 ENVIRONMENT

Most of the coral reefs surrounding the
islands are dead or dying. United Nations
sources estimate that the islands' forests
will be exhausted in 10–15 years. Some
42% of the islands' rural people, and 18%
of city dwellers do not have pure water.
Sources of pollution include sewage, pesticides, and mining byproducts. In 1994,
two mammal species and 20 bird species
were endangered, as well as 28 types of
plants.

6 POPULATION

The population was estimated at 470,000
in 2000 and was projected by the US Census Bureau at 544,000 in 2005. During the
1990s, the population grew about 3% per
year. The estimated overall population
density was 15 persons per square kilometer (39 per square mile) in 2000, but there
are significant variations from island to
island. Honiara, on Guadalcanal, is the
largest town and chief port, with an estimated 2000 population of 53,000.

7 MIGRATION

Since 1955, immigrants from the Gilbert
Islands (now Kiribati) have settled in
underpopulated areas. Movements from
the countryside to Honiara and north
Guadalcanal have created overcrowding in
those two areas.

8 ETHNIC GROUPS

According to 1999 figures, Melanesians
numbered 268,536, or 93% of the total
population. Also counted were Polynesians, 4%; Micronesians, 1%; Europeans,
0.4%; Chinese, 0.3%; and others, 0.4%.

9 LANGUAGES

Pidgin English is the common language,
but English is the official language. Some
120 local languages and dialects are spoken. Melanesian languages are spoken by
about 85% of the population, Papuan languages by 9%, and Polynesian languages
by 4%.

10 RELIGIONS

Christianity is the principal organized religion. As of 1999, 34% of the islanders were Anglicans, 43% were Protestants, and 19% were Roman Catholics. Native religions are practiced by up to 4% of the population, and there is a small Baha'i community.

11 TRANSPORTATION

In 1996 there were about 1,360 kilometers (845 miles) of roads in the Solomons. Honiara is the principal port. Government vessels provide interisland connections and handle freight. There are two permanent-surface air runways. Solomon Airlines provides regular flights between islands and to nearby Papua New Guinea and Vanuatu.

12 HISTORY

The Solomons were first sighted in 1567 by the Spanish explorer Alvaro de Mendaña, who named them Islas de Salomon for King Solomon's gold mines. The islands were visited by the English navigator Philip Carteret in 1767. The period 1845–93 saw the arrival of missionaries, traders, and "blackbirders," who captured native people and sold them into forced labor, often on colonial sugar plantations in Fiji, Hawaii, Tahiti, or Queensland.

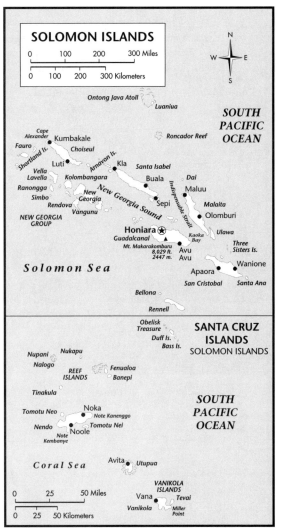

LOCATION: 5° to 12°30′s; 155° to 170°E. **TERRITORIAL SEA LIMIT:** 12 miles.

In 1893, the British government established a protectorate over parts of the Solomons, including Guadalcanal, Malaita, San Cristobal, and the New Georgia group. The remainder had by this time fallen under German dominion; some of these, including Choiseul and Santa Isabel, were transferred by treaty to the United Kingdom in 1900.

During World War II (1939–45), the Solomons saw some of the most bitter fighting of the Pacific war after Japanese troops invaded and occupied Guadalcanal

Photo credit: Cory Langley.

Three boys on a beach in the Solomon Islands. Melanesians account for almost 95% of the total population. Polynesians, Micronesians, Europeans, and Chinese are the other prominent ethnic groups.

in 1942. The Battle of Guadalcanal cost the lives of about 1,500 American soldiers and 20,000 Japanese.

In the decades after the war, the Solomons moved gradually toward independence. The islands achieved internal self-government in 1976 and became an independent member of the Commonwealth of Nations on 7 July 1978.

Francis Billy Hilly became the Solomon Islands' new prime minister in June 1993. Hilly has worked with the Melanesian Spearhead Conference to ease tension between the Solomon Islands and Papua New Guinea. In 1994, the parliament voted to replace Hilly with Solomon Mamaloni, leader of the Group for National Unity and Reconciliation (GNUR), the largest political party in the parliament.

In the 1997 parliamentary elections, GNUR retained its majority, and Bartholomew Ulufa'ala was chosen prime minister, while Queen Elizabeth II still remains the head of state. Manasseh Sogavare replaced Ulufa'ala in the 2000 elections as prime minister.

13 GOVERNMENT

The Solomon Islands are a parliamentary democracy with a prime minister and a single-chamber 47-member National Parliament. The islands are divided into eight administrative districts.

14 POLITICAL PARTIES

Parties have included the People's Alliance Party (PAP), the National Democratic Party (NDP), and the Nationalist Front for Progress. The Group for National Unity and Reconciliation (GNUR), led by Solomon Mamaloni, gained the most seats in the 1993 election. Other parties receiving seats were the National Action Party, the Labour Party, and the Christian Fellowship Group.

15 JUDICIAL SYSTEM

The judicial system consists of the High Court, magistrate courts, and local courts. Appeals from magistrate courts go to the High Court; customary land appeals courts hear appeals from the local courts.

16 ARMED FORCES

The Solomon Islands have no military forces.

17 ECONOMY

At least 90% of the population is tied to subsistence farming. The economy depends on the export of copra (dried coconut meat), timber, and fish. Production of other cash commodities—particularly cocoa, spices, and palm oil—has grown in recent years.

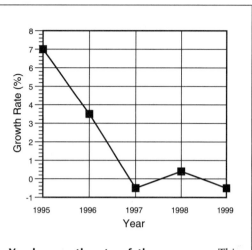

Yearly growth rate of the economy. This economic indicator tells by what percent the economy has increased or decreased when compared with the previous year.

18 INCOME

In 1998, Solomon Islands' gross domestic product (GDP) was $1.15 billion, or about $2,600 per person. In 1999, the average inflation rate was 9.7%, resulting in a decline in GDP of 0.5%.

19 INDUSTRY

The leading industries are fish processing and timber milling; soaps are made from palm oil and coconut oil. Small firms produce goods for local consumption, including biscuits, tobacco products, rattan furniture, and baskets and mats.

20 LABOR

Most of Solomon Islanders engage in subsistence farming. The wage labor force in 1992 totaled 26,842. The country suffers

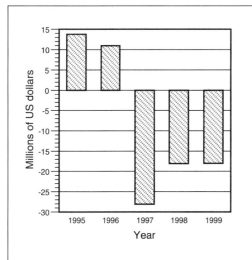

Yearly balance of trade measured in millions of US dollars. The balance of trade is the difference between what a country sells to other countries (its exports) and what it buys (its imports). If a country imports more than it exports, it has a negative balance of trade (a trade deficit). If exports exceed imports, there is a positive balance of trade (a trade surplus).

from an acute shortage of skilled workers. Minimum age laws regulate the use of child labor.

21 AGRICULTURE

Copra (dried coconut meat) is the dominant export and the economic lifeline of the Solomons; 1998 production was 66,000 tons. Other agricultural products in 1998 included cocoa, 4,000 tons; palm oil, 29,000 tons; and palm kernels, 7,000 tons.

The major food crops are coconuts, yams, taro, sweet potatoes, cassava, and green vegetables.

22 DOMESTICATED ANIMALS

There were 10,000 head of cattle and 57,000 pigs on the islands in 1998. About 3,000 tons of meat were produced in 1998.

23 FISHING

In 1997, the total catch was 53,765 tons. In the same year, the annual catch of skipjack tuna was 30,291 tons.

24 FORESTRY

Forests cover about 88% of the total area, providing an estimated timber yield in 1997 of 872,000 cubic meters (1.1 million cubic yards), of which about 700,000 cubic meters were exported as logs. Logging at current rates exceeds the rate for sustainable development by three times.

25 MINING

In addition to gold, deposits of bauxite, nickel, copper, chromite, and manganese ores have also been found.

26 FOREIGN TRADE

Leading exports in 1998 included rough timber, fresh and processed fish, palm oil, copra, and cocoa. Imports consist primarily of machinery and transport equipment, basic manufactures, food, fuels, and chemicals.

In 1998, Japan, the Solomons' most important trade partner, received close to 50% of the islands' exports. Other important trade partners are Australia, the United Kingdom, Thailand, Singapore, New Zealand, and China.

Selected Social Indicators

The statistics below are estimates for the period 1996 to 2000. For comparison purposes, data for the United States and averages for low-income countries and high-income countries are also given.

Indicator	Solomon Islands	Low-income countries	High-income countries	United States
Per capita gross national product (GNP)†	$2,050	$1,870	$25,690	$31,910
Population growth rate	3.2%	2.1%	0.7%	1.1%
People per square kilometer of land	15	73	29	30
Life expectancy in years	71	59	78	77
Number of physicians per 1,000 people	<1	1.0	2.5	2.5
Number of pupils per teacher (primary school)	24	41	17	14
Illiteracy rate (15 years and older)	40%	34%	<5%	3%
Television sets per 1,000 people	6	85	693	844
Energy consumed per capita (kg of oil equivalent)	156	550	5,366	7,937

† The GNP is the total dollar value of all goods and services produced by a country in a year. The per capita GNP is calculated by dividing a country's GNP by its population and adjusting for relative purchasing power. About 15% of the world's 6.1 billion people live in high-income countries, while 40% live in low-income countries.

n.a. = data not available   > = greater than   < = less than

Sources: World Bank. World Development Indicators. Washington, D.C.: The World Bank, 2001; Central Intelligence Agency. The World Factbook. Washington, D.C.: Government Printing Office, 2000.

27 ENERGY AND POWER

In 1998, electrical output was 30 million kilowatt hours. Honiara accounts for 90% of electricity consumption.

28 SOCIAL DEVELOPMENT

A National Provident Fund provides old age, disability, and survivor benefits. Most organized welfare services are provided by church missions. Much assistance is traditionally provided through the extended family.

29 HEALTH

Malaria and tuberculosis are widespread, because of poor hygiene and inadequate sanitation. Average life expectancy was 71 years and infant mortality rate was 23 deaths per 1,000 live births, in 2000.

30 HOUSING

The government has built low-cost housing projects in Honiara to help ease congestion. Outside Honiara, housing is primitive, with overcrowding a problem. As of 1990, 82% of urban and 58% of rural dwellers had access to a public water supply, while 73% of the urban population had access to sanitation services.

31 EDUCATION

About 60% of the adult population is estimated to be literate. Education is not compulsory, and many schools charge fees. In 1994 there were 60,493 students and

2,514 teachers in primary schools. Secondary schools had 7,811 pupils that year.

Higher education is provided by the Solomon Islands Teachers College, the Honiara Technical Institute, and the University of the South Pacific.

32 MEDIA

There were an estimated 80 radios and six televisions per 1,000 population in 2000. There are no daily newspapers. Periodicals include the weekly *Solomon Voice* (1995 circulation, 2,500), the biweekly *Solomon Star* (6,000), and the monthly *Solomon Nius* (2,000).

33 TOURISM AND RECREATION

In 1997, almost 16,000 tourists visited the Solomon Islands, the vast majority from East Asia and the Pacific. Popular pastimes include rugby football, soccer, and water sports.

34 FAMOUS SOLOMON ISLANDERS

Sir Peter Kenilorea (b.1943), Solomon Mamaloni (b.1943), and Ezekiel Alebua (b.1947) were the Solomons' political and government leaders from independence to the 1990s.

35 BIBLIOGRAPHY

Coffey, Maria. *Jungle Islands: My South Sea Adventure.* Toronto: Annick Press, 2000.

Diamond, J. *Solomon Islands.* Chicago: Children's Press, 1995.

White, Geoffrey M. *Identity through History: Living Stories in a Solomon Islands Society.* New York: Cambridge University Press, 1991.

SOMALIA

CAPITAL: Mogadishu (Muqdisho).

FLAG: The national flag is light blue with a five-pointed white star in the center.

ANTHEM: *Somalia Hanolato (Long Live Somalia).*

MONETARY UNIT: The Somali shilling (SH) of 100 cents is a paper currency. There are coins of 1, 5, 10, and 50 cents and 1 shilling, and notes of 5, 10, 20, 100, 500, and 1,000 shillings. SH1 = $0.00038 (or $1 = SH2,620).

WEIGHTS AND MEASURES: The metric system is in use.

HOLIDAYS: New Year's Day, 1 January; Labor Day, 1 May; National Independence Day, 26 June; Foundation of the Republic, 1 July. Muslim religious holidays include 'Id al-Fitr, 'Id al-Adha', 'Ashura, and Milad an-Nabi.

TIME: 3 PM = noon GMT.

1 LOCATION AND SIZE

Situated on the horn of East Africa, Somalia has an area of 637,660 square kilometers (246,202 square miles), slightly smaller than the state of Texas. It has a total boundary length of 5,391 kilometers (3,350 miles). Somalia's capital city, Mogadishu, is located on the Indian Ocean coast.

2 TOPOGRAPHY

The northern region is somewhat mountainous, and there are plateaus to the northeast, south, and west. The region between the Jubba and Shabeelle (Webi Shabeelle) rivers is low agricultural land. The Jubba and Shabeelle rivers originate in Ethiopia and flow toward the Indian Ocean. Despite its lengthy shoreline, Somalia has only one natural harbor, Berbera.

3 CLIMATE

Somalia has a tropical climate, and there is little seasonal change in temperature. In the low areas, the mean temperature ranges from about 24°C to 31°C (75°F to 88°F). Rain falls in two seasons of the year.

4 PLANTS AND ANIMALS

Acacia thorntrees, aloes, baobab, candelabra, and incense trees are native to the drier regions. Mangrove, kapok, and papaya grow along the rivers. Animal life includes the elephant, lion, wildcat, giraffe, zebra, hyena, and hippopotamus. The most common birds are the ostrich, duck, guinea fowl, partridge, green pigeon, sand grouse, and heron.

Geographic Profile

Geographic Features

Size ranking: 41 of 192
Highest elevation: 2,450 meters (8,038 feet) at Shimbiris
Lowest elevation: Sea level at the Indian Ocean

Land Use†

Arable land:	2%
Permanent crops:	0%
Permanent pastures:	69%
Forests:	26%
Other:	3%

Weather††

Average annual precipitation: 42.2 centimeters (16.6 inches)
Average temperature in January: 26.5°C (79.7°F)
Average temperature in July: 26°C (78.8°F)

†*Arable land:* Land used for temporary crops, like meadows for mowing or pasture, gardens, and greenhouses. *Permanent crops:* Land cultivated with crops that occupy its use for long periods, such as cocoa, coffee, rubber, fruit and nut orchards, and vineyards. *Permanent pastures:* Land used permanently for forage crops. *Forests:* Land containing stands of trees. *Other:* Any land not specified, including built-on areas, roads, and barren land.

††The measurements for precipitation and average temperature were taken at weather stations closest to the country's largest city. Precipitation and average temperature can vary significantly within a country, due to factors such as latitude, altitude, coastal proximity, and wind patterns.

5 ENVIRONMENT

Between 1983 and 1993, Somalia lost 6.7% of its forest and woodland. About 50% of the nation's city dwellers and 71% of the people living in rural areas do not have pure water. The nation's cities produce 500,000 tons of solid waste per year.

Somalia in the early 1980s still had one of the most abundant and varied stocks of wildlife in Africa. The hunting and trapping of antelopes and gazelles for their skins was banned in 1969. However, many species continued to be harmed by the advance of livestock and human settlement into their habitats, and the cutting of bush vegetation and tree cover. In 1994, 17 of the country's mammal species and seven bird species were endangered; 52 types of plants were threatened with extinction.

6 POPULATION

In 2000, Somalia had a population estimated at 7.4 million. But the United Nations, which apparently included refugees in its count while the Census Bureau did not, estimated the 1998 population at nearly 10.7 million. A population of 8.8 million is projected by the Census Bureau for 2005. The largest city and its estimated 2000 population is Mogadishu, the capital, with 1,227,000.

7 MIGRATION

Since about half of all Somalis are nomadic herdsmen, there is much movement back and forth across the frontiers as a normal part of grazing activities. By 1993, it was estimated that three-quarters of the population had been driven from their homes by civil war and severe drought since 1988. The political violence in Somalia was so extreme that about 700,000 people fled the country between 1988 and 1991. As of mid-1997, there were still 285,000 Somali refugees in Ethiopia, 131,000 in Kenya, 20,000 in Djibouti, and 10,000 in Yemen. Repatriation from Libya and Ethiopia has begun.

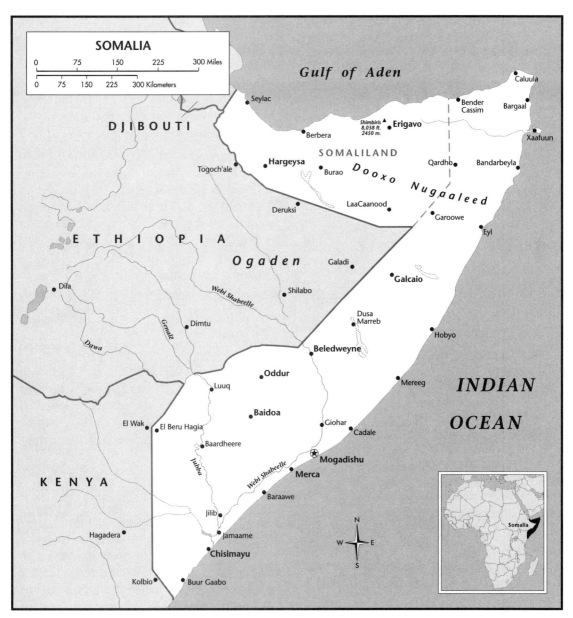

SOMALIA

0   75   150   225   300 Miles

0   75   150   225   300 Kilometers

Gulf of Aden

DJIBOUTI

Seylac

Caluula

Bender Cassim

Bargaal

Berbera

Shimbiris 8,038 ft. 2450 m.

Erigavo

Xaafuun

SOMALILAND

Togoch'ale

Hargeysa

Burao

Qardho

Bandarbeyla

Dooxo Nugaaleed

Deruksi

LaaCaanood

Garoowe

Eyl

ETHIOPIA

Ogaden

Galadi

Galcaio

Dila

Webi Shabeelle

Shilabo

Dusa Marreb

Hobyo

Dimtu

Genale

Dawa

Beledweyne

Oddur

Mereeg

INDIAN OCEAN

Luuq

Baidoa

Giohar

Cadale

El Wak

El Beru Hagia

Baardheere

Jubba

Mogadishu

Merca

KENYA

Webi Shabeelle

Baraawe

Jilib

Hagadera

Jamaame

Chisimayu

N
W   E
S

Somalia

Kolbio

Buur Gaabo

LOCATION: 12°N to 1°39′s; 41°30′ to 51°E. **BOUNDARY LENGTHS:** Total coastline, 3,025 kilometers (1,874 miles); Kenya, 682 kilometers (424 miles); Ethiopia, 1,626 kilometers (1,016 miles); Djibouti, 58 kilometers (36 miles). **TERRITORIAL SEA LIMIT:** 200 miles.

8 ETHNIC GROUPS

The Somalis are classified as a Hamitic people with a Cushitic culture. Ethnic Somalis, who made up about 85% of the population in 1998, are divided into two main clan families: the Samaal, who are principally nomadic herdsmen, and the Saab, who are primarily farmers and settled herders. The nonnative population consists primarily of Arabs, Italians, Pakistanis, and Indians.

9 LANGUAGES

Somali, classified as a lowland Eastern Cushitic language, is spoken by all Somalis, with dialectal differences that follow clan divisions. In 1973, a written form of Somali, with a script based on the Latin alphabet, was adopted as the nation's main official language, with Arabic a secondary language. However, Arabic, English, and Italian are all widely spoken and understood.

10 RELIGIONS

The Somalis are Sunni Muslims of the Shafi'i sect, and Islam is the religion of the state. Christian mission schools closed in 1972, and foreign Protestant missionaries were expelled in 1976. Protestants and Catholics make up less than 1% of the population. The practice of radical Islam is growing, making its way into social and governmental activities.

11 TRANSPORTATION

Of 22,100 kilometers (13,733 miles) of roads in Somalia in 1999, only 11% were paved. Motor vehicles in use in 1995 numbered 24,000. There are no railways and no commercial water transport facilities. The ports of Mogadishu, Chisimayu, and Berbera are served by vessels from many parts of the world. The major airfields are in Mogadishu and Berbera.

12 HISTORY

Ancient Egyptians came to Somalia's northern shores for incense and aromatic herbs. In the ninth or tenth century, Somalis began pushing south from the Gulf of Aden coast. About this time, Arabs and Persians established settlements along the Indian Ocean coast.

European Influence

During the fifteenth and sixteenth centuries, Portuguese explorers attempted without success to establish Portuguese rule over the Somali coast. After the British armed forces occupied Aden in 1839, they developed an interest in the northern Somali coast, and the British signed a number of treaties with Somali chiefs of the northern area to make Somalia a British protectorate. From 1899 to 1920, British rule was constantly disrupted by the "holy war" waged by 'Abdallah bin Hasan (generally known in English literature as the "Mad Mullah").

Italian expansion in Somalia began in 1885, and by 1889 Italy established protectorates over the eastern territories that were officially ruled by the sultans of Obbia and of Alula. Direct administrative control of the territory known as Italian Somaliland was not established until 1905. Italy's Fascist (dictatorial) government, which came to power under Benito Mussolini in 1922, increased Italian

Photo credit: AP/Wide World Photos/Kathy Willens.

Hassan Riyole, left, plays on a tree branch with other children from his tiny village of Dheeray, Somalia.

authority by its extensive military operations. During the Italian-Ethiopian conflict (1934–36), Somalia was a staging area for Italy's invasion and conquest of Ethiopia. From 1936 to 1941, Somalia and the Somali-inhabited portion of Ethiopia, the Ogaden, were combined in an enlarged province of Italian East Africa.

In 1940–41, the British conquered Italian Somaliland from Italian troops, who were allied with Nazi Germany. The Ogaden was returned to Ethiopia in 1948, and British administration over the rest of Italian Somaliland continued until 1950, when Italy, through the United Nations, gained administrative control again. However, in 1949 the UN General Assembly

resolved that Italian Somaliland would receive its independence in 1960.

A United Somalia

By the end of 1956, Somalis were in almost complete charge of domestic affairs. Meanwhile, Somalis in British Somaliland were demanding self-government. As Italy agreed to grant independence on 1 July 1960 to its trust territory, the United Kingdom gave its protectorate independence on 26 June 1960, thus enabling the two Somali territories to join in a united Somali Republic on 1 July 1960. On 20 July 1961, the Somali people ratified a new constitution, drafted in 1960, and one month later confirmed

Aden 'Abdullah Osman Daar as the nation's first president.

Military Rule

Somalia was involved in many border clashes with Ethiopia and Kenya. Soviet influence in Somalia grew after Moscow agreed in 1962 to provide substantial military aid. Abdirashid 'Ali Shermarke, who was elected president in 1967, was assassinated on 15 October 1969. Six days later, army commanders seized power with the support of the police. The military leaders dissolved parliament, suspended the constitution, arrested members of the cabinet, and changed the name of the country to the Somali Democratic Republic. Major General Jalle Mohamed Siad Barre, commander of the army, was named chairman of a 25-member Supreme Revolutionary Council (SRC) that assumed the powers of the president, the Supreme Court, and the National Assembly. Siad Barre was later named president.

In 1970, President Siad Barre proclaimed "scientific socialism" as the republic's guiding ideology. Controversy arose in the mid-1970s over Somalia's links to the Soviet Union and its support of the Western Somali Liberation Front in Ethiopia's Ogaden region.

In January 1986, Siad Barre met three times with Ethiopia's head of state in an effort to improve relations between the two countries, but no agreement was reached. In addition, internal dissent continued to mount.

Civil War Leads to Mass Starvation

In February 1987, relations between Somalia and Ethiopia worsened following an Ethiopian attack. By 1990, the Somali regime was losing control. Armed resistance from guerrilla groups was turning the Somali territory into a death trap.

In 1990, Barre was ousted and, in January 1991, he fled Mogadishu. The United Somali Congress (USC) seized the capital. The economy broke down and the country turned into chaos as armed groups terrorized the population and disrupted shipments of food. Several hundred thousand people were killed, and far more were threatened by starvation. More than a half million fled to Kenya. As the starvation and total breakdown of public services was publicized in the western media, calls for the United Nations to intervene mounted.

The United Nations Intervenes

Late on 3 December 1992, the UN Security Council passed a resolution to deploy a massive US-led international military intervention (UNITAF-United Task Force) to safeguard relief operations. By the end of December, faction leaders Muhammad Farah Aideed and Ali Maludi Muhammad had pledged to stop fighting. The UNITAF spread throughout the country, and violence decreased dramatically.

Although the problem of relief distribution had largely been solved, there was no central government, few public institutions, and local warlords and their forces became increasingly bold. By early 1993, more than 34,000 troops from 24 United

Nations members—75% from the United States—were deployed. Starvation was virtually ended, and some order had been restored. Yet, little was done to achieve a political solution or to disarm the factions. From January 1993 until 27 March, 15 armed factions met in Addis Ababa, Ethiopia, to end hostilities and form a transitional National Council for a two-year period to serve as the political authority in Somalia.

On 4 May 1993, Operation Restore Hope, as the relief effort was labeled, was declared successful, and US force levels were sharply reduced. A second relief effort, UNOSOM II, featured Pakistani, American, Belgian, Italian, Moroccan, and French troops, commanded by a Turkish general. On 23 June 1993, 23 Pakistani solders were killed in an ambush. General Aideed's forces were blamed and a $25,000 bounty was placed on Aideed's head. Mogadishu became a war zone.

In early October 1993, 18 US Army Rangers were killed and 75 were wounded in a firefight. American public opinion and politicians pressured President Bill Clinton to withdraw American troops, which was completed in March of 1995. New discussions in Kenya and in Mogadishu reached agreements that teetered on collapse. After the withdrawal of the foreign peacekeeping troops, General Muhammad Farah Aideed became Somalia's "self-declared" president. Fighting continued in 1995 and 1996.

The hope for an end to the violence came with the death of General Aideed on 1 August 1996. Aideed's rivals declared a ceasefire, although his son and successor, Hussein Muhammad Aideed, promised to renew the fight. Despite the lack of a functioning central government, Somalia's economy was still functioning at the end of 1996, and harvests have even improved since the early 1990s. The factional splits between warlord rivals are not based on ideology, religion, or political issues. Their ongoing struggle for power and riches provides little chance for national unity and the restoration of a central government.

In December 1997 the leaders of the main rival factions met in Cairo and agreed on a plan that would end the civil war and restore the national government. The plan was supposed to establish a conference on national reconciliation by 15 May 1998, but there were delays. In April 1998, the Red Cross pulled its personnel out of Somalia after ten of its workers were abducted in Mogadishu.

As of 2001, the country continued in a state of anarchy, disintegrating into regional governments. This problem will worsen with the continuing threat of drought. Tribal confrontations have also led to many deaths. In 2000, the transitional president Abdiqasim Salad Hassan was elected. His is the first internationally recognized administration in nearly ten years. Despite supporters of the new administration, fighting continues.

13 GOVERNMENT

Since the overthrow of President Siad Barre in 1990, Somalia has had no viable central government. Some 15 armed factions have been fighting for control. The United Nations' UNOSOM II was technically in control until March 1995, when troops were withdrawn. General Aideed's death in August 1996 offered the chance for a resolution, and there was a ceasefire. However, his successor and son, Hussein Muhammad Aideed, renewed the fight against his father's rivals.

Although it is unrecognized as an independent nation, Somalia's northern province declared its independence on 18 May 1993. The state of "Somaliland" (its name during British colonial rule) has its own army, police force, currency, and judicial system. Rebels and armed gangs also battle throughout the region, however, and the self-declared government only controls half of the "republic."

14 POLITICAL PARTIES

President Siad Barre's SRSP (Somali Revolutionary Socialist Party) was the sole legal party at the time of his overthrow in January 1991. The Somali National Movement (SNM) has seized control of the north. Armed factions have divided up the territory as they fight and negotiate to expand their influence. Although many of them bear the titles of political parties, such as the Somali Democratic Movement, the Somali National Union, and the United Somali Congress (USC), they do not have national bases of support. The USC controlled Mogadishu and much of central Somalia until late in 1991 when it split into two major factions, Aideed's Somali National Alliance (SNA) and Ali Mahdi's Somali Salvation Alliance.

15 JUDICIAL SYSTEM

As a result of the civil disorder in recent years, most of the structure for the administration of justice has collapsed. Islamic law and traditional courts continue to be applied to settle disputes over property and criminal offenses. In the northwest, the self-declared Republic of Somaliland uses the pre-1991 penal code.

16 ARMED FORCES

The regular armed forces disintegrated in the revolution of 1991, and as of 1999 had not been reconstituted. Clan gangs armed with imported weapons terrorized the country and continue to fight among themselves. United Nations troops withdrew in 1995.

17 ECONOMY

Since 1990, Somalia's primarily agricultural economy has fallen apart due to drought and a drawn-out civil war, which has left the country without central authority. By early 1992, virtually all trade, industry, and agriculture had stopped, large numbers of people were forced from their homes, and more than six million were at risk of starvation. In 1993 donors pledged $130 million toward Somalia's reconstruction, and good rains and increased stability eased the food situation. The aid, together with good harvests and increased stability, helped ease the food situation so that few communities were at risk of widespread famine in 1997. Continued fighting and lack of a central authority in 1999 prevented significant improvement in economic conditions.

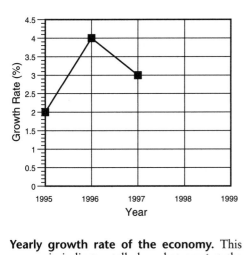

Yearly growth rate of the economy. This economic indicator tells by what percent the economy has increased or decreased when compared with the previous year.

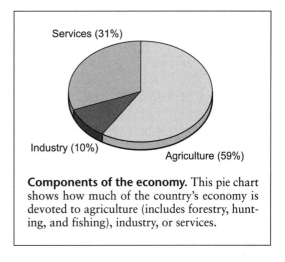

Components of the economy. This pie chart shows how much of the country's economy is devoted to agriculture (includes forestry, hunting, and fishing), industry, or services.

18 INCOME

In 1998, Somalia's gross domestic product (GDP) per person was $600 per capita.

19 INDUSTRY

Industries mainly serve the domestic market and, to a lesser extent, provide some of the needs of Somalia's agricultural exports, such as the manufacture of crates for packing bananas. The most important industries are the petroleum refinery, the state-owned sugar plants, an oilseed-crushing mill, and a soap factory. Newer industries manufacture corrugated iron, paint, cigarettes and matches, aluminum utensils, cardboard boxes and polyethylene bags, and textiles.

20 LABOR

In 1992, workers' rights vanished amid the civil chaos and fighting. Nomadic shepherds made up about 70% of the working population in the early 1990s; while industry, government, trade, and services employed the remaining 30%.

While children are not generally employed, they often are part of the armed militia groups that are fighting for control of Somalia.

21 AGRICULTURE

In 1998, less than 2% of Somalia's total land area was cultivated, and 69% was permanent pasture. There are two main types of agriculture, one native and the other introduced by European settlers. Somali and Italian farmers operating the banana farms practice modern European-style techniques, as do some of the newly created Somali cooperatives. Bananas constitute the nation's major commercial crop; output was 53,000 tons in 1998. Sugarcane production in 1998 totaled some 190,000 tons. Somalia is the world's leading producer of frankincense.

22 DOMESTICATED ANIMALS

The majority of Somalis raise livestock; in some areas, particularly in the north, this is the only livelihood. The national cattle herd was estimated at 5.3 million head at the end of 1998. At that time, Somalia also had 13.5 million sheep, 12.5 million goats, and 6.1 million camels. Total meat production in 1998 was 166,000 tons. The export of hides and skins also is important.

23 FISHING

The catch in 1997 was 15,700 tons. Fish-processing plants produce fish flour, inedible oil, and semirefined edible oil. Exports of fish products amounted to $10.9 million in 1997.

24 FORESTRY

Somalia is one of the few areas in the world where frankincense is produced; incense trees of the genus *Boswellia* are found in the northeast. Gum arabic in small quantities also is produced. Round-wood production was estimated at 9.7 million cubic meters, with 99% of it burned as fuel.

25 MINING

In 1996, the only nonfuel minerals being exploited were materials quarried for construction—cement, gypsum, and limestone—and one million tons of marine salt. Six thousand tons of sepiolite (meerschaum) also were reportedly extracted in 1996.

26 FOREIGN TRADE

Bananas, livestock, fish, and hides are the main exports. Food, chemicals, machinery, textiles, and petroleum are the main imports. The single greatest purchaser of Somalia's exports in 1998 was Sa'udi Arabia. The leading import supplier was Djibouti.

27 ENERGY AND POWER

Installed electrical capacity in 1998 was 70,000 kilowatts, almost entirely thermal; total production was 265 million kilowatt hours. There were four 200 kilowatt windmills in operation in 1991. Somalia is entirely dependent on imports to fill its oil needs. The only immediately exploitable domestic sources of energy are firewood and charcoal.

28 SOCIAL DEVELOPMENT

The internal fighting and widespread drought conditions between 1989 and late 1995 have totally destroyed the government's provision of social services. Because Somolia has no central government, current data is unavailable. Private humanitarian agencies tried to fill the needs but fighting, extortion, and the activities of armed factions and looters chased many of them away. Civilians are often the victims of indiscriminate attacks.

29 HEALTH

Because of the ongoing civil strife, hospitals are without drugs and illnesses are on the rise. Malaria and intestinal parasites are widespread. Water has been cut off to the capital city of Mogadishu leaving the

Selected Social Indicators

The statistics below are estimates for the period 1996 to 2000. For comparison purposes, data for the United States and averages for low-income countries and high-income countries are also given.

Indicator	Somalia	Low-income countries	High-income countries	United States
Per capita gross national product (GNP)†	**$600**	$1,870	$25,690	$31,910
Population growth rate	**3.9%**	2.1%	0.7%	1.1%
People per square kilometer of land	**15**	73	29	30
Life expectancy in years	**48**	59	78	77
Number of physicians per 1,000 people	**n.a.**	1.0	2.5	2.5
Number of pupils per teacher (primary school)	**n.a.**	41	17	14
Illiteracy rate (15 years and older)	**76%**	34%	<5%	3%
Television sets per 1,000 people	**18**	85	693	844
Energy consumed per capita (kg of oil equivalent)	**7**	550	5,366	7,937

† The GNP is the total dollar value of all goods and services produced by a country in a year. The per capita GNP is calculated by dividing a country's GNP by its population and adjusting for relative purchasing power. About 15% of the world's 6.1 billion people live in high-income countries, while 40% live in low-income countries.

n.a. = data not available   > = greater than   < = less than

Sources: World Bank. *World Development Indicators.* Washington, D.C.: The World Bank, 2001; Central Intelligence Agency. *The World Factbook.* Washington, D.C.: Government Printing Office, 2000.

people to rely on well water, which is scarce and often contaminated. Major operations are often performed without anesthetic. Average life expectancy in 2000 was only 48 years.

30 HOUSING

Development schemes aided by United Nations and foreign assistance programs have helped alleviate housing shortages in Mogadishu and Hargeysa. The typical Somali house is either a round or a rectangular hut with a thatched or metal roof.

31 EDUCATION

Somalia's educational system collapsed with the government in 1992. Few schools kept operating, and even the Somali National University was closed in 1991. Some schools began reopening in 1996. In 1990, the United Nations Educational, Scientific and Cultural Organization (UNESCO) estimated the adult literacy rate to be 24% (males, 36% and females, 14%).

32 MEDIA

As of 1999, the government published a daily newspaper in Somali, *Xiddigta Oktobar,* and a weekly newspaper in English, *Heegan.* The Somali National News Agency (SONNA) provides news information for radio and press, supplies information to foreign correspondents in Somalia, and publishes a daily news bulletin, *October Star,* in Somali and English.

Photo credit: AP/Wide World Photos/Kathy Willens.

Ten-year-old Hassan Riyole, right, walks with his best friend Osman Abdow, also ten, in the village of Dheeray, Somalia. Disruption of food supplies during Somalia's civil war brought Hassan to the brink of starvation. He was rescued by the Red Cross and placed in a hospital in Lafoole. He has since returned to his village with his father and his friends.

Somalia had an estimated 9,000 telephones in 1995. As of 1992, it had 5 radio stations, of which Radio Mogadishu and Radio Hargeisa are government-owned, and an estimated 40 radios per 1,000 population. A television service, limited to the Mogadishu area, was inaugurated in 1983; it broadcast in Somali and Arabic until the station was demolished in 1991. Freedom of press and speech is severely limited.

33 TOURISM AND RECREATION

Somalia's modest tourist industry has been stagnant since the civil war began. Before the war, Somalia offered lovely beaches, excellent skin diving, and numerous species of East African wildlife. About 15,000 tourists visited Somalia from abroad in 1994.

34 FAMOUS SOMALIS

The most important historical figure in Somali history was Muhammad 'Abdallah bin Hasan (known popularly in the English-speaking world as the "Mad Mullah"), who resisted British rule and also was one of Somalia's greatest poets. Aden 'Abdullah Osman Daar (b.1908) is regarded as the Somali most responsible for bringing about the transition of the Somali territory from dependence to independence; he was the nation's first president.

35 BIBLIOGRAPHY

Burton, Richard F. *First Footsteps in Eastern Africa.* London, England: Routledge & K. Paul, 1966.

Fox, Mary Virginia. *Somalia.* New York: Children's Press, 1996.

Hassig, Susan M. *Somalia.* Cultures of the World. New York: Marshall Cavendish, 1998.

Jardine, D. *The Mad Mullah of Somaliland.* Westport, Conn.: Negro Universities Press, 1969 (orig. 1924).

Loughran, Katheryne S. et al., eds. *Somalia in Word and Image.* Bloomington: Indiana University Press, 1986.

Nnoromele, Salome. *Somalia.* San Diego, CA: Lucent Books, 2000.

SOUTH AFRICA

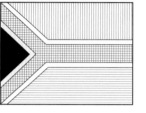

Republic of South Africa
Republiek van Suid-Afrika

CAPITAL: Pretoria (administrative); Cape Town (legislative); Bloemfontein (judicial).

FLAG: The national flag, adopted in 1994, consists of a blue-black triangle placed vertical to the hoist and bordered in gold-yellow. Bands of red, white, green, white, and blue appear horizontally.

ANTHEM: Two anthems are currently in use: the official anthem, *Die Stem van Suid-Afrika (The Call of South Africa),* and *Nkosi Sikelel' Afrika (God Bless Africa),* a hymn adopted by most liberation groups.

MONETARY UNIT: The South African rand (R) is a paper currency of 100 cents. It is used throughout the South African monetary area. There are coins of 1, 2, 5, 10, 20, and 50 cents and 1 rand, and notes of 2, 5, 10, 20, and 50 rand. R1 = $0.16328 (or $1 = R6.12439).

WEIGHTS AND MEASURES: The metric system is in use.

HOLIDAYS: New Year's Day, 1 January; Republic Day, 31 May; Kruger Day, 10 October; Day of the Vow, 16 December; Christmas, 25 December; Goodwill Day, 26 December. Movable religious holidays include Good Friday and Ascension; Family Day is a movable secular holiday.

TIME: 2 PM = noon GMT.

1 LOCATION AND SIZE

The area of South Africa is 1,321,219 square kilometers (510,125 square miles). Comparatively, the area occupied by South Africa is slightly less than twice the size of the state of Texas.

South Africa also controls two small islands, Prince Edward and Marion, which lie some 1,920 kilometers (1,200 miles) southeast of Cape Town.

South Africa's capital city, Pretoria, is located in the northeastern part of the country.

2 TOPOGRAPHY

South Africa has a mean altitude of about 1,200 meters (3,900 feet). Parts of Johannesburg are more than 1,800 meters (6,000 feet) above sea level. There are three major zones: the outside regions, including the eastern and western plateau slopes; a vast saucer-shaped interior plateau, separated from the outside regions by an area of higher elevation, and a desert in the northcentral region near the border with Botswana. The land rises steadily from west to east to the Drakensberg Mountains, the tallest of which is Mount Injasuti (3,408 meters/11,181 feet), on the border with Lesotho.

The two most important rivers draining the interior plateau are the Orange, which flows into the Atlantic Ocean, and the Limpopo, which empties into the Indian Ocean through Mozambique.

3 CLIMATE

South Africa lies almost wholly within the southern temperate zone. In February, the average daily minimum temperature at Durban, on the east coast, ranges from 11°C (52°F) in July to 21°C (70°F), while on the west coast, at Port Nolloth, the range is from 7°C (45°F) to 12°C (54°F). Temperatures are cooler in the highlands: at Johannesburg, the average daily minimum is 4°C (39°F) in June and July and 14°C (57°F) in January. While the mean annual rainfall is 46 centimeters (18 inches), 21% of the country receives less than 20 centimeters (8 inches) and 31% gets more than 60 centimeters (24 inches).

4 PLANTS AND ANIMALS

The variety of South Africa's climate and altitude accounts for its diversified plant and animal life. Of the 200 natural orders of plants in the world, more than 140 are represented, and South Africa has more than 25,000 species of plants, including a plant kingdom found nowhere else. There are more than 500 species of grass in the Cape Province alone. Wildflowers (including the protea, South Africa's national flower) abound throughout the Cape region.

Aardvark, jackal, lion, elephant, wild buffalo, hippopotamus, and various kinds of antelope are still found in some parts of the country. So great is the variety both of smaller mammals and of plants that they have not yet all been identified. The number of different kinds of birds is approximately 900; that of snakes, 200. The number of species of insects is estimated at 40,000, and there are about 1,000 kinds of fish.

5 ENVIRONMENT

Industry and urban life have taken their toll on the South African environment, as

---

Geographic Profile

Geographic Features

Size ranking: 24 of 192
Highest elevation: 3,408 meters (11,181 feet) at Mount Injasuti (Njesuthi)
Lowest elevation: Sea level at the Atlantic Ocean

Land Use†

Arable land:	10%
Permanent crops:	1%
Permanent pastures:	67%
Forests:	7%
Other:	15%

Weather††

Average annual precipitation: 46 centimeters (18 inches)
Average temperature in January: 21°C (69.8°F)
Average temperature in July: 10.3°C (50.5°F)

†*Arable land:* Land used for temporary crops, like meadows for mowing or pasture, gardens, and greenhouses. *Permanent crops:* Land cultivated with crops that occupy its use for long periods, such as cocoa, coffee, rubber, fruit and nut orchards, and vineyards. *Permanent pastures:* Land used permanently for forage crops. *Forests:* Land containing stands of trees. *Other:* Any land not specified, including built-on areas, roads, and barren land.

††Average annual temperatures are fairly uniform in South Africa. The average annual temperature of Cape Town is 17°C (62.6°F), and 17.5°C (63.5°F) for Pretoria. Temperatures above 32°C (89.6°F) frequently occur in the summer.

SOUTH AFRICA

0 75 150 225 300 Miles
0 75 150 225 300 Kilometers

LOCATION: 16°28′ to 32°54′E; 22°8′ to 34°50′S. **BOUNDARY LENGTHS:** Botswana, 1,778 kilometers (1,105 miles); Zimbabwe, 225 kilometers (140 miles); Mozambique, 491 kilometers (305 miles); Swaziland, 449 kilometers (279 miles); total coastline, 2,954 kilometers (1,836 miles); Namibia, 1,078 kilometers (670 miles); Lesotho, 909 kilometers (565 miles). **TERRITORIAL SEA LIMIT:** 12 miles.

have such agricultural practices as veld fires, overgrazing of livestock, and intensive use of pesticides. Three hundred to four hundred million tons of soil per year are lost due to erosion and the expansion of the desert into farm land. Mine drainage has endangered South Africa's limited water resources. The country has 12 cubic miles of water, of which 67% is used for farming and 17% for industrial activity.

Photo credit: Cynthia Bassett.

Lionesses at Kruger National Park, Africa's first wildlife reserve.

The country's cities produce 4.2 million tons of solid waste per year. Air pollution in urban areas stems primarily from coal burning and motor vehicle exhausts. The level of emissions per person is twice the world average.

As of 1994, 25 mammal species and 13 bird species were endangered. Plant species numbering 1,116 also were endangered. About 5% of the total land area is allocated to wildlife preservation, and there are numerous nature and game reserves and national parks. Some 120 rare Addo elephants are protected in Addo Elephant National Park, 56 kilometers (35 miles) north of Port Elizabeth; Mountain

Zebra National Park (near Cradock, in Cape Province) is a refuge for several hundred rare mountain zebras and springbok; and Kruger National Park has almost every species of South African wildlife in its natural habitat.

6 POPULATION

South Africa's 2000 population was estimated at 44 million. The projected population is 46.2 million for 2005. Estimated average population density in 1998 was 34 persons per square kilometer (88 per square mile). However, more than a third of the people live on only 4% of the land area.

In 1995, KwaZulu-Natal had the largest population of South Africa's nine provinces, at 8.7 million. Other provinces with populations greater than five million that year included the following: Gauteng, 7 million; Eastern Cape, 6.5 million; and Northern Province, 5.4 million.

The largest city, the commercial and industrial center of Johannesburg, had a 2000 metropolitan population of 2.4 million; the legislative capital, Cape Town, had 2.7 million; and Pretoria, the administrative capital, had 1.5 million.

7 MIGRATION

Between 1980 and 1984, some 72,528 residents of Zimbabwe (formerly Rhodesia) emigrated to South Africa, after black rule was instituted in Zimbabwe. Since then, immigration has fallen, and, perhaps as a consequence, the white population actually dropped between 1980 and 1991. Of the 63,495 immigrants between 1986 and

1991, 16,815 came from other African countries, 16,056 from the United Kingdom, 16,512 from other European countries, and 14,112 from other parts of the world. Emigration came to 46,541 during these years.

In 1986, it was estimated that between 1.5 million and two million black Africans migrate temporarily to South Africa each year to fulfill work contracts. South Africa was providing informal sanctuary to perhaps 200,000 refugees from Mozambique in 1992. All but 90,000 had returned to Mozambique by 1995.

Between 1994 and 1997, an estimated 39,000 skilled laborers emigrated, resulting in a shortage of trained workers. Emigration since the end of apartheid has been motivated by fear from rising crime levels in South Africa.

Photo credit: Corel Corporation.

Zulu village women in Natal, South Africa.

8 ETHNIC GROUPS

South Africa has one of the world's most complex ethnic patterns. Legal separation of the racial communities—called apartheid—was a cornerstone of government policy through most of the twentieth century and created one of the most rigidly segregated societies in the world. During the 1970s and 1980s, enforcement of separatist policies eased, but the division of the population into four racial communities remained. In 1991, parliament passed measures to repeal the apartheid laws.

As of the 1998 estimates, blacks formed the largest segment of the population, constituting 75.2% of the total. Whites accounted for 13.6% of the population; Cape Coloureds (persons of mixed race), 8.6% ; and Asians, 2.6%.

The black population includes a large number of peoples. According to a 1985 estimate, the largest groups were the Zulu, about 5.3 million; Xhosa, 2.1 million; Northern Sotho, 2.6 million; Southern Sotho, 1.6 million; and Tswana, 1.1 million. The four homelands contained another 3.5 million Xhosa and 1.6 million Tswana.

About 60% of the whites are descendants of Dutch, French Huguenot, and German settlers, and about 40% are of British descent. South Africans of European, especially Dutch, descent are called Afrikaners. The Cape Coloureds are a long-established racial amalgam of white, Hottentot, and other African, Indian, and Malay lineage. The Asians include descendants of Indian, East Indian, and Chinese indentured laborers.

9 LANGUAGES

The interim constitution adopted in 1993 recognized 11 languages as official at the national level: Afrikaans, English, Ndebele, Pedi, Sotho, Swazi, Tsonga, Tswana, Venda, Xhosa, and Zulu. The African languages spoken in South Africa are of the Niger-Congo family. In general, English is more commonly spoken in the cities, and Afrikaans in the rural areas.

Afrikaans is a variant of the Dutch spoken by the seventeenth-century colonists, and it includes words and phrases from Malay, Portuguese, the Bantu group, Hottentot, and other African languages, as well as from English, French, and German. Afrikaans has borrowed from English words such as *gelling* (gallon), *jaart* (yard), *sjieling* (shilling), and *trippens* (three pence), while English has taken over *kraal, veld,* and other Afrikaans words.

More than 70% of South African whites are bilingual. Afrikaans was the mother tongue of 58%, and English of 39%, in 1991. Some 83% of Coloureds spoke Afrikaans as their first language. Asians mostly (95%) spoke English as their first language. Zulu was the most common language of the blacks, and 39% spoke it as their first language.

10 RELIGIONS

In the early 1998, nearly 77% of the population was Christian, and about 15% followed native tribal religions. Black Christians were found in large numbers in all the European denominations, as well as in some 3,000 separatist sects under their own leaders. Nearly half of white South Africans, including almost all the Afrikaans-speaking population, belonged to the Dutch Reformed churches. The next-largest denomination was the Anglican (Episcopal), with 10% of the white population. About 9% was Methodist, 8% Roman Catholic, and 3% Presbyterian. About 3% of the white population was Jewish.

Most Christian nonwhites were members of the Dutch Reformed, Anglican, Roman Catholic, and other Christian churches. Most Asians retained their Asian religions, principally Hinduism (1%) and Islam (1%). In 1998, Jews accounted for about 0.4% of the total population in South Africa; and small numbers of Buddhists, Confucianists, and Baha'is.

11 TRANSPORTATION

South Africa's transportation network is among the most modern and extensive on the continent. In 1999, there were 331,265 kilometers (205,848 miles) of national and provincial roads, of which 137,475 kilometers (85,427 miles) were paved. There were four million automobiles and two million commercial vehicles in 1995.

The South African Transport Service, a government department under the minister of transport affairs, operates the railways, principal harbors, South African Airways, and some road transportation services. In 1999 there were 21,431 route-kilometers (13,316 route-miles) of track. South Africa's seven ports, owned and operated by the government, include the deepwater ports of Durban, Port Elizabeth, and Table Bay (at Cape Town).

The government-owned South African Airways operates both international and domestic flights. Jan Smuts Airport, near Johannesburg, is the major international airport; other international airports are located at Cape Town and Durban. In 1997, nearly 7.3 million passengers were carried on scheduled domestic and international flights.

12 HISTORY

Fossil skulls suggest that South Africa may have been one of the earliest scenes of human evolution. Little is known of the original settlers, but when Europeans first arrived, there were two distinct groups of peoples—the Bushmen, primitive nomadic hunters of the western desert, and the Hottentots, herdsmen who occupied the southern and eastern coastal areas.

European Exploration

Before AD 100, Bantu-speaking peoples entered the Transvaal area (northern region between the Vaal and Limpopo rivers). In 1488, the Portuguese sailor Bartholomeu Dias discovered the Cape of Good Hope, and on Christmas Day of 1497, Vasco da Gama discovered Natal, the area between the Drakensberg Mountains and the Indian Ocean.

The first European settlement at the Cape was made in 1652 under Jan van Riebeeck on behalf of the Dutch East India Company. Because there was a shortage of farm labor, the Dutch imported slaves from West Africa, Madagascar, and the East Indies, and because of the scarcity of European women, mixed marriages took place, eventually producing the Cape Coloured people.

The demand for meat encouraged the development of cattle farming, which in turn led to the need for more grazing land. Settlements were established on the coastal plain, along the valleys, and on the Great Karroo, a plateau in the south. The European population multiplied, but the Bushmen and Hottentots declined in numbers. In 1778, the Cape authorities proclaimed the Great Fish River the boundary between the colonists and the Africans. In 1779, invading Xhosa tribesmen were driven back across the river border. Three more frontier wars were fought by 1812.

British Influence

In 1814, the Cape of Good Hope was turned over to Britain by the Treaty of Vienna. Throughout the rest of the nineteenth century, the United Kingdom expanded its territory to include Natal, Kaffraria (south of Natal on the Indian Ocean), Griqualand West (north of the Orange River), Zululand (northeast of Natal on the Indian Ocean), Tongaland, and Basutoland (now Lesotho). The Transvaal was annexed (incorporated) in

1877 but returned to independence after a revolt in 1880–81.

Because of severe droughts and in reaction to British policy, about 6,000 Boers (Dutch farmers) undertook the Great Trek in 1834–36, migrating northward into the present Orange Free State (between the Orange and Vaal rivers) and the Transvaal.

In 1860, indentured Indians were brought into Natal to work on the sugarcane plantations; by 1911, when India halted the emigration because of what it called "poor working conditions," more than 150,000 Indians had come to South Africa as contract laborers. While pursuing the Indians' claims of injustice in South Africa, Mohandas (Mahatma) Gandhi, a young lawyer who later became famous for leading India to independence, developed his philosophy of nonviolent resistance.

The Boer War

Tension between the Boers and outsiders attracted to Transvaal by the discovery of gold in 1866 was increased by an unsuccessful attempt to capture Johannesburg by Dr. Leander Starr Jameson (Jameson Raid) in 1895–96 and culminated in the South African (or Boer) War in 1899–1902. Ultimately, the Boer republics of Transvaal and the Orange Free State gave up their independence by the Treaty of Vereeniging on 31 May 1902, but shortly thereafter were granted self-government by the British.

The Union of South Africa

A constitution for a united South Africa, which passed the British Parliament as the South Africa Act in 1909, provided for a union of all four territories or provinces, to be known as the Union of South Africa. South Africa fought with the Allies (United States, United Kingdom, and their allies) in World War I (1914–18), signed the Treaty of Versailles, and became a member of the League of Nations. Mining and industrialization advanced in the period between the two wars and led to higher living standards. South Africa sent troops to fight the German Nazis in World War II (1939–45), although many Afrikaners (as the Boers had come to be called) favored neutrality. In 1948, the National Party (NP) took power, enforcing the policy of apartheid, or racial separation of whites and nonwhites.

Apartheid

South Africa became a republic on 31 May 1961, and the president replaced the British monarch as head of state. There were mounting pressures on the government because of its apartheid policies. On 21 March 1960, a black demonstration had been staged against the "pass laws," laws requiring blacks to carry identification enabling the government to restrict their movement into urban areas. The demonstration resulted in the killing of 69 black protesters by government troops at Sharpeville in Soweto, and provided a focus for local black protests and for widespread international expressions of outrage. During this period, many black leaders were jailed, including Nelson

Mandela, the leader of the African National Congress (ANC), a black nationalist group. The ANC was banned as a political party.

In the mid-1970s, the Portuguese colonial empire disbanded and blacks came to power in Mozambique and Angola. The new black-controlled governments in these countries gave aid and political support to the ANC in South Africa. In response, South Africa aided rebel movements in the two former Portuguese territories.

In June 1976, the worst domestic confrontation since Sharpeville took place in Soweto, where blacks violently protested the compulsory use of the Afrikaans language in schools. Suppression of the riots by South African police left at least 174 blacks dead and 1,139 injured.

During the late 1970s, new protest groups and leaders emerged among the young blacks. After one of these leaders, 30-year-old Steven Biko, died while in police custody on 12 September 1977, there were renewed protests. On 4 November, the United Nations Security Council approved a mandatory arms embargo against South Africa—the first ever imposed on a member nation.

In an effort to satisfy nonwhite and international opinion, the government scrapped many aspects of apartheid in the mid-1980s, including the "pass laws" and the laws barring interracial sexual relations and marriage. These measures failed to satisfy blacks, however, and as political violence mounted the government imposed states of emergency in July 1985 and again in June 1986.

Further repression in the late 1980s included the banning of the United Democratic Front (UDF) and 16 other anti-apartheid organizations, suppression of the alternative newspapers *New Nation* and *Weekly Mail*, and assassination of anti-apartheid leaders by secret hit squads identified with the police and military intelligence.

De Klerk and the End of Apartheid

In 1989, President P.W. Botha resigned as head of the NP (National Party) and was replaced by F. W. de Klerk, who also was named acting state president. After the 6 September general election, de Klerk was elected to a five-year term as president. De Klerk launched a series of reforms in September 1989 that led to the release of ANC leader Nelson Mandela and others on 10 February 1990.

The African National Congress (ANC) and other resistance militants, including the Communist Party, were legalized. Mandela had been in prison 27 years and had become a revered symbol of resistance to apartheid. At that point, the ANC began to organize within South Africa and, in August 1990, suspended its armed struggle. Most leaders of the ANC returned from exile. Still, fighting continued, largely between ANC activists and supporters of the Zulu-dominated Inkatha Freedom Party, strongest in Natal province. More than 6,000 people were killed in political violence in 1990 and 1991. In 1991, parliament passed measures to repeal the apartheid laws—the Land Acts (1913 and 1936), the Group Areas Act

(1950), and the Population Registration Act (1950).

Mandela becomes President

In July, the ANC convened its first full conference in South Africa in 30 years. Mandela was elected president, and Cyril Ramaphosa was elected secretary general. Meanwhile, negotiations continued through 1991 and 1992 over a transition to majority rule and an end to factional fighting between the ANC and Inkatha, mostly through the Convention for a Democratic South Africa (CODESA), which began in December 1991.

In February 1993, the government and the ANC reached agreement on plans for a transition to democracy. The broad guidelines were agreed upon by the government, the ANC, and other parties in late December 1993. The Conservative Party and Inkatha boycotted the talks on multiparty government, but just a few days before the scheduled elections, Inkatha agreed to participate. The white right was divided on whether to participate in preelection talks, in the election itself, or whether to take up arms as a last resort. The elections proceeded relatively peacefully and with great enthusiasm, and they were pronounced "free and fair" by international observers.

The ANC was awarded 252 of the 400 seats in parliament. It became the governing party in all but two of the nine regions. Mandela became president and the ANC's Thabo Mbeki and the NP's de Klerk were made deputy presidents. Zulu leader Mangosuthu Buthelezi was persuaded to take a ministerial post in the cabinet. In May

Photo credit: EPD/Embassy of South Africa.

Name:	Thabo Mvuyelwa Mbeki
Position:	President of a republic
Took office:	16 June 1999
Birthplace:	Mbewuleni, South Africa
Birth date:	18 June 1942
Education:	London University, degree in economics; Sussex University, master's degree in economics; Lenin International School, guerilla training and lessons in Marxist ideology, 1970
Spouse:	Zanele Dlamini (director of the Women's Development Bank)
Of interest:	Kwanda Mpahlwa, Mbeki's son from a previous relationship, remains missing after going into exile in 1980.

1994, the Constitutional Assembly met to lay the groundwork for the new constitution. South Africa's new constitution was ratified in February 1997. Local elections were held in November 1995.

The Truth and Reconciliation Commission was established in early 1996 to expose apartheid crimes and abuses committed during the years of white rule.

In June 1999, President Mandela retired and his deputy president, Thabo Mbeki, was chosen as president and chief of state for a five-year term; the new deputy president is Jacob Zuma.

13 GOVERNMENT

The terms of the new constitution in February 1997 were determined before the elections of April 1994. There is a 400-seat National Assembly chosen by proportional representation. There also is a Senate of 90 members, 10 from each province or region, who serve as a legislature and also elect the president and deputy presidents. The president names a cabinet, divided proportionally between parties that have gained at least 5% of the vote. The nine provinces have assemblies based on the total number of votes cast in the general election.

14 POLITICAL PARTIES

Banned in 1960, the African National Congress (ANC) was legalized in 1987 in return for renouncing violence. Headed by Nelson Mandela, it received 62.5% of the vote in the April 1994 elections, making it the ruling party in South Africa.

The National Party (NP), first formed in 1910, was the last party of white rule in South Africa before the 1994 elections, in which it received 20.4% of the vote.

The Inkatha Freedom Party (IFP), headed by Zulu Chief Mangosuthu Buthelezi, captured more than 10% of the national vote and won the election for the provincial government in Natal.

Other parties participating in the elections were the Freedom Front (2.2%), the Democratic Party (1.7%), and the Pan-Africanist Congress (1.2%).

15 JUDICIAL SYSTEM

The Supreme Court has a supreme appeals division and provincial and local divisions with both original and appeals jurisdictions. The Court of Appeals, with its seat in Bloemfontein, normally consists of the chief justice and a variable number of appeals judges. Judges are appointed by the state president. Trial by jury was abolished in 1969. Black tribal chiefs have limited jurisdiction to hear cases in traditional courts.

16 ARMED FORCES

In 2000, South Africa had 70,000 active personnel; the draft has been abolished. The army had 37,970 troops, and the total strength of the navy was 5,150. The air force, with 9,400 personnel, had 116 combat aircraft and several armed helicopters. There also is a medical corps of 5,500. In 2000, South Africa spent $2 billion on defense. In 1995, there were 140,000 active members of the South African Police Service.

17 ECONOMY

The opening of the political process to all South Africans and the election of a new

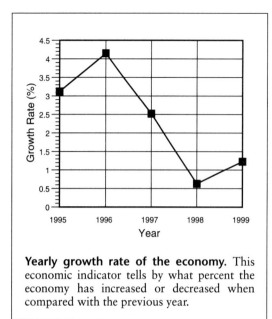

Yearly growth rate of the economy. This economic indicator tells by what percent the economy has increased or decreased when compared with the previous year.

multiracial government in 1994 marked a turning point in South Africa's economic history. With modest agriculture, fabulous mineral wealth, and diverse manufacturing, South Africa's influence extends well beyond its borders.

Real economic growth in the gross domestic product (GDP) was about 1.7% in 1999. The unemployment rate was estimated at 30%, which hampers economic growth.

18 INCOME

In 1998 South Africa's gross domestic product (GDP) was $291 billion, or about $6,800 per person. In 1999, the average annual inflation rate was 9%, resulting in a growth of GDP of about 1.3%.

19 INDUSTRY

Manufacturing is the largest contributor to South Africa's economy. Industry is located mainly in Gauteng, Western Cape, the Durban-Pinetown area of KwaZulu-Natal, and the Port Elizabeth-Uitenhage area of Eastern Cape. The largest industrial area is the metal products and engineering sector. The steel industry supplies a large motor vehicle sector. The chemical sector centers on fertilizer production and an explosives factory. The synthetic fuels production industry, with three plants in operation, serves 40% of the nation's motor fuels demand.

20 LABOR

In 1992, unemployment was an estimated 42%, with more than 100,000 jobs lost in manufacturing, mining, and construction. As of 1998, 16 million persons were classified as economically active; the labor force was expected to grow during the rest of the decade, reaching 18 million by 2000. In 1991, there were 1.4 million workers in manufacturing, the majority of whom were nonwhite. In that year, of the 840,747 persons employed in mining, the great majority was black.

At the end of 1996, there were 227 registered trade unions and about 40 unregistered unions. Total membership was about 3.2 million, or 42% of the workforce. Black trade unions were not officially recognized until 1979, when the law was modified to allow blacks not assigned to black homelands to join black trade unions. In 1993, there were 784 strikes involving 158,981 workers.

Hours of work vary from 40 to 46 per week. Employers must provide satisfactory working conditions and accident prevention measures. Workers' compensation, financed by employers, covers employees killed or injured at work, and compensation is payable in the case of occupational diseases. Unemployment insurance is paid to some contributing employees.

Minimum age laws regulate the use of child labor in business and industry but not in agriculture or the informal economy, where abuses are common.

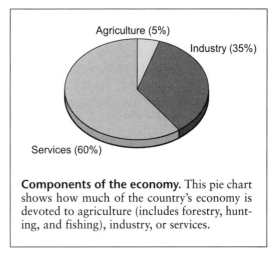

Components of the economy. This pie chart shows how much of the country's economy is devoted to agriculture (includes forestry, hunting, and fishing), industry, or services.

21 AGRICULTURE

About 80% of the total land area is available for farming, but only about 12% is cultivated. Many areas do not receive regular rainfall. The worst drought of this century in southern Africa resulted in near to total crop failure in 1991–92. Many farmers subsequently abandoned the countryside for urban areas. There was abundant rainfall in the 1996 growing season. Except for rice, tea, coffee, and cocoa, the country is typically self-sufficient in essential food production.

The principal crop is corn ("mealies"). Output totaled 4.7 million tons in 1995. Wheat can be grown only in winter; production of wheat totaled 2.1 million tons in 1995. A native sorghum ("Kaffir corn") is used to make beer and is an important source of protein. Less important, but planted in considerable quantities, are the other winter cereals—barley, oats, and rye. Potatoes are produced in large quantities. Sugarcane production totaled 16.8 million tons in 1995. That year, South Africa produced 1.7 million tons of grapes.

22 DOMESTICATED ANIMALS

The country's sheep breeds consist mainly of Merino for wool and Dorpes for mutton. Cattle breeds include the Hereford and Aberdeen Angus as well as the indigenous Afrikaner. Dairy cows are mostly Fresian, forming a well-developed dairy industry. The livestock in 1998 included 30 million sheep, 13.8 million head of cattle, 7 million goats, 1.6 million hogs, and 59 million chickens. Total estimated output of livestock products in 1998 included cow's milk, 2.8 million tons; eggs, 285,000 tons; and wool, 54,000 tons. Meat production that year included 676,000 tons of beef, 27,000 tons of pork, 120,000 tons of mutton and lamb, and 445,000 tons of poultry.

23 FISHING

South Africa is Africa's most important fishing nation. In 1995, about 28,000 people were employed in the fishing industry. In 1997, the fish catch amounted to 520,081 tons. Hake accounts for 70% of all deep-sea landings. Anchovy, pilchard, mackerel, round herring, snook, abalone, kingklip, rock lobster, oysters, and mussels are other important species. Major fishery products are fish meal, canned fish, and fish oil. About 1,310 tons of rock lobster were caught in 1997, with 75% of it processed into frozen lobster tails for export.

24 FORESTRY

South Africa is sparsely wooded, with a wooded and forested area of about 8.2 million hectares (20.3 million acres), or about 7% of the land area. Commercial forestry covers 1.2 million hectares (three million acres), with pine and commercial softwoods, eucalyptus, and wattle the principal timbers produced. The timber cut was 25.3 million cubic meters (33.1 million cubic yards) in 1997, with 28% used as fuel. Domestic timber production satisfies 90% of domestic needs.

25 MINING

Since the latter part of the nineteenth century, the South African economy has been based on the production and export of minerals. Taxation of mining enterprises has supported South African agriculture and financed many of the country's administrative and social needs. The railways were built mainly to transport mineral products, and minerals still form a major part of rail freight.

As of 1994, South Africa produced 25% of the world's gold metal, 37% of its chrome ore, 12% of manganese, and 10% of diamonds. It also is a leading producer of platinum-group metals, vermiculite, antimony, uranium, and asbestos. Other minerals produced include corundum, nickel, talc, copper, tin, and silver. The country also has much coal and iron ore and all the materials needed for alloying steel, a factor of great importance for its industrial development.

In 1996, the leading minerals by value were as follows: gold, 497,853 kilograms; platinum-group metals, 188,959 kilograms; iron ore, 30.8 million tons; copper, 152,595 tons; nickel, 33,613 tons; manganese ore, 3.2 million tons; and chrome ore, five million tons.

The value of all exported minerals in 1995 represented more than 48% of total exports.

26 FOREIGN TRADE

Gold, diamonds, and other metals and minerals are the most valuable export commodities. Exports of gold alone accounted for 27% of foreign exchange earnings in 1994. Gold exports are directly linked to the international gold price. Other leading exports include diamonds, chemicals, and machinery and equipment.

The largest expenditures on imports are for machinery, motor vehicles, consumer goods, and chemicals. The leading buyers of South African exports in 1998 were Italy, Germany, Japan, the United Kingdom, and the United States. Imports came mostly from Germany, Italy, the United States, and Japan.

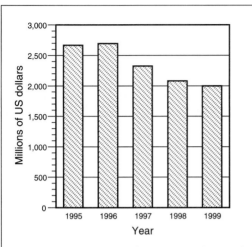

Yearly balance of trade measured in millions of US dollars. The balance of trade is the difference between what a country sells to other countries (its exports) and what it buys (its imports). If a country imports more than it exports, it has a negative balance of trade (a trade deficit). If exports exceed imports there is a positive balance of trade (a trade surplus).

27 ENERGY AND POWER

South Africa produces at least half of all electricity generated on the African continent. Coal supplied about 75% of the country's primary energy needs in 1998. Electric generation totaled 192 billion kilowatt hours in 1998, of which 176.8 billion kilowatt hours were thermal. Seventeen coal-fired plants accounted for 95% of installed capacity with nuclear power, and hydroelectric power providing the balance. Net generating capacity totaled 36.5 gigawatts at the beginning of 1998.

South Africa was the world's third largest exporter of coal in 1998, at 246.8 million tons. About 65% of annual pro-duction comes from underground mines. South Africa produces no crude oil, but does have four crude oil refineries whose combined annual distillation capacity was 466,547 barrels per day in 1999. Africa's only nuclear power station, at Koeburg near Cape Town, began operating in 1984.

28 SOCIAL DEVELOPMENT

South Africa has a comprehensive system of social legislation, which includes unemployment insurance, industrial accident insurance, old age pensions, disability pensions, war veterans' pensions, pensions for the blind, and maternity grants. In addition, there are about 25 major private welfare organizations partly subsidized by government funds. A variety of pension funds also have been established by railways, commercial and business firms, and the gold-mining industry for the protection of employees and their families.

The current African National Congress (ANC) "government of national unity" is seeking to provide more social services for its black constituents within the context of the constraints of a weakened economy. Its first priorities are housing, health, education, and the creation of more jobs in the formal economic sector.

29 HEALTH

As of 1992, the South African government increased its spending in the public and private sectors of health care.

South Africa's governmental policy has been directed toward a more streamlined and equitable public health service to

Photo credit: Cynthia Bassett.

A typical early 19th century house with black thatch roofing and wood doors and trim.

bridge the country's social and ideological divisions. With apartheid dissolved and a new 1994 government in place, other new programs may come into being. Provincial administrations maintain most major hospitals and receive subsidies from the national government. Hospital care is free for those unable to bear the costs, including nonwhites, but medical treatment is generally conducted on a private basis.

In 1990, there were 684 hospitals, with Baragwanath Hospital near Johannesburg the largest in southern Africa (nearly 3,000 beds). Total health care expenditures in 1990–97 was 7.9% of GDP. In 2000 there were 0.6 physicians per 1,000 population. There are medical schools at six universities in South Africa.

The most prevalent infectious diseases reported in South Africa are tuberculosis, measles, typhoid, malaria, and viral hepatitis. Circulatory disorders are the leading causes of death. By 1990, leprosy had been reduced to less than one per 100,000, but malaria and tuberculosis still cause serious problems. In 1996, there were 240 cases of tuberculosis per 100,000 people. In 1997, 12.9% of the adult population was infected with HIV, and there were 10,351 new cases of AIDS reported in 1995. Average life expectancy was 48 years in 2000.

30 HOUSING

In 1994, the housing backlog was estimated to be 1.2 million homes for the black population, while there is a surplus of white housing units of 83,000. Experts in South Africa forecast that almost three million homes will have to be provided by the year 2000 in the urban areas of the country. Recently, there has been an explosive growth of shacks and shantytowns surrounding South Africa's major urban areas. An estimated 66% of the country's population have no access to electricity, and in most black townships there is only one water tap per several thousand people.

31 EDUCATION

Systems of primary, secondary, and university education are generally provided in separate English-language and Afrikaans-language institutions. Adult literacy was about 82%. In 1995, 20,863 primary schools had a total student enrollment of nearly 8.2 million. Secondary education lasts an additional seven years.

In 1994, there were 21 universities and 15 other higher education institutions with 617,897 students.

32 MEDIA

The government operates the postal, telegraph, and telephone services through the Department of Posts and Telecommunications. In 1997, there were more than 4.5 million telephones. The South African Broadcasting Corporation (SABC), a semi-governmental organization, offers transmissions in English, Afrikaans, and nine Bantu languages. The country's first television service was begun in January 1976 under government auspices. In 1981, a separate channel began broadcasting in native languages. In 1999, there were 556 television broadcasting services, with transmissions in English, Afrikaans, and four Bantu languages. There were an estimated 129 television sets and 316 radios per 1,000 population in 2000. South Africa had 34 Internet hosts per 1,000 population in 1998.

The English and Afrikaans populations have their own newspapers, distinguished not only by language but also by the variety and slant of news. Two Sunday newspapers are published in Johannesburg and two in Durban, of which one is in Afrikaans and three are in English. About 150 local newspapers appear weekly or biweekly. Magazines and general periodicals are divided equally between Afrikaans and English.

33 TOURISM AND RECREATION

In 1991, international sanctions against tourism were lifted with the support of the ANC. In 1997, there were 5.4 million tourist arrivals.

In addition to the principal cities and many ocean beaches, popular attractions include the Kruger National Park, situated in the northeast on the Mozambique and Zimbabwe borders, and several game reserves; the Castle of Good Hope fortress at Cape Town (built during 1666–82); and the Kimberley Mine Museum at the site of the famous Big Hole diamond mine. Entertainment facilities include symphony halls, theaters, movies, nightclubs, and discos. Among popular pastimes are golf, tennis, bowls, hunting, horse racing, rugby, soccer, cricket, and water sports.

Selected Social Indicators

The statistics below are estimates for the period 1996 to 2000. For comparison purposes, data for the United States and averages for low-income countries and high-income countries are also given.

Indicator	South Africa	Low-income countries	High-income countries	United States
Per capita gross national product (GNP)†	$8,710	$1,870	$25,690	$31,910
Population growth rate	2.2%	2.1%	0.7%	1.1%
People per square kilometer of land	34	73	29	30
Life expectancy in years	48	59	78	77
Number of physicians per 1,000 people	0.6	1.0	2.5	2.5
Number of pupils per teacher (primary school)	37	41	17	14
Illiteracy rate (15 years and older)	14%	34%	<5%	3%
Television sets per 1,000 people	129	85	693	844
Energy consumed per capita (kg of oil equivalent)	2,681	550	5,366	7,937

† The GNP is the total dollar value of all goods and services produced by a country in a year. The per capita GNP is calculated by dividing a country's GNP by its population and adjusting for relative purchasing power. About 15% of the world's 6.1 billion people live in high-income countries, while 40% live in low-income countries.

n.a. = data not available   > = greater than   < = less than

Sources: World Bank. *World Development Indicators.* Washington, D.C.: The World Bank, 2001; Central Intelligence Agency. *The World Factbook.* Washington, D.C.: Government Printing Office, 2000.

34 FAMOUS SOUTH AFRICANS

Among the most famous tribal leaders in what is now South Africa were Shaka (1773–1828), who built the Zulu into a powerful nation, and Cetewayo (d.1884), who led the Zulu in an unsuccessful war against the British in 1879. Jan Christiaan Smuts (1870–1950) was a renowned statesman and military leader.

Among the best-known South African writers in the English language was Olive (Emily Albertina) Schreiner (1855–1920), whose *Story of an African Farm* has become a classic. Well-known authors and poets in the Afrikaans language are Cornelis Jacob Langenhoven (1873–1932), author of the national anthem; and N.P.

van Wyk Louw (1906–70). Breyten Breytenbach (b.1939) has earned international recognition as an important Afrikaans poet. V. (J.E.A.) Volschenck (1853–1935) is sometimes called the "father of South African art." Christiaan Neething Barnard (1922–2001) pioneered open heart surgery.

South Africa's first Nobel Prize winner (for peace in 1961) was Chief Albert John Luthuli (1898–1967), a former president of the ANC. Desmond Mpilo Tutu (b.1931), the secretary general of the South African Council of Churches during 1979–84 and an outspoken foe of apartheid, received the 1984 Nobel Prize for peace. Nelson R. Mandela (b.1918), a prominent leader of the ANC, was sentenced to life imprisonment in 1964; he was released in 1990 and elected president of South Africa in April 1994.

35 BIBLIOGRAPHY

Brink, André. "The Afrikaners." *National Geographic,* October 1988, 556–585.

Clark, Domini. *South Africa, the Land.* New York: Crabtree, 2000.

Cobb, Charles E., Jr. "The Twilight of Apartheid." *National Geographic,* February 1993, 66–94.

Davenport, T. R. H. *South Africa: A Modern History.* 3d ed. Toronto: University of Toronto Press, 1987.

Fish, Bruce. *South Africa: 1880 to the Present: Imperialism, Nationalism, and Apartheid.* Philadelphia: Chelsea House, 2001.

Green, Jen. *South Africa.* Austin, TX: Raintree Steck-Vaughn, 2001.

Haskins, J., et al. *From Afar to Zulu.* New York: Walker and Company, 1995.

Mandela, Nelson. *The Struggle Is My Life.* Rev. ed. New York: Pathfinders, 1986.

Park, Ted. *South Africa.* Austin, TX: Steadwell Books, 2001.

Reader's Digest Illustrated History of South Africa. Cape Town: Reader's Digest Association, 1994.

Smith, David Marshall. *Apartheid in South Africa, 3d ed.* Cambridge; New York: Cambridge University Press, 1990.

Thompson, Leonard Monteath. *A History of South Africa.* New Haven: Yale University Press, 1990.

Woods, Donald. *Biko.* 3d rev. ed. New York: H. Holt, 1991.

GLOSSARY

abdicate: To formally give up a claim to a throne; to give up the right to be king or queen.

aboriginal: The first known inhabitants of a country. A species of animals or plants which originated within a given area.

acid rain: Rain (or snow) that has become slightly acid by mixing with industrial air pollution.

adobe: A brick made from sun-dried heavy clay mixed with straw, used in building houses. A house made of adobe bricks.

adult literacy: The ability of adults to read and write.

agrarian economy: An economy where agriculture is the dominant form of economic activity. A society where agriculture dominates the day-to-day activities of the population is called an agrarian society.

air link: Refers to scheduled air service that allows people and goods to travel between two places on a regular basis.

airborne industrial pollutant: Pollution caused by industry that is supported or carried by the air.

allies: Groups or persons who are united in a common purpose. Typically used to describe nations that have joined together to fight a common enemy in war.

In World War I, the term Allies described the nations that fought against Germany and its allies. In World War II, Allies described the United Kingdom, United States, the USSR and their allies, who fought against the Axis Powers of Germany, Italy, and Japan.

aloe: A plant particularly abundant in the southern part of Africa, where leaves of some species are made into ropes, fishing lines, bow strings, and hammocks. It is also a symbolic plant in the Islamic world; anyone who returns from a pilgrimage to Mecca (Mekkah) hangs aloe over his door as a token that he has performed the journey.

Altaic language family: A family of languages spoken in portions of northern and eastern Europe, and nearly the whole of northern and central Asia, together with some other regions. The family is divided into five branches: the Ugrian or Finno-Hungarian, Smoyed, Turkish, Mongolian, and Tunguse.

althing: A legislative assembly.

amendment: A change or addition to a document.

Amerindian: A contraction of the two words, American Indian. It describes native peoples of North, South, or Central America.

amnesty: An act of forgiveness or pardon, usually taken by a government, toward persons for crimes they may have committed.

Anglican: Pertaining to or connected with the Church of England.

animal husbandry: The branch of agriculture that involves raising animals.

animism: The belief that natural objects and phenomena have souls or innate spiritual powers.

annex: To incorporate land from one country into another country.

annual growth rate: The rate at which something grows over a period of 12 months.

annual inflation rate: The rate of inflation in prices over the course of a year.

anthracite coal: Also called hard coal, it is usually 90 to 95 percent carbon, and burns cleanly, almost without a flame.

anti-Semitism: Agitation, persecution, or discrimination (physical, emotional, economic, political, or otherwise) directed against the Jews.

apartheid: The past governmental policy in the Republic of South Africa of separating the races in society.

appeasement: To bring to a state of peace.

appellate: Refers to an appeal of a court decision to a high authority.

aquaculture: The culture or "farming" of aquatic plants or other natural produce, as in the raising of catfish in "farms."

aquatic resources: Resources that come from, grow in, or live in water, including fish and plants.

aquifer: An underground layer of porous rock, sand, or gravel that holds water.

arable land: Land that can be cultivated by plowing and used for growing crops.

arbitration: A process whereby disputes are settled by a designated person, called the arbitrator, instead of by a court of law.

archipelago: Any body of water abounding with islands, or the islands themselves collectively.

archives: A place where records or a collection of important documents are kept.

arctic climate: Cold, frigid weather similar to that experienced at or near the north pole.

aristocracy: A small minority that controls the government of a nation, typically on the basis of inherited wealth.

armistice: An agreement or truce which ends military conflict in anticipation of a peace treaty.

artesian well: A type of well where the water rises to the surface and overflows.

ASEAN *see* Association of Southeast Asian Nations

Association of Southeast Asian Nations: ASEAN was established in 1967 to promote political, economic, and social cooperation among its six member countries: Indonesia, Malaysia, the Philippines, Singapore, Thailand, and Brunei. ASEAN headquarters are in Jakarta, Indonesia. In January

1992, ASEAN agreed to create the ASEAN Free Trade Area (AFTA).

asylum: To give protection, security, or shelter to someone who is threatened by political or religious persecution.

atoll: A coral island, consisting of a strip or ring of coral surrounding a central lagoon.

atomic weapons: Weapons whose extremely violent explosive power comes from the splitting of the nuclei of atoms (usually uranium or plutonium) by neutrons in a rapid chain reaction. These weapons may be referred to as atom bombs, hydrogen bombs, or H-bombs.

austerity measures: Steps taken by a government to conserve money or resources during an economically difficult time, such as cutting back on federally funded programs.

Australoid: Pertains to the type of aborigines, or earliest inhabitants, of Australia.

Austronesian language: A family of languages which includes practically all the languages of the Pacific Islands—Indonesian, Melanesian, Polynesian, and Micronesian sub-families. Does not include Australian or Papuan languages.

authoritarianism: A form of government in which a person or group attempts to rule with absolute authority without the representation of the citizens.

autonomous state: A country which is completely self-governing, as opposed to being a dependency or part of another country.

autonomy: The state of existing as a self-governing entity. For instance, when a country gains its independence from another country, it gains autonomy.

average inflation rate: The average rate at which the general prices of goods and services increase over the period of a year.

average life expectancy: In any given society, the average age attained by persons at the time of death.

Axis Powers: The countries aligned against the Allied Nations in World War II, originally applied to Nazi Germany and Fascist Italy (Rome-Berlin Axis), and later extended to include Japan.

Baha'i: The follower of a religious sect founded by Mirza Husayn Ali in Iran in 1863.

Baltic states. The three formerly communist countries of Estonia, Latvia, and Lithuania that border on the Baltic Sea.

Bantu language group: A name applied to the languages spoken in central and south Africa.

Baptist: A member of a Protestant denomination that practices adult baptism by complete immersion in water.

barren land: Unproductive land, partly or entirely treeless.

barter: Trade practice where merchandise is exchanged directly for other merchandise or services without use of money.

bedrock: Solid rock lying under loose earth.

bicameral legislature: A legislative body consisting of two chambers, such as the U.S. House of Representatives and the U.S. Senate.

bill of rights: A written statement containing the list of privileges and powers to be granted to a body of people, usually introduced when a government or other organization is forming.

bituminous coal: Soft coal; coal which burns with a bright-yellow flame.

black market: A system of trade where goods are sold illegally, often for excessively inflated prices. This type of trade usually develops to avoid paying taxes or tariffs levied by the government, or to get around import or export restrictions on products.

bloodless coup: The sudden takeover of a country's government by hostile means but without killing anyone in the process.

boat people: Used to describe individuals (refugees) who attempt to flee their country by boat.

bog: Wet, soft, and spongy ground where the soil is composed mainly of decayed or decaying vegetable matter.

Bolshevik Revolution. A revolution in 1917 in Russia when a wing of the Russian Social Democratic party seized power. The Bolsheviks advocated the violent overthrow of capitalism.

bonded labor: Workers bound to service without pay; slaves.

border dispute: A disagreement between two countries as to the exact location or length of the dividing line between them.

Brahman: A member (by heredity) of the highest caste among the Hindus, usually assigned to the priesthood.

broadleaf forest: A forest composed mainly of broadleaf (deciduous) trees.

Buddhism: A religious system common in India and eastern Asia. Founded by and based upon the teachings of Siddhartha Gautama, Buddhism asserts that suffering is an inescapable part of life. Deliverance can only be achieved through the practice of charity, temperance, justice, honesty, and truth.

buffer state: A small country that lies between two larger, possibly hostile countries, considered to be a neutralizing force between them.

bureaucracy: A system of government that is characterized by division into bureaus of administration with their own divisional heads. Also refers to the inflexible procedures of such a system that often result in delay.

Byzantine Empire: An empire centered in the city of Byzantium, now Istanbul in present-day Turkey.

CACM *see* Central American Common Market.

canton: A territory or small division or state within a country.

capital punishment: The ultimate act of punishment for a crime, the death penalty.

capitalism: An economic system in which goods and services and the means to produce and sell them are privately owned, and prices and wages are determined by market forces.

Caribbean Community and Common Market (CARICOM): Founded in 1973 and with its headquarters in Georgetown, Guyana, CARICOM seeks the establishment of a common trade policy and increased cooperation in the Caribbean region. Includes 13 English-speaking Caribbean nations: Antigua and Barbuda, the Bahamas, Barbados, Belize, Dominica, Grenada, Guyana, Jamaica, Montserrat, Saint Kitts-Nevis, Saint Lucia, St. Vincent/Grenadines, and Trinidad and Tobago.

CARICOM *see* Caribbean Community and Common Market.

carnivore: Flesh-eating animal or plant.

carob: The common English name for a plant that is similar to and sometimes used as a substitute for chocolate.

cartel: An organization of independent producers formed to regulate the production, pricing, or marketing practices of its members in order to limit competition and maximize their market power.

cash crop: A crop that is grown to be sold rather than kept for private use.

cassation: The reversal or annulling of a final judgment by the supreme authority.

cassava: The name of several species of stout herbs, extensively cultivated for food.

caste system: One of the artificial divisions or social classes into which the Hindus are rigidly separated according to the religious law of Brahmanism. Membership in a caste is hereditary, and the privileges and disabilities of each caste are transmitted by inheritance.

Caucasian or Caucasoid: The white race of human beings, as determined by genealogy and physical features.

cease-fire: An official declaration of the end to the use of military force or active hostilities, even if only temporary.

censorship: The practice of withholding certain items of news that may cast a country in an unfavorable light or give away secrets to the enemy.

census: An official counting of the inhabitants of a state or country with details of sex and age, family, occupation, possessions, etc.

Central American Common Market (CACM): Established in 1962, a trade alliance of five Central American nations. Participating are Costa Rica, El Salvador, Guatemala, Honduras, and Nicaragua.

Central Powers: In World War I, Germany and Austria-Hungary, and their allies, Turkey and Bulgaria.

centrally planned economy: An economic system all aspects of which are supervised and regulated by the government.

centrist position: Refers to opinions held by members of a moderate political group; that is, views that are somewhere in the middle of popular thought between conservative and liberal.

cession: Withdrawal from or yielding to physical force.

chancellor: A high-ranking government official. In some countries it is the prime minister.

cholera: An acute infectious disease characterized by severe diarrhea, vomiting, and, often, death.

Christianity: The religion founded by Jesus Christ, based on the Bible as holy scripture.

Church of England: The national and established church in England. The Church of England claims continuity with the branch of the Catholic Church that existed in England before the Reformation. Under Henry VIII, the spiritual supremacy and jurisdiction of the pope were abolished, and the sovereign (king or queen) was declared head of the church.

circuit court: A court that convenes in two or more locations within its appointed district.

CIS *see* Commonwealth of Independent States

city-state: An independent state consisting of a city and its surrounding territory.

civil court: A court whose proceedings include determinations of rights of individual citizens, in contrast to criminal proceedings regarding individuals or the public.

civil jurisdiction: The authority to enforce the laws in civil matters brought before the court.

civil law: The law developed by a nation or state for the conduct of daily life of its own people.

civil rights: The privileges of all individuals to be treated as equals under the laws of their country; specifically, the rights given by certain amendments to the U.S. Constitution.

civil unrest: The feeling of uneasiness due to an unstable political climate, or actions taken as a result of it.

civil war: A war between groups of citizens of the same country who have different opinions or agendas. The Civil War of the United States was the conflict between the states of the North and South from 1861 to 1865.

climatic belt: A region or zone where a particular type of climate prevails.

Club du Sahel: The Club du Sahel is an informal coalition which seeks to reverse the effects of drought and the desertification in the eight Sahelian zone countries: Burkina Faso, Chad, Gambia, Mali, Mauritania, Niger, Senegal, and the Cape Verde Islands. Headquarters are in Ouagadougou, Burkina Faso.

CMEA *see* Council for Mutual Economic Assistance.

coalition government: A government combining differing factions within a country, usually temporary.

coastal belt: A coastal plain area of lowlands and somewhat higher ridges that run parallel to the coast.

coastal plain: A fairly level area of land along the coast of a land mass.

coca: A shrub native to South America, the leaves of which produce organic compounds that are used in the production of cocaine.

coke: The solid product of the carbonization of coal, bearing the same relation to coal that charcoal does to wood.

cold war: Refers to conflict over ideological differences that is carried on by words and diplomatic actions, not by military action. The term is usually used to refer to the tension that existed between the United States and the USSR from the 1950s until the breakup of the USSR in 1991.

collective bargaining: The negotiations between workers who are members of a union and their employer for the purpose of deciding work rules and policies regarding wages, hours, etc.

collective farm: A large farm formed from many small farms and supervised by the government; usually found in communist countries.

collective farming: The system of farming on a collective where all workers share in the income of the farm.

colloquial: Belonging to ordinary, everyday speech; often especially applied to common words and phrases which are not used in formal speech.

colonial period: The period of time when a country forms colonies in and extends control over a foreign area.

colonist: Any member of a colony or one who helps settle a new colony.

colony: A group of people who settle in a new area far from their original country, but still under the jurisdiction of that country. Also refers to the newly settled area itself.

COMECON *see* Council for Mutual Economic Assistance.

commerce: The trading of goods (buying and selling), especially on a large scale, between cities, states, and countries.

commercial catch: The amount of marketable fish, usually measured in tons, caught in a particular period of time.

commercial crop: Any marketable agricultural crop.

commission: A group of people designated to collectively do a job, including a government agency with certain law-making powers. Also, the power given to an individual or group to perform certain duties.

commodity: Any items, such as goods or services, that are bought or sold, or agricultural products that are traded or marketed.

common law: A legal system based on custom and decisions and opinions of the law courts. The basic system of law of England and the United States.

common market: An economic union among countries that is formed to remove trade barriers (tariffs) among those countries, increasing economic cooperation. The European Community is a notable example of a common market.

commonwealth: A commonwealth is a free association of sovereign independent states that has no charter, treaty, or constitution. The association promotes cooperation, consultation, and mutual assistance among members.

Commonwealth of Independent States: The CIS was established in December 1991 as an association of 11 republics of the former Soviet Union. The members include: Russia, Ukraine, Belarus (formerly Byelorussia), Moldova (formerly Moldavia), Armenia, Azerbaijan, Uzbekistan, Turkmenistan, Tajikistan, Kazakhstan, and Kyrgyzstan (formerly Kirghiziya). The Baltic states—Estonia, Latvia, and Lithuania—did not join. Georgia maintained observer status before joining the CIS in November 1993.

Commonwealth of Nations: Voluntary association of the United Kingdom and its present dependencies and associated states, as well as certain former dependencies and their dependent territories. The term was first used officially in 1926 and is embodied in the Statute of Westminster (1931). Within the Commonwealth, whose secretariat (established in 1965) is located in London, England, are numerous subgroups devoted to economic and technical cooperation.

commune: An organization of people living together in a community who share the ownership and use of property. Also refers to a small governmental district of a country, especially in Europe.

communism: A form of government whose system requires common ownership of property for the use of all citizens. All profits are to be equally distributed and prices on goods and services are usually set by the state. Also, communism refers directly to the official doctrine of the former U.S.S.R.

compulsory: Required by law or other regulation.

compulsory education: The mandatory requirement for children to attend school until they have reached a certain age or grade level.

conciliation: A process of bringing together opposing sides of a disagreement for the purpose of compromise. Or, a way of settling an international dispute in which the disagreement is submitted to an independent committee that will examine the facts and advise the participants of a possible solution.

concordat: An agreement, compact, or convention, especially between church and state.

confederation: An alliance or league formed for the purpose of promoting the common interests of its members.

Confucianism: The system of ethics and politics taught by the Chinese philosopher Confucius.

coniferous forest: A forest consisting mainly of pine, fir, and cypress trees.

conifers: Cone-bearing plants. Mostly evergreen trees and shrubs which produce cones.

conscription: To be required to join the military by law. Also known as the draft. Service personnel who join the military because of the legal requirement are called conscripts or draftees.

conservative party: A political group whose philosophy tends to be based on established traditions and not supportive of rapid change.

constituency: The registered voters in a governmental district, or a group of people that supports a position or a candidate.

constituent assembly: A group of people that has the power to determine the election of a political representative or create a constitution.

constitution: The written laws and basic rights of citizens of a country or members of an organized group.

constitutional monarchy: A system of government in which the hereditary sovereign (king or queen, usually) rules according to a written constitution.

constitutional republic: A system of government with an elected chief of state and elected representation, with a written constitution containing its governing principles. The United States is a constitutional republic.

consumer goods: Items that are bought to satisfy personal needs or wants of individuals.

continental climate: The climate of a part of the continent; the characteristics and peculiarities of the climate are a result of the land itself and its location.

continental shelf: A plain extending from the continental coast and varying in width that typically ends in a steep slope to the ocean floor.

copra: The dried meat of the coconut; it is frequently used as an ingredient of curry, and to produce coconut oil. Also written *cobra, coprah,* and *copperah.*

Coptic Christians: Members of the Coptic Church of Egypt, formerly of Ethiopia.

cordillera: A continuous ridge, range, or chain of mountains.

corvette: A small warship that is often used as an escort ship because it is easier to maneuver than larger ships like destroyers.

Council for Mutual Economic Assistance (CMEA): Also known as COMECON, the alliance of socialist economies was established on 25 January 1949 and abolished 1 January 1991. It included Afghanistan*, Albania, Angola*, Bulgaria, Cuba, Czechoslovakia, Ethiopia*, East Germany, Hungary, Laos*, Mongolia, Mozambique*, Nicaragua*, Poland, Romania, USSR, Vietnam, Yemen*, and Yugoslavia. Nations marked with an asterisk were observers only.

counterinsurgency operations: Organized military activity designed to stop rebellion against an established government.

county: A territorial division or administrative unit within a state or country.

coup d'ètat or coup: A sudden, violent overthrow of a government or its leader.

court of appeal: An appellate court, having the power of review after a case has been decided in a lower court.

court of first appeal: The next highest court to the court which has decided a case, to which that case may be presented for review.

court of last appeal: The highest court, in which a decision is not subject to review by any higher court. In the United States, it could be the Supreme Court of an individual state or the U.S. Supreme Court.

cricket (sport): A game played by two teams with a ball and bat, with two wickets (staked target) being defended by a batsman. Common in the United Kingdom and Commonwealth of Nations countries.

criminal law: The branch of law that deals primarily with crimes and their punishments.

crown colony: A colony established by a commonwealth over which the monarch has some control, as in colonies established by the United Kingdom's Commonwealth of Nations.

Crusades: Military expeditions by European Christian armies in the eleventh, twelfth, and thirteenth centuries to win land controlled by the Muslims in the middle east.

cultivable land: Land that can be prepared for the production of crops.

Cultural Revolution: An extreme reform movement in China from 1966 to 1976; its goal was to combat liberalization by restoring the ideas of Mao Zedong.

Cushitic language group: A group of Hamitic languages that are spoken in Ethiopia and other areas of eastern Africa.

customs union: An agreement between two or more countries to remove trade barriers with each other and to establish common tariff and nontariff policies with respect to imports from countries outside of the agreement.

cyclone: Any atmospheric movement, general or local, in which the wind blows spirally around and in towards a center. In the northern hemisphere, the cyclonic movement is usually counter-clockwise, and in the southern hemisphere, it is clockwise.

Cyrillic alphabet: An alphabet adopted by the Slavic people and invented by Cyril and Methodius in the ninth century as an alphabet that was easier for the copyist to write. The Russian alphabet is a slight modification of it.

decentralization: The redistribution of power in a government from one large central authority to a wider range of smaller local authorities.

deciduous species: Any species that sheds or casts off a part of itself after a definite period of time. More commonly used in reference to plants that shed their leaves on a yearly basis as opposed to those (evergreens) that retain them.

declaration of independence: A formal written document stating the intent of a group of persons to become fully self-governing.

deficit: The amount of money that is in excess between spending and income.

deficit spending: The process in which a government spends money on goods and services in excess of its income.

deforestation: The removal or clearing of a forest.

deity: A being with the attributes, nature, and essence of a god; a divinity.

delta: Triangular-shaped deposits of soil formed at the mouths of large rivers.

demarcate: To mark off from adjoining land or territory; set the limits or boundaries of.

demilitarized zone (DMZ): An area surrounded by a combat zone that has had military troops and weapons removed.

demobilize: To disband or discharge military troops.

democracy: A form of government in which the power lies in the hands of the people, who can govern directly, or can be governed indirectly by representatives elected by its citizens.

denationalize: To remove from government ownership or control.

deportation: To carry away or remove from one country to another, or to a distant place.

depression: A hollow; a surface that has sunken or fallen in.

deregulation: The act of reversing controls and restrictions on prices of goods, bank interest, and the like.

desalinization plant: A facility that produces freshwater by removing the salt from saltwater.

desegregation: The act of removing restrictions on people of a particular race that keep them socially, economically, and, sometimes, physically, separate from other groups.

desertification: The process of becoming a desert as a result of climatic changes, land mismanagement, or both.

détente: The official lessening of tension between countries in conflict.

devaluation: The official lowering of the value of a country's currency in relation to the value of gold or the currencies of other countries.

developed countries: Countries which have a high standard of living and a well-developed industrial base.

development assistance: Government programs intended to finance and promote the growth of new industries.

dialect: One of a number of regional or related modes of speech regarded as descending from a common origin.

dictatorship: A form of government in which all the power is retained by an absolute leader or tyrant. There are no rights granted to the people to elect their own representatives.

dike: An artificial riverbank built up to control the flow of water.

diplomatic relations: The relationship between countries as conducted by representatives of each government.

direct election: The process of selecting a representative to the government by balloting of the voting public, in contrast to selection by an elected representative of the people.

disarmament: The reduction or depletion of the number of weapons or the size of armed forces.

dissident: A person whose political opinions differ from the majority to the point of rejection.

dogma: A principle, maxim, or tenet held as being firmly established.

domain: The area of land governed by a particular ruler or government, sometimes referring to the ultimate control of that territory.

domestic spending: Money spent by a country's government on goods used, investments, running of the government, and exports and imports.

dominion: A self-governing nation that recognizes the British monarch as chief of state.

dormant volcano: A volcano that has not exhibited any signs of activity for an extended period of time.

dowry: The sum of the property or money that a bride brings to her groom at their marriage.

draft constitution: The preliminary written plans for the new constitution of a country forming a new government.

Druze: A member of a Muslim sect based in Syria, living chiefly in the mountain regions of Lebanon.

dual nationality: The status of an individual who can claim citizenship in two or more countries.

duchy: Any territory under the rule of a duke or duchess.

due process: In law, the application of the legal process to which every citizen has a right, which cannot be denied.

durable goods: Goods or products which are expected to last and perform for several years, such as cars and washing machines.

duty: A tax imposed on imports by the customs authority of a country. Duties are generally based on the value of the goods (*ad valorem* duties), some other factors such as weight or quantity (specific duties), or a combination of value and other factors (compound duties).

dyewoods: Any wood from which dye is extracted.

dynasty: A family line of sovereigns who rule in succession, and the time during which they reign.

earned income: The money paid to an individual in wages or salary.

Eastern Orthodox: The outgrowth of the original Eastern Church of the Eastern Roman Empire, consisting of eastern Europe, western Asia, and Egypt.

EC *see* European Community

ecclesiastical: Pertaining or relating to the church.

echidna: A spiny, toothless anteater of Australia, Tasmania, and New Guinea.

ecological balance: The condition of a healthy, well-functioning ecosystem, which includes all the plants and animals in a natural community together with their environment.

ecology: The branch of science that studies organisms in relationship to other organisms and to their environment.

economic depression: A prolonged period in which there is high unemployment, low production, falling prices, and general business failure.

economically active population: That portion of the people who are employed for wages and are consumers of goods and services.

ecotourism: Broad term that encompasses nature, adventure, and ethnic tourism; responsible or wilderness-sensitive tourism; soft-path or small-scale tourism; low-impact tourism; and sustainable tourism. Scientific, educational, or academic tourism (such as biotourism, archetourism, and geotourism) are also forms of ecotourism.

elected assembly: The persons that comprise a legislative body of a government who received their positions by direct election.

electoral system: A system of choosing government officials by votes cast by qualified citizens.

electoral vote: The votes of the members of the electoral college.

electorate: The people who are qualified to vote in an election.

emancipation: The freeing of persons from any kind of bondage or slavery.

embargo: A legal restriction on commercial ships to enter a country's ports, or any legal restriction of trade.

emigration: Moving from one country or region to another for the purpose of residence.

empire: A group of territories ruled by one sovereign or supreme ruler. Also, the period of time under that rule.

enclave: A territory belonging to one nation that is surrounded by that of another nation.

encroachment: The act of intruding, trespassing, or entering on the rights or possessions of another.

endangered species: A plant or animal species whose existence as a whole is threatened with extinction.

endemic: Anything that is peculiar to and characteristic of a locality or region.

Enlightenment: An intellectual movement of the late seventeenth and eighteenth centuries in which scientific thinking gained a strong foothold and old beliefs were challenged. The idea of absolute monarchy was questioned and people were gradually given more individual rights.

enteric disease: An intestinal disease.

epidemic: As applied to disease, any disease that is temporarily prevalent among people in one place at the same time.

Episcopal: Belonging to or vested in bishops or prelates; characteristic of or pertaining to a bishop or bishops.

ethnolinguistic group: A classification of related languages based on common ethnic origin.

EU *see* European Union

European Community: A regional organization created in 1958. Its purpose is to eliminate customs duties and other trade barriers in Europe. It promotes a common external tariff against other countries, a Common Agricultural Policy (CAP), and guarantees of free movement of labor and capital. The original six members were Belgium, France, West Germany, Italy, Luxembourg, and the Netherlands. Denmark, Ireland, and the United Kingdom became members in 1973; Greece joined in 1981;

Spain and Portugal in 1986. Other nations continue to join.

European Union: The EU is an umbrella reference to the European Community (EC) and to two European integration efforts introduced by the Maastricht Treaty: Common Foreign and Security Policy (including defense) and Justice and Home Affairs (principally cooperation between police and other authorities on crime, terrorism, and immigration issues).

exports: Goods sold to foreign buyers.

external migration: The movement of people from their native country to another country, as opposed to internal migration, which is the movement of people from one area of a country to another in the same country.

faction: People with a specific set of interests or goals who form a subgroup within a larger organization.

fallout: The precipitation of particles from the atmosphere, often the result of a ground disturbance by volcanic activity or a nuclear explosion.

family planning: The use of birth control to determine the number of children a married couple will have.

Fascism: A political philosophy that holds the good of the nation as more important than the needs of the individual. Fascism also stands for a dictatorial leader and strong oppression of opposition or dissent.

federal: Pertaining to a union of states whose governments are subordinate to a central government.

federation: A union of states or other groups under the authority of a central government.

fetishism: The practice of worshipping a material object that is believed to have mysterious powers residing in it, or is the representation of a deity to which worship may be paid and from which supernatural aid is expected.

feudal estate: The property owned by a lord in medieval Europe under the feudal system.

feudal society: In medieval times, an economic and social structure in which persons could hold land given to them by a lord (nobleman) in return for service to that lord.

final jurisdiction: The final authority in the decision of a legal matter. In the United States, the Supreme Court would have final jurisdiction.

Finno-Ugric language group: A subfamily of languages spoken in northeastern Europe, including Finnish, Hungarian, Estonian, and Lapp.

fiscal year: The twelve months between the settling of financial accounts, not necessarily corresponding to a calendar year beginning on January 1.

fjord: A deep indentation of the land forming a comparatively narrow arm of the sea with more or less steep slopes or cliffs on each side.

fly: The part of a flag opposite and parallel to the one nearest the flagpole.

fodder: Food for cattle, horses, and sheep, such as hay, straw, and other kinds of vegetables.

folk religion: A religion with origins and traditions among the common people of a nation or region that is relevant to their particular life-style.

foreign exchange: Foreign currency that allows foreign countries to conduct financial transactions or settle debts with one another.

foreign policy: The course of action that one government chooses to adopt in relation to a foreign country.

Former Soviet Union: The FSU is a collective reference to republics comprising the former Soviet Union. The term, which has been used as both including and excluding the Baltic republics (Estonia, Latvia, and Lithuania), includes the other 12 republics: Russia, Ukraine, Belarus, Moldova, Armenia, Azerbaijan, Uzbekistan, Turkmenistan, Tajikistan, Kazakhstan, Kyrgizstan, and Georgia.

fossil fuels: Any mineral or mineral substance formed by the decomposition of organic matter buried beneath the earth's surface and used as a fuel.

free enterprise: The system of economics in which private business may be conducted with minimum interference by the government.

free-market economy: An economic system that relies on the market, as opposed to government planners, to set the prices for wages and products.

frigate. A medium-sized warship.

fundamentalist: A person who holds religious beliefs based on the complete acceptance of the words of the Bible or other holy scripture as the truth. For instance, a fundamentalist would believe the story of creation exactly as it is told in the Bible and would reject the idea of evolution.

game reserve: An area of land reserved for wild animals that are hunted for sport or for food.

GDP *see* gross domestic product.

genocide: Planned and systematic killing of members of a particular ethnic, religious, or cultural group.

Germanic language group: A large branch of the Indo-European family of languages including German itself, the Scandinavian languages, Dutch, Yiddish, Modern English, Modern Scottish, Afrikaans, and others. The group also includes extinct languages such as Gothic, Old High German, Old Saxon, Old English, Middle English, and the like.

glasnost: President Mikhail Gorbachev's frank revelations in the 1980s about the state of the economy and politics in the Soviet Union; his policy of openness.

global greenhouse gas emissions: Gases released into the atmosphere that contribute to the greenhouse effect, a condition in which the earth's excess heat cannot escape.

global warming: Also called the greenhouse effect. The theorized gradual warming of the earth's climate as a result of the burning of fossil fuels, the use of man-made chemicals, deforestation, etc.

GMT *see* Greenwich Mean Time.

GNP *see* gross national product.

grand duchy: A territory ruled by a nobleman, called a grand duke, who ranks just below a king.

Greek Catholic: A person who is a member of an Orthodox Eastern Church.

Greek Orthodox: The official church of Greece, a self-governing branch of the Orthodox Eastern Church.

Greenwich (Mean) Time: Mean solar time of the meridian at Greenwich, England, used as the basis for standard time throughout most of the world. The world is divided into 24 time zones, and all are related to the prime, or Greenwich mean, zone.

gross domestic product: A measure of the market value of all goods and services produced within the boundaries of a nation, regardless of asset ownership. Unlike gross national product, GDP excludes receipts from that nation's business operations in foreign countries.

gross national product: A measure of the market value of goods and services produced by the labor and property of a nation. Includes receipts from that nation's business operation in foreign countries

groundwater: Water located below the earth's surface, the source from which wells and springs draw their water.

guano: The excrement of seabirds and bats found in various areas around the world. Gathered commercially and sold as a fertilizer.

guerrilla: A member of a small radical military organization that uses unconventional tactics to take their enemies by surprise.

gymnasium: A secondary school, primarily in Europe, that prepares students for university.

hardwoods: The name given to deciduous trees, such as cherry, oak, maple, and mahogany.

harem: In a Muslim household, refers to the women (wives, concubines, and servants in ancient times) who live there and also to the area of the home they live in.

harmattan: An intensely dry, dusty wind felt along the coast of Africa between Cape Verde and Cape Lopez. It prevails at intervals during the months of December, January, and February.

heavy industry: Industries that use heavy or large machinery to produce goods, such as automobile manufacturing.

hoist: The part of a flag nearest the flagpole.

Holocaust: The mass slaughter of European civilians, the vast majority Jews, by the Nazis during World War II.

Holy Roman Empire: A kingdom consisting of a loose union of German and Italian territories that existed from around the ninth century until 1806.

home rule: The governing of a territory by the citizens who inhabit it.

homeland: A region or area set aside to be a state for a people of a particular national, cultural, or racial origin.

homogeneous: Of the same kind or nature, often used in reference to a whole.

Horn of Africa: The Horn of Africa comprises Djibouti, Eritrea, Ethiopia, Somalia, and Sudan.

housing starts: The initiation of new housing construction.

human rights activist: A person who vigorously pursues the attainment of basic rights for all people.

human rights issues: Any matters involving people's basic rights which are in question or thought to be abused.

humanist: A person who centers on human needs and values, and stresses dignity of the individual.

humanitarian aid: Money or supplies given to a persecuted group or people of a country at war, or those devastated by a natural disaster, to provide for basic human needs.

hydrocarbon: A compound of hydrogen and carbon, often occurring in organic substances or derivatives of organic substances such as coal, petroleum, natural gas, etc.

hydrocarbon emissions: Organic compounds containing only carbon and hydrogen, often occurring in petroleum, natural gas, coal, and bitumens, and which contribute to the greenhouse effect.

hydroelectric potential: The potential amount of electricity that can be produced hydroelectrically. Usually used in reference to a given area and how many hydroelectric power plants that area can sustain.

hydroelectric power plant: A factory that produces electrical power through the application of water-power.

IBRD *see* World Bank.

illegal alien: Any foreign-born individual who has unlawfully entered another country.

immigration: The act or process of passing or entering into another country for the purpose of permanent residence.

imports: Goods purchased from foreign suppliers.

indigenous: Born or originating in a particular place or country; native to a particular region or area.

Indo-Aryan language group: The group that includes the languages of India; also called Indo-European language group.

Indo-European language family: The group that includes the languages of India and much of Europe and southwestern Asia.

industrialized nation: A nation whose economy is based on industry.

infanticide: The act of murdering a baby.

infidel: One who is without faith or belief; particularly, one who rejects the distinctive doctrines of a particular religion.

inflation: The general rise of prices, as measured by a consumer price index. Results in a fall in value of currency.

installed capacity: The maximum possible output of electric power at any given time.

insurgency: The state or condition in which one rises against lawful authority or established government; rebellion.

insurrectionist: One who participates in an unorganized revolt against an authority.

interim government: A temporary or provisional government.

interim president: One who is appointed to perform temporarily the duties of president during a transitional period in a government.

internal migration: Term used to describe the relocation of individuals from one region to another without leaving the confines of the country or of a specified area.

International Date Line: An arbitrary line at about the 180th meridian that designates where one day begins and another ends.

Islam: The religious system of Mohammed, practiced by Moslims and based on a belief in Allah as the supreme being and Mohammed as his prophet. The spelling variations, Muslim and Muhammad, are also used, primarily by Islamic people. Islam also refers to those nations in which it is the primary religion.

isthmus: A narrow strip of land bordered by water and connecting two larger bodies of land, such as two continents, a continent and a peninsula, or two parts of an island.

Judaism: The religious system of the Jews, based on the Old Testament as revealed to Moses and characterized by a belief in one God and adherence to the laws of scripture and rabbinic traditions.

Judeo-Christian: The dominant traditional religious makeup of the United States and other countries based on the worship of the Old and New Testaments of the Bible.

junta: A small military group in power of a country, especially after a coup.

khan: A sovereign, or ruler, in central Asia.

khanate: A kingdom ruled by a khan, or man of rank.

kwashiorkor: Severe malnutrition in infants and children caused by a diet high in carbohydrates and lacking in protein.

kwh: The abbreviation for kilowatt-hour.

labor force: The number of people in a population available for work, whether actually employed or not.

labor movement: A movement in the early to mid-1800s to organize workers in groups according to profession to give them certain rights as a group, including bargaining power for better wages, working conditions, and benefits.

land reforms: Steps taken to create a fair distribution of farmland, especially by governmental action.

landlocked country: A country that does not have direct access to the sea; it is completely surrounded by other countries.

least developed countries: A subgroup of the United Nations designation of "less developed countries;" these countries generally have no significant economic growth, low literacy rates, and per person gross national product of less than $500. Also known as undeveloped countries.

leeward: The direction identical to that of the wind. For example, a *leeward tide* is a tide that runs in the same direction that the wind blows.

leftist: A person with a liberal or radical political affiliation.

legislative branch: The branch of government which makes or enacts the laws.

leprosy: A disease that can effect the skin and/or the nerves and can cause ulcers of the skin, loss of feeling, or loss of fingers and toes.

less developed countries (LDC): Designated by the United Nations to include countries with low levels of output, living standards, and per person gross national product generally below $5,000.

literacy: The ability to read and write.

Maastricht Treaty: The Maastricht Treaty (named for the Dutch town in which the treaty was signed) is also known as the Treaty of European Union. The treaty creates a European Union by: (a) committing the member states of the European Economic Community to both European Monetary Union (EMU) and political union; (b) introducing a single currency (European Currency Unit, ECU); (c) establishing a European System of Central Banks (ESCB); (d) creating a European Central Bank (ECB); and (e) broadening EC integration by including both a common foreign and security policy (CFSP) and cooperation in justice and home affairs (CJHA). The treaty entered into force on November 1, 1993.

Maghreb states: The Maghreb states include the three nations of Algeria, Morocco, and Tunisia; sometimes includes Libya and Mauritania.

maize: Another name (Spanish or British) for corn or the color of ripe corn.

majority party: The party with the largest number of votes and the controlling political party in a government.

mangrove: A tree which abounds on tropical shores in both hemispheres. Characterized by its numerous roots which arch out from its trunk and descend from its branches, mangroves form thick, dense growths along the tidal muds, reaching lengths hundreds of miles long.

manioc: The cassava plant or its product. Manioc is a very important food-staple in tropical America.

maquis: Scrubby, thick underbrush found along the coast of the Mediterranean Sea.

marginal land: Land that could produce an economic profit, but is so poor that it is only used when better land is no longer available.

marine life: The life that exists in, or is formed by the sea.

maritime climate: The climate and weather conditions typical of areas bordering the sea.

maritime rights: The rights that protect navigation and shipping.

market access: Market access refers to the openness of a national market to foreign products. Market access reflects a government's willingness to permit imports to compete relatively unimpeded with similar domestically produced goods.

market economy: A form of society which runs by the law of supply and demand. Goods are produced by firms to be sold to consumers, who determine the demand for them. Price levels vary according to the demand for certain goods and how much of them is produced.

market price: The price a commodity will bring when sold on the open market. The price is determined by the amount of demand for the commodity by buyers.

Marshall Plan: Formally known as the European Recovery Program, a joint project between the United States and most Western European nations under which $12.5 billion in U.S. loans and grants was expended to aid European recovery after World War II.

Marxism *see* Marxist-Leninist principles.

Marxist: A follower of Karl Marx, a German socialist and revolutionary leader of the late 1800s, who contributed to Marxist-Leninist principles.

Marxist-Leninist principles: The doctrines of Karl Marx, built upon by Nikolai Lenin, on which communism was founded. They predicted the fall of capitalism, due to its own internal faults and the resulting oppression of workers.

massif: A central mountain-mass or the dominant part of a range of mountains.

matrilineal (descent): Descending from, or tracing descent through, the maternal, or mother's, family line.

Mayan language family: The languages of the Central American Indians, further divided into two subgroups: the Maya and the Huastek.

mean temperature: The air temperature unit measured by the National Weather Service by adding the maximum and minimum daily temperatures together and diving the sum by 2.

Mecca (Mekkah): A city in Saudi Arabia; a destination of pilgrims in the Islamic world.

Mediterranean climate: A wet-winter, dry-summer climate with a moderate annual temperature range.

mestizo: The offspring of a person of mixed blood; especially, a person of mixed Spanish and American Indian parentage.

migratory birds: Those birds whose instincts prompt them to move from one place to another at the regularly recurring changes of season.

migratory workers: Usually agricultural workers who move from place to place for employment depending on the growing and harvesting seasons of various crops.

military coup: A sudden, violent overthrow of a government by military forces.

military junta: The small military group in power in a country, especially after a coup.

military regime: Government conducted by a military force.

military takeover: The seizure of control of a government by the military forces.

militia: The group of citizens of a country who are either serving in the reserve military forces or are eligible to be called up in time of emergency.

millet: A cereal grass whose small grain is used for food in Europe and Asia.

minority party: The political group that comprises the smaller part of the large overall group it belongs to; the party that is not in control.

missionary: A person sent by authority of a church or religious organization to spread his religious faith in a community where his church has no self-supporting organization.

monarchy: Government by a sovereign, such as a king or queen.

money economy: A system or stage of economic development in which money replaces barter in the exchange of goods and services.

Mongol: One of an Asiatic race chiefly resident in Mongolia, a region north of China proper and south of Siberia.

Mongoloid: Having physical characteristics like those of the typical Mongols (Chinese, Japanese, Turks, Eskimos, etc.).

Moors: One of the Arab tribes that conquered Spain in the eighth century.

Moslem: A frequently used variation of the spelling of Muslim; a follower of Muhammad in the religion of Islam.

mosque: An Islam place of worship and the organization with which it is connected.

mouflon: A type of wild sheep characterized by curling horns.

Muhammad (or Muhammed or Mahomet): An Arabian prophet, known as the "Prophet of Allah" who founded the religion of Islam in 622, and wrote *The Koran*, the scripture of Islam. Also commonly spelled Mohammed.

mujahideen (mujahedin or mujahedeen): Rebel fighters in Islamic countries, especially those supporting the cause of Islam.

mulatto: One who is the offspring of parents one of whom is white and the other is black.

municipality: A district such as a city or town having its own incorporated government.

Muslim: A follower of the prophet Muhammad, the founder of the religion of Islam.

Muslim New Year: A Muslim holiday. Although in some countries 1 Muharram, which is the first month of the Islamic year, is observed as a holiday, in other places the new year is observed on Sha'ban, the eighth month of the year. This practice apparently stems from pagan Arab times. Shab-i-Bharat, a national holiday in Bangladesh on this day, is held by many to be the occasion when God ordains all actions in the coming year.

NAFTA (North American Free Trade Agreement): NAFTA, which entered into force in January 1994, is a free trade agreement between Canada, the United States, and Mexico. The agreement progressively eliminates almost all U.S.-Mexico tariffs over a 10–15 year period.

nationalism: National spirit or aspirations; desire for national unity, independence, or prosperity.

nationalization: To transfer the control or ownership of land or industries to the nation from private owners.

native tongue: One's natural language. The language that is indigenous to an area.

NATO *see* North Atlantic Treaty Organization

natural gas: A combustible gas formed naturally in the earth and generally obtained by boring a well. The chemical makeup of natural gas is principally methane, hydrogen, ethylene compounds, and nitrogen.

natural harbor: A protected portion of a sea or lake along the shore resulting from the natural formations of the land.

naturalize: To confer the rights and privileges of a native-born subject or citizen upon someone who lives in the country by choice.

nature preserve: An area where one or more species of plant and/or animal are protected from harm, injury, or destruction.

neutrality: The policy of not taking sides with any countries during a war or dispute among them.

Newly Independent States: The NIS is a collective reference to 12 republics of the former Soviet Union: Russia, Ukraine, Belarus (formerly Byelorussia), Moldova (formerly Moldavia), Armenia, Azerbaijan, Uzbekistan, Turkmenistan, Tajikistan, Kazakhstan, and Kirgizstan (formerly Kirghiziya), and Georgia. Following dissolution of the Soviet Union, the distinction between the NIS and the Commonwealth of Independent States (CIS) was that Georgia was not a member of the CIS. That distinction dissolved when Georgia joined the CIS in November 1993.

news censorship *see* censorship

Nonaligned Movement: The NAM is an alliance of third world states that aims to promote the political and economic interests of developing countries. NAM interests have included ending colonialism/neo-colonialism, supporting the integrity of independent countries, and seeking a new international economic order.

Nordic Council: The Nordic Council, established in 1952, is directed toward supporting cooperation among Nordic countries. Members include Denmark, Finland, Iceland, Norway, and Sweden. Headquarters are in Stockholm, Sweden.

North Atlantic Treaty Organization (NATO): A mutual defense organization. Members include Belgium, Canada, Denmark, France (which has only partial membership), Greece, Iceland, Italy, Luxembourg, Netherlands, Norway, Portugal, Spain, Turkey, United Kingdom, United States, and Germany.

nuclear power plant: A factory that produces electrical power through the application of the nuclear reaction known as nuclear fission.

nuclear reactor: A device used to control the rate of nuclear fission in uranium. Used in commercial applications, nuclear reactors can maintain temperatures high enough to generate sufficient quantities of steam which can then be used to produce electricity.

OAPEC (Organization of Arab Petroleum Exporting countries): OAPEC was created in 1968; members include: Algeria, Bahrain, Egypt, Iraq, Kuwait, Libya, Qatar, Saudi Arabia, Syria, and the United Arab Emirates. Headquarters are in Cairo, Egypt.

OAS (Organization of American States): The OAS (Spanish: Organizaciûn de los Estados Americanos,

OEA), or the Pan American Union, is a regional organization which promotes Latin American economic and social development. Members include the United States, Mexico, and most Central American, South American, and Caribbean nations.

oasis: Originally, a fertile spot in the Libyan desert where there is a natural spring or well and vegetation; now refers to any fertile tract in the midst of a wasteland.

occupied territory: A territory that has an enemy's military forces present.

official language: The language in which the business of a country and its government is conducted.

oligarchy: A form of government in which a few people possess the power to rule as opposed to a monarchy which is ruled by one.

OPEC *see* OAPEC

open economy: An economy that imports and exports goods.

open market: Open market operations are the actions of the central bank to influence or control the money supply by buying or selling government bonds.

opposition party: A minority political party that is opposed to the party in power.

Organization of Arab Petroleum Exporting Countries *see* OAPEC

organized labor: The body of workers who belong to labor unions.

Ottoman Empire: A Turkish empire founded by Osman I in about 1603, that variously controlled large areas of land around the Mediterranean, Black, and Caspian Seas until it was dissolved in 1918.

overfishing: To deplete the quantity of fish in an area by removing more fish than can be naturally replaced.

overgrazing: Allowing animals to graze in an area to the point that the ground vegetation is damaged or destroyed.

overseas dependencies: A distant and physically separate territory that belongs to another country and is subject to its laws and government.

Pacific Rim: The Pacific Rim, referring to countries and economies bordering the Pacific Ocean.

pact: An international agreement.

Paleolithic: The early period of the Stone Age, when rough, chipped stone implements were used.

panhandle: A long narrow strip of land projecting like the handle of a frying pan.

papyrus: The paper-reed or -rush which grows on marshy river banks in the southeastern area of the Mediterranean, but more notably in the Nile valley.

paramilitary group: A supplementary organization to the military.

parasitic diseases: A group of diseases caused by parasitic organisms which feed off the host organism.

parliamentary republic: A system of government in which a president and prime minister, plus other ministers of departments, constitute the executive branch of the government and the parliament constitutes the legislative branch.

parliamentary rule: Government by a legislative body similar to that of Great Britain, which is composed of two houses—one elected and one hereditary.

parochial: Refers to matters of a church parish or something within narrow limits.

partisan politics: Rigid, unquestioning following of a specific party's or leader's goals.

patriarchal system: A social system in which the head of the family or tribe is the father or oldest male. Kinship is determined and traced through the male members of the tribe.

patrilineal (descent): Descending from, or tracing descent through, the paternal or father's line.

pellagra: A disease marked by skin, intestinal, and central nervous system disorders, caused by a diet deficient in niacin, one of the B vitamins.

per capita: Literally, per person; for each person counted.

perestroika: The reorganization of the political and economic structures of the Soviet Union by president Mikhail Gorbachev.

periodical: A publication whose issues appear at regular intervals, such as weekly, monthly, or yearly.

petrochemical: A chemical derived from petroleum or from natural gas.

pharmaceutical plants: Any plant that is used in the preparation of medicinal drugs.

plantain: The name of a common weed that has often been used for medicinal purposes, as a folk remedy and in modern medicine. *Plaintain* is also the name of a tropical plant producing a type of banana.

polar climate: Also called tundra climate. A humid, severely cold climate controlled by arctic air masses, with no warm or summer season.

political climate: The prevailing political attitude of a particular time or place.

political refugee: A person forced to flee his or her native country for political reasons.

potable water: Water that is safe for drinking.

pound sterling: The monetary unit of Great Britain, otherwise known as the pound.

prefect: An administrative official; in France, the head of a particular department.

prefecture: The territory over which a prefect has authority.

prime meridian: Zero degrees in longitude that runs through Greenwich, England, site of the Royal Observatory. All other longitudes are measured from this point.

prime minister: The premier or chief administrative official in certain countries.

private sector: The division of an economy in which production of goods and services is privately owned.

privatization: To change from public to private control or ownership.

protectorate: A state or territory controlled by a stronger state, or the relationship of the stronger country toward the lesser one it protects.

Protestant: A member or an adherent of one of those Christian bodies which descended from the Reformation of the sixteenth century. Originally applied to those who opposed or protested the Roman Catholic Church.

Protestant Reformation: In 1529, a Christian religious movement begun in Germany to deny the universal authority of the pope, and to establish the Bible as the only source of truth. (*Also see* Protestant)

proved reserves: The quantity of a recoverable mineral resource (such as oil or natural gas) that is still in the ground.

province: An administrative territory of a country.

provisional government: A temporary government set up during time of unrest or transition in a country.

pulses: Beans, peas, or lentils.

purge: The act of ridding a society of "undesirable" or unloyal persons by banishment or murder.

Rastafarian: A member of a Jamaican cult begun in 1930 as a semi-religious, semi-political movement.

rate of literacy: The percentage of people in a society who can read and write.

recession. A period of reduced economic activity in a country or region.

referendum: The practice of submitting legislation directly to the people for a popular vote.

reforestation: Systematically replacing forest trees lost due to fire or logging.

Reformation *see* Protestant Reformation.

refugee: One who flees to a refuge or shelter or place of safety. One who in times of persecution or political commotion flees to a foreign country for safety.

revolution: A complete change in a government or society, such as in an overthrow of the government by the people.

right-wing party: The more conservative political party.

Roman alphabet: The alphabet of the ancient Romans from which the alphabets of most modern western European languages, including English, are derived.

Roman Catholic Church: The designation of the church of which the pope or Bishop of Rome is the head, and that holds him as the successor of St. Peter and heir of his spiritual authority, privileges, and gifts.

romance language: The group of languages derived from Latin: French, Spanish, Italian, Portuguese, and other related languages.

roundwood: Timber used as poles or in similar ways without being sawn or shaped.

runoff election: A deciding election put to the voters in case of a tie between candidates.

Russian Orthodox: The arm of the Orthodox Eastern Church that was the official church of Russia under the czars.

sack: To strip of valuables, especially after capture.

Sahelian zone: Eight countries make up this dry desert zone in Africa: Burkina Faso, Chad, Gambia, Mali, Mauritania, Niger, Senegal, and the Cape Verde Islands. *Also see* Club du Sahel.

salinization: An accumulation of soluble salts in soil. This condition is common in desert climates, where water evaporates quickly in poorly drained soil due to high temperatures.

Samaritans: A native or an inhabitant of Samaria; specifically, one of a race settled in the cities of Samaria by the king of Assyria after the removal of the Israelites from the country.

savanna: A treeless or near treeless plain of a tropical or subtropical region dominated by drought-resistant grasses.

schistosomiasis: A tropical disease that is chronic and characterized by disorders of the liver, urinary bladder, lungs, or central nervous system.

secession: The act of withdrawal, such as a state withdrawing from the Union in the Civil War in the United States.

sect: A religious denomination or group, often a dissenting one with extreme views.

segregation: The enforced separation of a racial or religious group from other groups, compelling them to live and go to school separately from the rest of society.

seismic activity: Relating to or connected with an earthquake or earthquakes in general.

self-sufficient: Able to function alone without help.

separation of power: The division of power in the government among the executive, legislative, and judicial branches and the checks and balances employed to keep them separate and independent of each other.

separatism: The policy of dissenters withdrawing from a larger political or religious group.

serfdom: In the feudal system of the Middle Ages, the condition of being attached to the land owned by a lord and being transferable to a new owner.

Seventh-day Adventist: One who believes in the second coming of Christ to establish a personal reign upon the earth.

shamanism: A religion of some Asians and Amerindians in which shamans, who are priests or medicine men, are believed to influence good and evil spirits.

shantytown: An urban settlement of people in flimsy, inadequate houses.

Shia Muslims: Members of one of two great sects of Islam. Shia Muslims believe that Ali and the Imams are the rightful successors of Muhammad (also commonly spelled Mohammed). They also believe that the last recognized Imam will return as a messiah. Also known as Shiites. (*Also see* Sunni Muslims.)

Shiites *see* Shia Muslims.

Shintoism: The system of nature- and hero-worship which forms the indigenous religion of Japan.

shoal: A place where the water of a stream, lake, or sea is of little depth. Especially, a sand-bank which shows at low water.

sierra: A chain of hills or mountains.

Sikh: A member of a politico-religious community of India, founded as a sect around 1500 and based on the principles of monotheism (belief in one god) and human brotherhood.

Sino-Tibetan language family: The family of languages spoken in eastern Asia, including China, Thailand, Tibet, and Burma.

slash-and-burn agriculture: A hasty and sometimes temporary way of clearing land to make it available for agriculture by cutting down trees and burning them.

slave trade: The transportation of black Africans beginning in the 1700s to other countries to be sold as slaves—people owned as property and compelled to work for their owners at no pay.

Slavic languages: A major subgroup of the Indo-European language family. It is further subdivided into West Slavic (including Polish, Czech, Slovak and Serbian), South Slavic (including Bulgarian, Serbo-Croatian, Slovene, and Old Church Slavonic), and East Slavic (including Russian Ukrainian and Byelorussian).

social insurance: A government plan to protect low-income people, such as health and accident insurance, pension plans, etc.

social security: A form of social insurance, including life, disability, and old-age pension for workers. It is paid for by employers, employees, and the government.

socialism: An economic system in which ownership of land and other property is distributed among the community as a whole, and every member of the community shares in the work and products of the work.

socialist: A person who advocates socialism.

softwoods: The coniferous trees, whose wood density as a whole is relatively softer than the wood of those trees referred to as hardwoods.

sorghum (also known as Syrian Grass): Plant grown in various parts of the world for its valuable uses, such as for grain, syrup, or fodder.

Southeast Asia: The region in Asia that consists of the Malay Archipelago, the Malay Peninsula, and Indochina.

staple crop: A crop that is the chief commodity or product of a place, and which has widespread and constant use or value.

state: The politically organized body of people living under one government or one of the territorial units that make up a federal government, such as in the United States.

steppe: A level tract of land more or less devoid of trees, in certain parts of European and Asiatic Russia.

student demonstration: A public gathering of students to express strong feelings about a certain situation, usually taking place near the location of the people in power to change the situation.

subarctic climate: A high latitude climate of two types: *continental subarctic*, which has very cold winters, short, cool summers, light precipitation and moist air; and *marine subarctic*, a coastal and island climate with polar air masses causing large precipitation and extreme cold.

subcontinent: A land mass of great size, but smaller than any of the continents; a large subdivision of a continent.

subsistence economy: The part of a national economy in which money plays little or no role, trade is by barter, and living standards are minimal.

subsistence farming: Farming that provides the minimum food goods necessary for the continuation of the farm family.

subtropical climate: A middle latitude climate dominated by humid, warm temperatures and heavy rainfall in summer, with cool winters and frequent cyclonic storms.

Sudanic language group: A related group of languages spoken in various areas of northern Africa, including Yoruba, Mandingo, and Tshi.

suffrage: The right to vote.

Sufi: A Muslim mystic who believes that God alone exists, there can be no real difference between good and evil, that the soul exists within the body as in a cage, so death should be the chief object of desire, and sufism is the only true philosophy.

sultan: A king of a Muslim state.

Sunni Muslims: Members of one of two major sects of the religion of Islam. Sunni Muslims adhere to strict orthodox traditions, and believe that the four caliphs are the rightful successors to Mohammed, founder of Islam. (Mohammed is commonly spelled Muhammad, especially by Islamic people.) (*Also see* Shia Muslims.)

Taoism: The doctrine of Lao-Tzu, an ancient Chinese philosopher (about 500 B.C.) as laid down by him in the *Tao-te-ching.*

tariff: A tax assessed by a government on goods as they enter (or leave) a country. May be imposed to protect domestic industries from imported goods and/or to generate revenue.

temperate zone: The parts of the earth lying between the tropics and the polar circles. The *northern temperate zone* is the area between the tropic of Cancer and the Arctic Circle. The *southern temperate zone* is the area between the tropic of Capricorn and the Antarctic Circle.

terracing: A form of agriculture that involves cultivating crops in raised banks of earth.

terrorism: Systematic acts of violence designed to frighten or intimidate.

thermal power plant: A facility that produces electric energy from heat energy released by combustion of fuel or nuclear reactions.

Third World: A term used to describe less developed countries; as of the mid-1990s, it is being replaced by the United Nations designation Less Developed Countries, or LDC.

topography: The physical or natural features of the land.

torrid zone: The part of the earth's surface that lies between the tropics, so named for the character of its climate.

totalitarian party: The single political party in complete authoritarian control of a government or state.

trachoma: A contagious bacterial disease that affects the eye.

trade unionism: Labor union activity for workers who practice a specific trade, such as carpentry.

treaty: A negotiated agreement between two governments.

tribal system: A social community in which people are organized into groups or clans descended from common ancestors and sharing customs and languages.

tropical monsoon climate: One of the tropical rainy climates; it is sufficiently warm and rainy to produce tropical rainforest vegetation, but also has a winter dry season.

tsetse fly: Any of the several African insects which can transmit a variety of parasitic organisms through its bite. Some of these organisms can prove fatal to both human and animal victims.

tundra: A nearly level treeless area whose climate and vegetation are characteristically arctic due to its northern position; the subsoil is permanently frozen.

undeveloped countries *see* least developed countries.

unemployment rate: The overall unemployment rate is the percentage of the work force (both employed and unemployed) who claim to be unemployed.

UNICEF: An international fund set-up for children's emergency relief: United Nations Children's Fund (formerly United Nations International Children's Emergency Fund).

universal adult suffrage: The policy of giving every adult in a nation the right to vote.

untouchables: In India, members of the lowest caste in the caste system, a hereditary social class system. They were considered unworthy to touch members of higher castes.

urban guerrilla: A rebel fighter operating in an urban area.

urbanization: The process of changing from country to city.

veldt: In South Africa, an unforested or thinly forested tract of land or region, a grassland.

Warsaw Pact: Agreement made 14 May 1955 (and dissolved 1 July 1991) to promote mutual defense between Albania, Bulgaria, Czechoslovakia, East Germany, Hungary, Poland, Romania, and the USSR.

Western nations: Blanket term used to describe mostly democratic, capitalist countries, including the United States, Canada, and western European countries.

wildlife sanctuary: An area of land set aside for the protection and preservation of animals and plants.

workers' compensation: A series of regular payments by an employer to a person injured on the job.

World Bank: The World Bank is a group of international institutions which provides financial and technical assistance to developing countries.

world oil crisis: The severe shortage of oil in the 1970s precipitated by the Arab oil embargo.

yaws: A tropical disease caused by a bacteria which produces raspberry-like sores on the skin.

yellow fever: A tropical viral disease caused by the bite of an infected mosquito, characterized by jaundice.

Zoroastrianism: The system of religious doctrine taught by Zoroaster and his followers in the Avesta; the religion prevalent in Persia until its overthrow by the Muslims in the seventh century.

Qatar

Romania

Russia

St. Vincent and
the Grenadines

San Marino

São Tomé and Príncipe

Sierra Leone

Singapore

Slovakia

South Africa